Global Catholicism

Global Catholicism

Profiles & Polarities

THOMAS P. RAUSCH, SJ

ORBIS BOOKS
Maryknoll, New York 10545

Founded in 1970, Orbis Books endeavors to publish works that enlighten the mind, nourish the spirit, and challenge the conscience. The publishing arm of the Maryknoll Fathers and Brothers, Orbis seeks to explore the global dimensions of the Christian faith and mission, to invite dialogue with diverse cultures and religious traditions, and to serve the cause of reconciliation and peace. The books published reflect the views of their authors and do not represent the official position of the Maryknoll Society. To learn more about Orbis Books, please visit our website at www.orbisbooks.com.

Manufactured in the United States of America
Manuscript editing and typesetting by Joan Weber Laflamme.

Library of Congress Cataloging-in-Publication Data

Names: Rausch, Thomas P., author.
Title: Global Catholicism : profiles and polarities / Thomas P. Rausch, SJ.
Description: Maryknoll, New York : Orbis Books, 2021. | Includes bibliographical refeences and index. | Summary: "A critical analysis of the Catholic Churches around the world by areas (North America, Latin America, Africa, Asia, the Pacific, Europe), with attention to their origins, internal challenges, and external pressures"— Provided by publisher.
Identifiers: LCCN 2020031300 (print) | LCCN 2020031301 (ebook) | ISBN 9781626983960 (trade paperback) | ISBN 9781608338603 (epub)
Subjects: LCSH: Globalization—Religious aspects—Catholic Church. | Catholic Church—History—21st century.
Classification: LCC BX1795.G66 R38 2021 (print) | LCC BX1795.G66 (ebook) | DDC 282.09/05—dc23
LC record available at https://lccn.loc.gov/2020031300
LC ebook record available at https://lccn.loc.gov/2020031301

For Sister Jean Dolores Schmidt, BVM
Teacher, Mentor, Friend

Contents

Acknowledgments

The idea for this book came from one of my former teachers at Duke University, Jill Raitt, founder of the Department of Religious Studies at the University of Missouri and longtime professor there. I've learned much from the research in preparing it and am grateful to her for the suggestion. Thanks also to my longtime editor and friend, Paul McMahon, for his encouragement and always helpful suggestions, and to Joan Laflamme, whose careful copyediting makes this a much better book.

Various friends reviewed different chapters on their homelands or places of origin and made suggestions, among them colleagues Jina Kang, Simon Kim, and Stanislaw Obirek, as well as fellow Jesuits Ernald Andal, Allan Figueroa Deck, Dominic Irudayaraj, Paul Mariani, Lan Ngo, Amaechi Ugwu, Ramesh Vanan, and Yves Vendé. The responsibility for the text is my own.

Introduction

Of the 2.5 billion Christians in the world as of 2018, Catholics number more than 50 percent, over 1.2 billion. According to current estimates, Protestants represent about 37 percent, with another 12 percent belonging to the various Orthodox churches. Other less mainstream communities identifying as Christian (Christian Scientists, Mormons, Jehovah's Witnesses) represent about 1 percent. Also remarkable is the growth of Pentecostal, charismatic, or renewalist churches today, with over 682 million members.[1] Catholics and Pentecostal/charismatics together constitute three quarters of global Christianity.

Yet demographic shifts are changing the face of world Christianity. The mainline churches of Europe and North America continue to lose members, while Christianity is exploding in Africa, Asia, and Latin America, usually referred to as the Global South. According to the Pew Forum, more than 1.3 billion Christians (61 percent) live in the Global South, compared with about 860 million in Europe and North America (39 percent).[2]

There are more Christians in the United States than in any other country in the world, some 173 million according to a 2015 Pew Research Center study, meaning that roughly seven in ten Americans identify with some Christian tradition. However, that population continues to decline, especially among Catholics and mainline Protestants, with the drop greatest among mainline Protestants. In 2007, there were an estimated 41 million mainline Protestant adults in the United States. As of 2014, there were roughly 36 million, a decline of 5 million. Evangelicals have also suffered some losses.[3]

---

[1]Todd M. Johnson, et al., "Christianity 2018: More African Christians and Counting Martyrs," *International Bulletin of Mission Research* 42, no. 1 (2018): 23–24.

[2]Pew Research Center, "Global Christianity—A Report on the Size and distribution of the World's Christian Population, December 19, 2011.

[3]Pew Research Center, "America's Changing Religious Landscape," May 12, 2015.

According to the latest Pew study (2018–19), 65 percent of Americans describe themselves as Christian, down 12 percentage points from a decade ago, while the number describing themselves as atheist, agnostic, or "nothing in particular" is now at 26 percent of the population, up from 17 percent a decade ago. Some 43 percent of adults identify as Protestants, down from 51 percent in 2009, while Catholics went from 23 percent to 20 percent during the same period. Only 47 percent of Hispanics identify as Catholics, down from 57 percent ten years ago.[4]

Although the Catholic Church has the largest net loss, it is also the largest Christian community in the United States. According to a 2008 CARA study, its numbers would be even worse if it were losing members at the rate of the mainline Protestant churches.[5] Regardless, the latest numbers from the Pew Research Center are not good news. They show Catholics losing 12.9 percent of adults raised Catholics, compared to losses of 10.4 percent for mainline Protestants and 8.4 for evangelicals. Nearly 13 percent of all Americans are former Catholics.[6] The Southern Baptist Convention (SBC), the largest Protestant denomination in the United States, has suffered the largest drop in membership in more than a century. According to surveys conducted between 2015 and 2018, "just over half of those raised Southern Baptist were still with the SBC. In other words, nearly half of Southern Baptists kids leave and never come back."[7]

However, if Christianity is in trouble in Europe and North America, it is exploding in the Global South. The growth of Christianity in Africa has been extraordinary, from 9 million in 1900 to an estimated 380 million today. The number of African Christians has already surpassed that of Christians in Latin America. According to Todd Johnson and his associates, "By 2050 there will likely be more Christians in Africa (1.25 billion) than in Latin America (705 million) and Europe (490 million) combined."[8] This means that Europe will not dominate global Christianity as it did in the past.

---

[4] Pew Research Center, "In US, Decline of Christianity Continues at Rapid Pace," October 17, 2019.

[5] Mark M. Gray, "The Impact of Religious Switching and Secularization on the Estimated size of the US Adult Catholic Population," Center for Applied Research in the Apostolate (CARA), Georgetown University, 2008.

[6] Pew Research Center, "America's Changing Religious Landscape: Chapter 2: Switching and Intermarriage," May 12, 2015.

[7] Ryan P. Burge, "Only Half of Kids Raised Southern Baptist Stay Southern Baptist," *Christianity Today*, May 24, 2019.

[8] Johnson, et al., "Christianity 2018," 21.

In Asia, Christianity continues to grow, driven by mushrooming evangelical and Pentecostal churches. In 1970, there were 17 million Asian evangelicals and Pentecostals; today, the number is over 200 million. The largest congregations are in South Korea and the Philippines, with megachurches in the tens of thousands of members. Christianity is growing also in Indonesia and Malaysia among Buddhists and Confucians. The City Harvest Church in Singapore has a weekly attendance of just under sixteen thousand. The service involves music from a rock group, prayer in tongues, and witness. Many of these megachurches preach the "prosperity gospel." In Singapore, the Christian population, most of it evangelical or Pentecostal, has increased from 2 percent in 1970 to 8 percent in 2015.

Christianity in China continues to grow despite the efforts of the Chinese government to limit its growth. Estimates put the Catholic population at between 10 and 12 million, while those of evangelical and Pentecostal Christians range from 40 to 60 million, with some suggesting numbers as high as 100 million.

The Catholic Church today, with its enormous numbers and worldwide presence, is truly a global church, at once the world's oldest institution and a transnational actor. My intention in this book is to survey global Catholicism in an effort to give a brief profile of the church's dimensions, state of health, polarities both internal and external, and emerging trends by looking at Catholic churches around the world. These churches exist in very different cultures and face different challenges. Some with long histories are showing their age with a loss of vitality. Others are new churches, moving beyond their missionary or colonial past; they struggle with questions of inculturation, developing their own spiritualities, finding their own voices, or learning how best to proclaim the gospel in the pluralistic and sometimes hostile cultures in which they are rooted.

The Second Vatican Council was an effort to renew the church, trying to move beyond its long battle with modernity and bring it into the twentieth century. But we are now in the twenty-first century, and the challenges facing the church are considerable. An increasing number of people are leaving the church, not just in Europe and the United States but in other parts of the world as well. A pluralism of nontraditional spiritual practices presents options for some, while a considerable pluralism of theologies, liturgical tastes, spiritual practices, and social commitments exists within the church itself. Many Catholics experience a disconnection between their lives and official teachings, especially in the areas of marriage and sexuality, but they remain active in pastoral or educational ministries and do not consider themselves any less Catholic. Apart from India and Islamic countries, secularism prevails. In some countries religious liberty is at risk and Christians are persecuted.

So how does the church find new ways to make its message heard? How can it continue to mediate an experience of the Holy? How does it renew itself for the sake of its mission? Cultural individualism finds expression even within the church, as many of those still practicing do so on their own terms. Authority, institutions, and traditional metanarratives are suspect. Without cultural supports for religious practice, the few devotional practices that remain, at least in the West, are generally not valued. What is respected is experience.

A global Catholic Church will no longer be served by a highly centralized, institutional authority, and a Eurocentric theology will not suffice. Nor will patriarchal structures. The structures of the church need reform; they need to be less focused on Rome, open to greater diversity and the participation of previously excluded voices. In Africa and Asia inculturation becomes increasingly important. Many of those still in the church want models and inspirational figures, not teachers. Others are "seekers," not churchgoers but still not free of a cultural or residual Christianity. They long for some spiritual key to unlock the conflicting values and ideas mediated by digital media, for some illuminating vision.

Vatican II is an important reference point, but not the final word; it is better understood as the point of departure for a renewed church.[9] Or as Johanna Rahner says, "The comfortable identity of the 'stronghold of eternal truths,' which the Catholic Church displayed in the 19th century by using the image of a hierarchical ordered *societas perfecta*, is being replaced by the uncomfortable and unsettling situation of a continuous journey."[10] But it is a journey into a future yet unknown; it means reading the signs of the times to discern what the Spirit might be saying.

Pope Francis, the first non-European pontiff, is seeking to carry through that renewal and reform in the twenty-first century. His ecclesial vision sees the church as a church of and for the poor, a welcoming church no longer centered in Europe, but one that goes to the peripheries without losing its gospel identity. His influence will be seen in the pages that

---

[9] See Staf Hellemans and Peter Jonkers, eds., *Envisioning Futures for the Catholic Church* (Washington, DC: Council for Research in Values and Philosophy, 2018).

[10] Johanna Rahner, "A Less Eurocentric Theology: Advantages, Tasks, and Challenges," in Hellemans and Jonkers, *Envisioning Futures for the Catholic Church*, 164.

follow. In the final chapter I suggest what this survey might mean for the church's future.

Naturally, with more than 1.2 billion Catholics, such a survey can be little more than an overview; not every church or country can be included. I apologize for those I have omitted. Nevertheless, what emerges is a sketch of a global church, often struggling, sometimes polarized or persecuted, but rich in its diversity, its peoples, and its lives of faith.

1

A Global Church

The Catholic Church is the world's oldest institution. It is truly a world church, at once a global institution united in faith and life under the guidance of the bishop of Rome, the Roman pontiff, and at the same time a communion of different churches around the world, each under the authority of its bishop.

The church has also felt the effects of the shift of the Christian population to the Global South. Estimates put 75 percent of the world's Catholics south of the equator by 2050, so the Catholic Church is no longer a church with members largely from Europe and North America. And with the election of Jorge Mario Bergoglio to the Chair of Peter, the church has a pope from the Global South. Francis's agenda, spelled out in his apostolic letter *Evangelii gaudium*, is clearly different from that of his predecessors.

In terms of percentages, the number of Catholics remains highest in North and South America. Europe is 48 percent Catholic, 32 percent Orthodox (including Russia, with its huge population), and about 19 percent Protestant. However, with a meager 0.1 percent growth rate, the percentage of European Catholics continues to decline.[1]

Latin America has traditionally been Catholic, with Catholics constituting 90 percent of the population in the period from 1900 to 1960. Yet the number of Catholics has diminished substantially, with tens of millions joining evangelical and especially Pentecostal congregations or dropping out entirely. A Pew Research survey of eighteen countries and

---

[1] *Catholics and Cultures*, with its focus on global Catholic practices and beliefs, is a helpful website. See also global Catholicism at https://www.catholicsandcultures.org/about-site/authors; and the site's online *Journal of Global Catholicism*, https://crossworks.holycross.edu/jgc/.

one territory, Puerto Rico, shows that only 69 percent of adults across the region identify as Catholics today. In most of the countries surveyed, at least one-third of current Protestants were raised in the Catholic Church, and one-half or more say they were baptized as Catholics. Nearly 20 percent of Latin Americans describe themselves as Protestant, with the majority identifying with Pentecostal or neo-Pentecostal congregations.

At the same time, according to the *Annuario Pontifico* for 2016, the overall number of Catholics continues to grow faster than the rate of the world's population. In Africa, the number of Catholics increased by 41 percent and in Asia by 20 percent. Still, the fastest growing religious community today is Islam, which in the last quarter of the twentieth century displaced Catholicism as the world's largest religious community. Its numbers increased from 571 million in 1970 to 1.7 billion.[2]

Some scholars are now raising an interesting picture of the future of Christianity. Discouraged by the failure of formal dialogue to produce any real ecumenical progress, Lutheran theologian Robert Jenson asks if perhaps God is not winding down the Protestant experiment, suggesting that, if things continue as they are, God "will carry on the *ecumene* with the Roman Catholic Church, Eastern churches, and Pentecostal groups."[3] Pentecostal scholar Cheryl Bridges Johns cites with approval a 1969 projection by John Mackay, "The Christian future may lie with a reformed Catholicism and a mature Pentecostalism."[4]

Cecil M. Robeck, Jr., a Pentecostal scholar and ecumenist, likes to imagine Pentecostals/charismatics in three hundred years, not in terms of a church but as "a uniquely powerful form of spirituality *within* the one, holy, catholic, and apostolic Church."[5] In an address at the Gregorian University in Rome, Robeck attributes his suggestive vision to a conversation with another scholar some years ago. Reflecting on the large losses experienced by churches in the West, in comparison to the remarkable growth of Christianity in the Global South, the professor stated his belief

---

[2] George Weigel, "World Christianity by the Numbers," *First Things*, February 25, 2015.

[3] Robert W. Jenson, "The Strange Future of 'the Ecumenical Movement,'" *The Living Church*, January 19, 2014, 24.

[4] Cheryl Bridges Johns, "Of Like Passion: A Pentecostal Appreciation of Benedict XVI," in *The Pontificate of Benedict XVI*, ed. William G. Rush (Grand Rapids, MI: Eerdmans, 2009), 113; for Mackay's statement, see John Mackay, *Christian Reality and Appearance* (Richmond, VA: John Knox Press, 1969), 88–89.

[5] Cecil M. Robeck, Jr., "Can We Imagine an Ecumenical Future Together? A Pentecostal Perspective," *Gregorianum* 100, no. 1 (2019): 66.

that in three hundred years the only church left would be the Catholic Church. When Robeck raised the question of the remarkable growth of Pentecostal and charismatic Christians, his friend's response was, "If the Church is to have any future at all, then *it must* and eventually *it will* be reformed and renewed. Pentecostals and Charismatics will find their home in a renewed and revitalized Catholic Church that will look quite different from the one currently led from Rome."[6]

The Second Vatican Council

The Second Vatican Council (1962–65) was an effort to *renew* and *revitalize* the Catholic Church, using these terms as another way of translating Pope John XXIII's *aggiornamento*. Renewal and revitalization was one of his primary goals in calling the church into council. The other was to commit not just Catholics but all Christians to the search for Christian unity, to strive for the "unity and grace to which so many souls aspire in all part of the earth."[7]

The council was largely successful. In many ways, it moved a previously immobile, fortress church beyond its long defensiveness against Protestantism and modernity and into the twentieth century. The council replaced a monarchical, juridical ecclesiology with a biblical, communal model based on its doctrine of collegiality, and it developed a theology of all the baptized, giving them an explicit share in the mission of the church (*Lumen gentium*). It broadened the church's understanding of its mission, placing it at the service of the world and especially of those who were poor or afflicted (*Gaudium et spes*). Acknowledging the Catholic Church's share in the sin of division, the council committed the church to the search for reconciliation and Christian unity (*Unitatis redintegratio*). It acknowledged that other religions can reflect some of the truth that enlightens all people (*Nostra aetate*) and established a positive theological approach to the Jewish people. For the first time, it proclaimed that religious freedom was a fundamental human right (*Dignitatis humanae*). And it took important steps toward renewing the church's liturgy, making it more at home in the church's many diverse cultures (*Sacrosanctum concilium*). In this way the council set the agenda for the church's future.

---

[6] Robeck, "Can We Imagine an Ecumenical Future Together?" 64.

[7] "Pope John's Announcement of Ecumenical Council," *Council Daybook*, Session 1–2 (Washington, DC: National Catholic Welfare Conference, 1965), 2.

Not all of its efforts were successful. Some, even some in high places, resisted the changes the council called for. Some sought to idealize the past. A few broke communion with the universal church, establishing schismatic communities. Others, impatient with the process of renewal, formed radical communities or joined other churches. Thus, the council's agenda is still unfinished. None of this should be surprising. As church historians have pointed out, the process of "receiving" and incorporating the results of a council is lengthy and sometimes painful, often extending over a century. Nevertheless, the process of renewal and revitalization is ongoing.

In a powerful address Dominican John Markey wrote that Vatican II began a revolution, still in its early stages, of "deep, social, political, cultural, and religious transformation that may take many, many more years to complete and is beyond the power of anyone to control or stop."[8] Thus, it represented a Copernican revolution in the church's life, one leading to four fundamental ecclesial insights or breakthroughs. First, the council meant that the Catholic Church for the first time truly began to exist as a world church. Second, it recognized that God's grace is abundantly present beyond the structures of Catholicism. Third, it stressed the primacy of baptism and the universal call to holiness. Finally, it represented a rediscovery of the grace of the Holy Spirit, present not just in the church's sacramental life and magisterial authority, but also in different times, places, and peoples.[9] Let me examine and expand somewhat on Markey's four headings.

A World Church

Karl Rahner was one of the first to recognize that Vatican II represented the transformation of the Western church into a world church. "For the first time a world-wide Council with a world-wide episcopate came into existence and functioned independently."[10] While representatives of the Asian and African episcopates were present at Vatican I, they were largely missionary bishops of European and North American origin. But

---

[8] John J. Markey, "George Washington, Napoleon, John Paul II and the Future of the Vatican II Revolution," in *Seattle Theology and Ministry Review* 3 (2003): 15.

[9] Markey, "Future of the Vatican II Revolution," 15–19.

[10] Karl Rahner, "Towards a Fundamental Theological Interpretation of Vatican II," *Theological Studies* 40, no. 4 (1979): 718.

at Vatican II, the bishops came from 116 countries, most of them native born; 36 percent came from Europe, 23 percent from Latin America, 12 percent from North America, 20 percent from Asia and Oceania, and 10 percent from Africa.[11]

By the 1985 Extraordinary Synod of Bishops in Rome, 74 percent of the bishops came from countries other than those in Europe or North America, as do more than 70 percent of the world's Catholics today. This means that the Catholic Church can no longer be identified with Europe or North America. What are the implications of the church being truly global?

Vatican II made clear that the church's bishops are not simply vicars of the Roman pontiff. As members of the episcopal college, they share with the bishop of Rome in the government of the whole church, while as bishops in their own right, they govern the churches assigned to them (LG, no. 27). That means that the church is not a single, monolithic institution, but a communion of churches, embedded not just in the West but also in the hundreds of different cultures of Africa, Asia, Latin America, and the Pacific. These local or regional churches, some long established, others new and still growing, will have to find ways to relate to their different cultures and still maintain communion with the universal church, presided over by the bishop of Rome. The nature of the church as a communion of churches has important implications for governance. It implies a more decentralized church, with more local decision-making power. "The whole Church grows, changes and develops over time in response to the needs of people and cultures that shape and form people's daily lives."[12] Unity is more than uniformity.

Even before his election to the Chair of Peter, Pope Francis called the church to move beyond a comfortable complacency, a "self-referentiality" or theological narcissism that lives within itself rather than coming out with the message of the gospel that is its mission to proclaim. Just eight months after his election to the Chair of Peter (2013), he set forth his agenda for renewal and reform in his apostolic letter *Evangelii gaudium*. In it he called for a missionary transformation of the church involving every Christian, every community, and the church itself in both the papacy and its central structures (EG, nos. 20–31).

---

[11] See John W. O'Malley, *What Happened at Vatican II* (Cambridge, MA: Harvard University Press, 2008), 23; also Massimo Faggioli, *Vatican II: The Battle for Meaning* (New York: Paulist Press, 2012), 183.

[12] Markey, "Future of the Vatican II Revolution," 16.

Abundant Grace

A second revolutionary insight was the recognition of the abundance of God's grace in the world. No longer restricted to the Catholic Church and its sacraments, as so many neo-Scholastic textbooks seem to suggest, the council recognized that grace was present in other churches and religions. It is not limited, nor is it a thing. Grace is a relationship with God, a share in God's life. The church should be a sign of God's love for all people. Other churches and ecclesial communities also mediate salvific grace.

A recognition of the abundance of grace changes the church's relationship to other churches and religions. *Nostra aetate* acknowledged that other religions often reflect some of the truth that enlightens all people (NA, no. 2). *Lumen gentium* taught that God's saving grace was available to those who even without knowing Christ or his church respond to that grace (LG, no. 16). Grace is present in other religions, in different cultures, and in nature itself, as we will see below.

Primacy of Baptism

The council's emphasis on the primacy of baptism implied important changes in the church's internal life. It meant that all the faithful, not just the ordained, participate in the mission of the church. Lay men and women are not just "helpers." They are commissioned by baptism and confirmation to an apostolate that shares in the church's saving mission (LG, no. 33). From this perspective the fundamental sacrament of ministry is not ordination but baptism. "That the ordained no longer have a monopoly on holiness, the charisms, and power remains the most subversive and threatening 'architectonic' shift made by the Council."[13]

Furthermore, the call to holiness is universal. Members of the laity too are called to holiness. Thus, speaking of priesthood or the religious life as a "higher way" or "the state of perfection" is no longer appropriate. A famous picture in the *Baltimore Catechism* shows a couple celebrating their marriage and a young sister on her vow day. Over the first is written, "This Is Good," while over the second, "This Is Better."

The emphasis on the primacy of baptism and the share of all the baptized in the "*threefold munera*" of Christ's priestly, prophetic, and kingly office was to lead in the postconciliar church to an explosion of lay ministries. Without taking anything away from the office of the ordained, this

---

[13] Markey, "Future of the Vatican II Revolution," 18.

means that ordained and lay ministers become partners in the mission of the church. The council's recovery of the theology of the charismata or charismatic gifts was another important step in this direction (LG 4, 7, 12).

Rediscovery of the Holy Spirit

Perhaps one of the most important breakthroughs of the council was its "rediscovery" of the Spirit's role in the life of the church; Markey calls it "revolutionary." He writes that at the council "the Holy Spirit was recovered as the very presence of God acting in every human life, in the Christian community and throughout the whole world. The Spirit is the source of life and unity for the Church. The hierarchy only aids the Spirit which cannot be contained within any one place or time or people."[14]

While Eastern Christianity has always been more pneumatological in its theology and liturgy, Western Christianity, with its roots in Roman law, government, and culture, has tended to emphasize christological foundations at the expense of the Spirit. Positively, Jesus has a body and a voice. The scriptures witness to his teaching and the development of his body, the church, grounding Catholic ecclesiology.

At the same time, important as it is, an exclusive focus on Christology can be too narrow, not recognizing the Spirit's freedom. The Spirit is more difficult to identify; without a "face," the Spirit lacks concreteness. It is more affect than subject, not a noun but a verb. The Spirit warms and comforts. It blows where it will; like the wind, "you do not know where it comes from or where it goes" (Jn 3:8). It cannot be programmed or controlled. Most of all, it brings about novelty and must be discerned.

Contemporary Challenges

While Vatican II helped in many ways to revitalize, renew, and move the Catholic Church forward, the Catholic Church today still faces many challenges. The tragic sight of the fire burning through the roof of Paris's iconic cathedral, Notre Dame, at the beginning of Holy Week in 2019, is symbolic of a church under threat. One challenge is declining numbers, a function of both an advancing secularism in many countries as well as the loss of Catholics to evangelical and especially Pentecostal communities.

---

[14] Markey, "Future of the Vatican II Revolution," 18.

Another is the sexual abuse scandal, now recognized as a global problem. The shortage of priests is another challenge not yet faced. So too is the challenge of how to be church in an increasingly intercultural and religiously diverse world, one that will demand a decentralization that gives greater authority to national and regional churches. Finally, there is the unpredictable fallout from global and regional pandemics that we have experienced in recent years.

There are other issues not adequately addressed. There is the perennial problem of internal tensions and external conflicts. Some are conflicts with governments, with changing cultures, other churches, or other religions; others are polarities that divide Catholics internally, threatening the church's unity. We need to consider these challenges.

Declining Numbers

Latin America is home to 425 million Catholics. But with the growth of evangelical and Pentecostal Christianity, the Catholic Church began losing tens of millions of members, radically changing the religious demographics of Latin America. Pentecostals now claim 70 percent of all Latin American Protestants. David Stoll's 1990 book, *Is Latin America Turning Protestant?*—though more measured than that of some commentators—is symptomatic of this change.[15]

With its emphasis on the supernatural, expressive worship, prayers for healing, and often preaching the so-called prosperity gospel (which promises financial reward for following Jesus), Pentecostalism in its various forms has proved particularly attractive to the poor of Latin America. Pentecostals have a zeal for evangelism usually foreign to Catholics, who are often more reticent about sharing their faith. With an emphasis on charismatic giftedness rather than theological education, Pentecostals are more easily able to provide pastors than the Catholic Church with the long training it requires of its priests. The Catholic Church, secure in its cultural monopoly, has tended to wait "for nominal Catholics to come to them for assistance or spiritual support rather than actively recruiting new members to their ranks."[16] Chilean Jesuit Renate Poblete acknowledged

---

[15] David Stoll, *Is Latin America Turning Protestant? The Politics of Evangelical Growth* (Berkeley and Los Angeles: University of California Press, 1990).

[16] See Brian H. Smith, *Religious Politics in Latin America: Pentecostal vs. Catholic* (Notre Dame, IN: University of Notre Dame Press, 1998), 76.

the superficiality of the church's mode of evangelization, attributing the effectiveness of Pentecostals to their emphasis on a subjective experience of God, something long lost sight of in Western theology[17]

However, Catholic losses are not confined to Latin America. The percentage of US Catholics has dropped from 23 percent to 20 percent, with the greatest losses in the Northeast, where 36 percent identified as Catholic in 2009, compared with 27 percent today.[18] Losses are most dramatic among young adults. Fully 36 percent of millennials (those between the ages of eighteen and twenty-four), are disconnected from any religious tradition. They are often called *nones,* for their negative response to questions about their religious affiliation. Just 16 percent of millennials are Catholic, and only 11 percent identify with mainline Protestantism. Evangelical Protestants are roughly one in five.[19] Cardinal Michael Czerny points to "the distance, the non-communication or the gap between the church—the organized church, the institutional church—and the young generation" as the number one challenge faced by the church today.[20]

A new study published by Saint Mary's Press reports that among those Catholics who choose to leave the church, 74 percent do so between the ages of ten and twenty. The study listed three preliminary categories of disaffiliation. "The injured" point to negative experiences with family or church, for example, the death of a loved one, a divorce, long-term illness, or other family issues that caused disruption in their lives. "The drifters" ultimately dropped out because of uncertain faith, lack of engagement with a faith community, or the lack of spiritual companions, whether family or peers. The third group, "the dissenters," are those who disagree with church teachings, particularly on same-sex marriage, birth control, and abortion, though this last reason is complex because many oppose abortion but support a woman's right to choose.[21]

European Christianity is also experiencing significant losses, both in numbers and in general population; Europe is the only region in the

---

[17] Renato Poblete, "The Catholic Church and Latin America's Pentecostals," *Origins* 27, no. 43 (1998): 719–20.

[18] Pew Research Center, "In US, Decline of Christianity Continues at Rapid Pace," October 17, 2019.

[19] Pew Research Center, "America's Changing Religious Landscape," May 12, 2015.

[20] In Gerald O'Connell, "A Jesuit Cardinal-Designate Says Pope Francis Is Making Vatican II Real," *America,* October 3, 2019.

[21] Robert J. McCarty and John M. Vitek, *Going, Going, Gone: The Dynamics of Disaffiliation in Young Catholics* (Winona, MN: Saint Mary's Press, 2017), 13–24.

world where the population continues to decline. The Pew Research Center predicts a population loss of almost 50 million between 2010 and 2050, while predictions see the number of Christians dropping by about 100 million, from roughly 553 million to 454 million. In many European countries church membership and attendance continue to drop. For example, according to the *Guardian,* weekly church attendance in the Church of England has fallen for the first time to less than 1 million, that is, to less than 2 percent of the population.[22] In Germany, the Catholic Church lost over 215,000 members in 2018; Protestant churches lost some 220,000 members.

In the period between 2010 and 2015, Christian deaths in Europe outnumbered births by nearly 6 million. "This natural *decrease* in Europe's aging Christian population was unique compared with Christians in other parts of the world and other religious groups."[23] Reasons for the decline include the low fertility rate across the continent, the fact that most Christians are older—with a median age of forty-two as of 2010—and the increasing number of those leaving Christianity. The number of those not identifying with any religious group is expected to grow from 19 percent in 2010 to 23 percent by 2050.[24]

European Christianity has the lowest annual growth rate (0.16 percent), while its share of the world's Christian population has shrunk from 66 percent in 1900 to 23 percent today. This means that Europe no longer dominates global Christianity as it did in the past. However, as the churches in Europe and North America continue to lose members, the growth of the church in the Global South—Asia, Africa, and Latin America—is remarkable, as we have noted. Much of this growth has been in the church's evangelical, Pentecostal, and neo-Pentecostal expressions, though in European countries (except Portugal), they remain a small minority, less than 2 percent. These renewalist communities continue to grow in the rest of the world; yet even here, according to the Pew Forum, there are signs of the disaffiliation of adults under forty, especially evident in Australia, Latin America, South Korea, and Japan.

---

[22] Harriet Sherwood, "Church of England Weekly Attendance Falls Below 1M for First Time," *Guardian,* January 12, 2015.

[23] Conrad Hacket and David McClendon, "Christians Remain World's Largest Religious Group, But They Are Declining in Europe," Pew Research Center, April 5, 2017.

[24] David Masci, "Europe Projected to Retain Its Christian Majority, But Religious Minorities Will Grow," Pew Research Center, April 15, 2015.

Clergy Sexual Abuse

Beyond its declining numbers in Europe and North America, the sexual abuse of minors by clergy has seriously damaged the Catholic Church, a scandal that will surface repeatedly in this study.[25] The worst crisis the church has faced since the Reformation, it has made evident the detrimental effects of the clerical culture that so characterizes the Catholic Church.

One of the first to report on the crisis, long before the 2002 *Boston Globe* exposé, was Jason Barry, a Georgetown University graduate and journalist based in New Orleans. In 1985, he published an article in the *National Catholic Reporter* on sexual abuse by clergy, focusing on Louisiana. His book, *Lead Us Not into Temptation,* appeared in 1992.[26] Other stories followed.

Pressure, especially from the media, forced bishops in the United States to confront the scandal from at least the late 1980s, though they were slow to respond. Initially, they sent offending priests to various treatment centers specializing in alcoholism and other addictive behaviors, including sexual abuse, only to learn from tragic experience that psychological interventions were not sufficient. The pathology was much deeper. After their meeting in Dallas in 2002, they put in place the "Charter for the Protection of Children and Young People," known as the Dallas Charter. One of its provisions was "zero tolerance" for any church minister, priest, or deacon credibly accused of sexual abuse of a minor, permanently removing him from ministry. Though cases of abuse began to drop significantly after 1985, the results of the Dallas Charter were dramatic. However, it did not deal with bishops who reassigned offending priests or covered up their offenses. The full body of bishops approved the Dallas Charter in 2002, revising it in 2005, 2011, and 2018.[27] The church in Canada

---

[25] The September 2019 issue of *Theological Studies* is entirely dedicated to the sexual abuse crisis.

[26] Jason Barry, "Priest Child Abuse Cases Victimizing Families; Bishops Lack Policy Response," *National Catholic Reporter,* June 7, 1985; idem, *Lead Us Not into Temptation: Catholic Priests and the Sexual Abuse of Children* (New York: Doubleday, 1994).

[27] United States Conference of Catholic Bishops, "Charter for the Protection of Children and Young People," 2002–18, available at usccb.org. See also the two studies done by the John Jay College of Criminal Justice, commissioned by the USCCB: *The Nature and Scope of Sexual Abuse by Minors by Catholic Priests and Deacons in the United States, 1950–2002* (February 2004), and *The Causes and Context of Sexual Abuse of Minors by Catholics Priests in the United States, 1950–2010* (March 2011).

has a similar policy in place. In the United States at least fifteen dioceses have had to declare bankruptcy after paying out millions of dollars to compensate victims.

Though originally dismissed by some in Rome as "an American problem," reports of sexual abuse surfaced in Germany in 2010 at the exclusive Jesuit prep school in Berlin, Canisius College; and then it appeared in Belgium, France, Holland, Austria, Ireland, and Australia. Four different studies since 2005 in Ireland report thousands of children suffering various kinds of abuse. The damage to the once dominant Irish church has been devastating. The crisis also surfaced in Chile, after Pope Francis appointed Bishop Juan Barros bishop of Osorno against the advice of several Chilean bishops. They opposed Barros's appointment because of his relationship with Father Fernando Karadima, a popular priest forced into retirement in 2011 for abusing children. Because the Vatican continued to support Barros, so did Francis until an investigation by Archbishop Charles Scicluna of Malta, the Vatican's expert on clergy sexual abuse, forced him to change his position. He subsequently apologized to the Chilean church.

The various studies on the numbers of children injured were overwhelming. In Ireland, four separate reports concluded that thousands of children suffered various kinds of abuse in Catholic institutions or at the hands of clergy. Released in 2018, a report commissioned by the German Bishops' Conference documents the abuse of more than thirty-six hundred children between 1946 and 2014. Some 4.4 percent of the clergy were involved. Still another report in the same year reveals that more than half of the Dutch bishops had covered up the sexual abuse of children between 1945 and 2010, though the bishops stated that this had been public knowledge since 2011 and a strict code of conduct had been in place since then. In Australia, a 2017 report from the Royal Commission in Australia found 4,444 cases of abuse at more than 1,000 Catholic institutions between 1950 and 2010. Canada has also had many cases of abuse, particularly in schools for its First Nations students.

The sexual abuse of others, not just minors but sometimes religious sisters, is a global problem. However, because of cultural differences, reluctance to talk about issues of sexuality, and the lack of media attention in some countries, the crisis is not as obvious in other parts of the world. One hears little about it in Asia.

Shortage of Priests

Another challenge facing the Catholic Church is the shortage of priests. In the United States the number of priests active in ministry is rapidly diminishing. The statistics are alarming. In 1965, there were 58,632 priests in the United States, with 94 percent of them in active ministry. By 2014, the number had dropped to 38,275, with only 68 percent active. By 2019, half of all these active priests had reached the minimum retirement age of seventy. Simply put, the church is running out of priests.

Nor are many coming after them. The number of graduate-level seminarians is almost half of what it was in 1970, dropping from 6,602 then to 3,650 in 2015. That year, 3,533 out of 17,337 parishes lacked a resident pastor. This is especially a problem in the Northeast and Upper Midwest, as the Catholic population continues to diminish in these regions and grows in the South and Southwest. For example, in 2015, the Diocese of Green Bay, Wisconsin, had sixty-four active diocesan priests and 157 parishes. Parishes in the United States are increasingly dependent on foreign-born priests, today some 30 percent of them. While many are fine priests, cultural differences or difficult accents can make them less effective in their ministry.

Bishops in the United States have done little to address the problem beyond stopgap measures such as combining parishes, requiring some priests to pastor several different communities, or building larger churches, resulting in "megachurches" when most Catholics want smaller, more intimate communities. Appointing lay parish life directors gives lay people more significant roles in parish life, and many are gifted pastorally. But it also risks reducing priests to sacramental functionaries, diminishing their role of pastoral leadership.

Compared to the rest of the world, the United States is relatively rich in priests; the situation in many other countries is far worse. In Germany, an acute priest shortage is leading to the clustering of parishes. In Ireland, the average age of priests is seventy, and of the country's eight seminaries, all but one have closed since 1993. Parishes in at least one diocese in Ireland can celebrate mass only on alternating Sundays. In Italy, foreign born, clergy are pastors or administrators for up to 40 percent of the country's parishes. In Australia, 51 percent of the priests in parish ministry are foreign-born and ordinations of those native to Australia is very low. Brazil has only one priest for every ten thousand Catholics, Mexico one for every seven thousand. In the United States, the ratio is about one for every two thousand. In Poland, admission to the country's seminaries is falling, with bishops beginning to worry about a future priest shortage.

Increasing Cultural and Religious Pluralism

The church today lives in a world marked by cultural and religious pluralism. Many of those cultures are increasingly secular, and not all religions are open to dialogue. In an age of social media many of the young are ignorant of the mysteries of their faith, with so much of their information coming from blogs and postings on social media. All of this makes a life of faith increasingly difficult.

Catholic churches in Africa struggle to move beyond their colonial roots to develop a genuine African Christianity. Asian churches, often dismissed as serving "foreign religions," are committed to a threefold dialogue with other religions, cultures, and the poor. In Latin America, Catholics are often divided on how to deal with the poverty of so many, and how to relate to the burgeoning Pentecostal churches, many of them not Catholic friendly. In some countries, especially China, India, and some Islamic countries, Catholic churches must contend with hostile governments, political pressure, lack of religious freedom, or even persecution. They do not always find ecumenical partners, and interreligious contact can lead to violence rather than dialogue. In some countries Catholics are dying for their faith.

These are only some of the challenges the church faces today. Some conflicts come from within. Catholics around the world are frequently polarized between conservatives and liberals, traditionalists and Vatican II Catholics, culture warriors and reformers. They battle over issues of authority, sexuality, liturgy, and politics. Some advocate development and reform on questions of marriage and sexuality; others see this as attempting to change doctrine, accusing those they disagree with of being lacking in orthodoxy. A small but significant number are opposed to Pope Francis's efforts at reform.

The Pandemic

Then, in December 2019, people in Wuhan, China, began falling ill and dying of a respiratory disease subsequently identified as COVID-19, a coronavirus closely related to SARS. Though both China and the United States were slow to respond to the rapid spread of the disease, by March it was recognized as a global pandemic, affecting people in at least 155 countries and territories. By June, Latin America had become the epicenter. As governments struggled to respond, ordering people to self-quarantine and closing schools, restaurants, and businesses, a new vocabulary emerged: *sheltering in place, social distancing, flattening the curve.* Stores and factories closed, streets emptied of traffic, schools began teaching online, and church services were canceled. International travel was greatly reduced, and some countries virtually closed their borders. A cover on the *Economist* showed the blue and white earth against the blackness of space with a sign on it that simply said: "CLOSED."

The poor especially have suffered during the pandemic. In Africa and Latin America they have often been trapped between going out in search of food and being exposed to the virus or staying at home and dying of hunger. In their densely populated communities, working in informal settings, social distancing, and frequent handwashing are often not possible. Some governments have enforced remaining at home, preventing them from going out to buy food.[28] Even before the pandemic, many countries were facing the threat of hunger.[29]

The economic impact of the pandemic will be devastating. With people quarantined, unemployment skyrocketed, with millions out of work. Economies and gross domestic products (GDPs) plunged. People not working cannot spend. With growing fears of a depression, governments faced the burden of providing cash to households and businesses through stimulus programs, tax relief, and guaranteed loans. Families without insurance needed healthcare. Countries with substandard health services struggled to provide adequate care. Even developed countries like the United States and Britain found themselves short of sufficient hospital beds, face masks, ventilators, and specialists. Many health systems were simply overwhelmed. The need for government investment in healthcare has never been more obvious. Furthermore, there are no guarantees that the pandemic won't return once restrictions are lifted. The best hope for control is mass testing until a vaccine can be developed, but sufficient instruments for testing are not yet available.

Church life has also been changed. Around the world, bishops and episcopal conferences suspended public masses in an effort to stem the pandemic. Some proposed creative ways for liturgical participation. For

---

[28] Francis McDonagh et al., "Urban Poor Endure Hunger and Oppression during Lockdown," *Tablet*, May 7, 2020.

[29] World Food Program, "2020 Global Report on Food Crisis," April 20, 2020.

example, on Palm Sunday, one suggestion was to hang green boughs on one's front door in lieu of psalms; another was to read the passion as a family, with members taking on the various parts. Others developed domestic liturgies, prayer services based on readings from scripture, more extended table prayers, or singing psalms together, sometimes setting up home worship spaces. Pastoral ministers have developed creative online services to reach out to parishioners. Some encouraged them to watch and then discuss films with significant religious themes or invited them to conduct their own "liturgies" using the daily readings. Some took a more active part in the church's liturgy by praying the Liturgy of the Hours, either privately or in groups.

As the faithful mourned their inability to take part in the Eucharist, priests and bishops began to celebrate solitary masses, "virtual liturgies," which were then broadcasted on television or live-streamed on the internet. But while these online liturgies have brought some comfort to the isolated or shut-ins, they fail to realize the meaning of the word *liturgy* itself, a work of the people. They are solitary celebrations, clerical, done by a priest alone; the worshiping community is absent.[30]

The Vision of Pope Francis

In his apostolic letter *Evangelii gaudium* Pope Francis sees humanity as at a turning point in history, a period of "epochal change" with rapid advances in science and technology and new information systems leading often to anonymous kinds of power (EG, no. 52).[31] As Massimo Faggioli argues, Francis is both a product of globalization and a pope whose ministry is shaped by the often challenging relationships between a global church and the process of globalization. The church over which he presides is turning toward the Global South and the poor. It will be a church less European, more distant from American Catholicism, more cosmopolitan and pluralist. In some parts of the church this has engendered not insignificant opposition.[32]

---

[30] For a different perspective, see Felix Just, "Real Presence and Virtual Liturgies," Parts I and II, *La Croix International*, April 28–29, 2020.

[31] See Gerard Mannion, ed., *Pope Francis and the Future of Catholicism:* Evangelii Gaudium *and the Papal Agenda* (New York: Cambridge University Press, 2017).

[32] Massimo Faggioli, *The Liminal Papacy of Pope Francis: Moving toward Global Catholicism* (Maryknoll, NY: Orbis Books, 2020).

This calls for new efforts by the church in its mission of evangelization. In his apostolic exhortation Francis calls for a missionary church and for all Catholics to be missionary disciples, demanding a pastoral conversion of all that includes the papacy and the central structures of the universal church. In an October 17, 2015, address marking the fiftieth anniversary of the institution of the Synod of Bishops, he spoke of a "synodal" church: "A synodal Church is a Church which listens, which realizes that listening 'is more than simply hearing' [EG, no. 171]. It is a mutual listening in which everyone has something to learn."

Francis has also made it clear that theology must remain open to the Spirit, as he recently outlined in a remarkable address in 2019. He argued that Catholicism needs to develop a charismatic, evangelical, welcoming theology, a discerning theology that moves beyond the "decadent scholasticism," defensive apologetics, and rigid schemes of the past, what Faggioli describes as "a shift towards a theology shaped by pastorality."[33] Interdisciplinarity should be one of its criteria, with a commitment to *"continually revisit and reconsider tradition,"* remaining open to what Francis calls "the inexhaustible novelties of the Spirit." It should enter into "a sincere dialogue with social and civil institutions, with university and research centers, with religious leaders and with all women and men of good will, for the construction in peace of an inclusive and fraternal society, and also for the care of creation."[34] This means that the church not only evangelizes but may sometimes need to be evangelized itself.

No one can predict the work of the Spirit. Nevertheless, careful attention to the signs of the times may yield some clues. The enormous growth of Pentecostalism today is suggestive. The 1.2 billion Catholics in the world make up about 50 percent of all Christians. Pentecostal or charismatic Christians constitute the next largest group, some 25 percent.[35] And churches in this tradition are the most rapidly growing. Clearly, Pentecostal/charismatic Christianity will play a significant role in the church's future, even affecting what some call a Pentecostalization of Christianity. There are already signs of this in Latin America.[36] According to the Pew Research Center, a

---

[33] Faggioli, 9.

[34] See Pope Francis, "Theology after *Veritatis Gaudium* in the Context of the Mediterranean," June 21, 2019.

[35] Todd M. Johnson et al., "Christianity 2018: More African Christians and Counting Martyrs," *International Bulletin of Mission Research* 42, no. 1 (2018): 22–24.

[36] Thomas M. Landy, "Charismatic Practice Draws Half of Brazilian Catholics," *Catholics and Culture*, July 27, 2018.

median of 40 percent of Latin American Catholics say they are charismatic, incorporating beliefs and practices associated with Pentecostalism into their worship.[37] Robeck's vision, mentioned earlier, may well come true.

In his 1990 encyclical *Redemptoris missio*, Pope John Paul II teaches that "the Spirit's presence and activity affect not only the individuals but also society and history, peoples, cultures and religions," sowing the "seeds of the word" in their existential and religious questioning (RM, no. 28). This means that entering into dialogue with representatives of another religious tradition can no longer be seen as bringing the truth to those in error; it becomes itself a religious act, coming with respect to encounter whatever reflections of God's truth may be present there. It means being open to the Spirit's presence in one's dialogue partners and in their religions. This will be particularly important in Africa and Asia, where interreligious tensions frequently lead to violence.

Pope Francis sees the Spirit working also in nature. In his encyclical *Laudato si'*, he describes nature as "God's art," moving it to a determinate end, dwelling in every living creature, inviting us into relationship (LS, nos. 80, 88). His vision in some ways echoes that of Teilhard de Chardin and is shared by theologians like Elizabeth Johnson and John Haught.[38]

The pope shows his Jesuit formation in his continual emphasis on conscience and discernment. In his apostolic exhortation *Amoris laetitia* he refers eleven times to conscience and twenty-nine times to discernment. In writing about marriage and family life, including his efforts to include those in what he calls "irregular" situations, he calls attention to a "pedagogy of grace" made possible by the power of the Holy Spirit (AL, no. 297), and he places great emphasis on experience. In the English translation of *Amoris laetitia* the word *experience* appears more than eighty times. Neither discernment nor the correct exercise of conscience is possible without paying careful attention to experience. This is in keeping with his principle that "realities are more important than ideas" (EG, no. 231).[39] Faith and the Gospel are more important than rules and doctrines.

Discernment and attention to experience are critical in the efforts to address the problems the church faces as it seeks to inculturate the

---

[37] Pew Research Center, "Religion in Latin America: Widespread Change in a Historically Catholic Region," November 13, 2014.

[38] Elizabeth A. Johnson, *Ask the Beasts: Darwin and the God of Love* (London: Bloomsbury, 2014); John F. Haught, *Making Sense of Evolution: Darwin, God, and the Drama of Life* (Louisville, KY: Westminster John Knox, 2010), 61–65.

[39] "Pope Talks about Tradition, Criticizes Traditionalists," *La Croix International*, June 3, 2019.

gospel in the many and varied cultures in which it now lives, as well as to continue its work for Christian unity. If Christianity today is global, it is often a result of multiple Christianities, not a reconciled church. Attention to the movements of the Spirit may help Catholics to respond to this new situation; they may discover that the church has far more freedom in renewing and shaping its life, even its structures, sacraments, and doctrines, than those whose limited imagination Bernard Lonergan once described as a static, "classicist" worldview.[40]

Of course, Pope Francis's efforts to read the signs of the times and discern where the Spirit may be leading the church have generated considerable opposition from a small group of traditionalist bishops and theologians who accuse him of trying to change doctrine, and even of heresy. In an interview with journalists on his flight back from Romania in June 2019, he criticized those Catholic traditionalists for wanting to "return to the ashes" of the past, rather than use the deep roots of the church's tradition in order to grow, flourish, and move forward. He has even been asked by journalists about a possible schism in the American church, from where much of the opposition is coming.

Conclusion

How can the Catholic Church move toward Pope Francis's vision of the church as a community of missionary disciples? How can it bring the transforming, liberating vision of the gospel to a world so much in need when the church itself is so often polarized and facing so many challenges?

The contemporary church is faced with a diminished authority, brought on at least in part by the scandal of the sexual abuse of minors and women by clergy. It also faces a shortage of priests, internal conflicts, and, in some countries, persecution. Other challenges include new questions in a world increasingly marked by cultural and religious pluralism. Catholic churches in Africa and Asia struggle to find their own voices; they want to develop theologies reflective of their own contexts and spiritualities, to be more at home in their cultures. But despite the significant losses in Western countries and others where new Pentecostal churches continue

---

[40] Bernard J. F. Lonergan, "The Transition from a Classicist World View to Historical Mindedness," in *A Second Collection*, ed. William F. J. Ryan and Bernard J. Tyrrell (London: Darton, Longman and Todd, 1974), 1–9.

to attract millions of Catholics into their congregations, the Catholic Church continues to grow.

The Second Vatican Council initiated a renewal, both in the church's inner life and in its outward mission, rediscovering the presence of the Spirit not just in the hierarchy but in the entire people of God as well as in other cultures, religions, and the world itself. Francis has worked to better realize that vision in a church now truly global. Certainly, the coronavirus pandemic that overtook the world in 2020 has helped demonstrate how closely we are related to one another. In a much quoted phrase, Francis sees the church as a "field hospital after a battle," concerned not so much with diagnosis but with healing the wounds and warming the hearts of the faithful.[41] Instead of a defensive apologetics, he speaks of the inexhaustible novelties of the Spirit. He continues to stress the importance of ecumenical and interreligious relations. His special concerns include the poor, the marginal, migrants, and efforts to heal our damaged planet. In his encyclical, *Laudato si'* he calls on all to protect our "common home," described by Saint Francis of Assisi as "Our Sister, Mother Earth," who now cries out to us because of the harm we have inflicted on her by our irresponsible use and abuse of the goods with which God has endowed her (LS, nos. 1–2).

---

[41] See Antonio Spadaro, "A Big Heart Open to God: An Interview with Pope Francis," *America*, September 30, 2013.

2

North America

The Catholic roots of the North American continent are not always recognized today, even by Catholics. As the late Kevin Starr points out in *Continental Ambitions,* the establishment of the Catholic colonies of New Spain, New France, and Maryland means that Catholics were not so much immigrants as founding members of the American experience. Catholicism was not a Johnny-come-lately to North America.

Starr argues that the Spanish founding of New Spain brought European urbanism to North America, and it was to spread. Catholic missionaries in New Spain, New France, as well as Texas, New Mexico, Arizona, and California sought to bring the indigenous peoples into the faith and established churches. In many cases they succeeded, though Starr does not ignore the violence, destabilizing of native cultures, and disease that often accompanied their efforts. The intermarriage of Spaniards and Native Americans in lands under Spanish administration produced a new, mixed-race people, while the short-lived Catholic colony of Maryland established Catholic culture in the Chesapeake region.[1] Today, the Catholic Church is the largest in the three nations that are at least in part the inheritors of this tradition, Canada, Mexico, and the United States.

Canada

Catholics in Canada make up the country's largest church, with 40 percent of the population, some 13 million members. The faith arrived in 1497

---

[1] Kevin Starr, *Continental Ambitions: Roman Catholics in North America: The Colonial Experience* (San Francisco: Ignatius Press, 2016).

with John Cabot, who landed in Newfoundland and claimed the land for England's King Henry VII. In 1608, Samuel de Champlain, a French explorer and colonist, founded the first Catholic colony at Quebec. With French influence came missionaries, including in 1610, a secular priest, Jessé Fleché, who apparently baptized native peoples indiscriminately. A year later the Jesuits arrived and sought to learn the native peoples' languages and properly instruct them. After the French and Indian War (1754–63), New France became a British colony, though British sovereigns protected the rights of Catholics in Canada, and the church continued to grow.

During the nineteenth century considerable anti-Catholic feeling surfaced from Presbyterian and Protestant Irish immigrants, much of it over the continued use of the French language, reflecting differences in language and culture. This led to a struggle for control of the church, pitting French-speaking Catholics in Quebec against Irish-speaking Catholics based in Ontario who joined with Protestants over the language to be used in schools. Gradually the Irish gained the upper hand over the churches in all the provinces except Quebec. The Official Languages Acts of 1969 gave normative status to both languages, making the country officially bilingual.

Canadian Catholicism flourished after the Second Vatican Council; the country produced a number of outstanding theologians, among them Gregory Baum, J. M. R. Tillard, R. A. F. MacKenzie, David Stanley, and Bernard Lonergan. After the promulgation of Pope Paul VI's encyclical *Humanae vitae* in 1968, Catholicism began a slide into decline and polarization, though in a typically Canadian nonconfrontational fashion.

Francophone Canada was once the greatest center of French Catholic piety outside France. Everywhere in Quebec it has left its mark on street and place names, monuments, and churches. Today, however, little is left save for these reminders. In the province of Quebec, mass attendance is about 11 percent, but in Montreal, the largest city in the province, it drops to 2–4 percent. Few French-speaking Canadians celebrate their marriages in the church. An anticlerical movement beginning in the 1960s, the Quiet Revolution, sought to disconnect the union of Catholicism and culture so long dominant. Schools and hospitals were virtually secularized. One article's author argues that progressive Catholics, including members of the Jesuit and Dominican orders, were in part responsible for a more independent laity "where people thought and acted more freely."[2] Nor is

---

[2] M. D. and Erasmus, "Why Francophone Canada Is So Post-Catholic a Place," *Economist*, September 23, 2016.

the weakening of the Canadian religious practice limited to Francophone Canada or just to Catholics.

A 2015 study by the Angus Reid Institute reports that 30 percent of Canadians are inclined to embrace religion, 26 percent are inclined to reject it, and 44 percent lie somewhere in between. More than half of those in the "inclined to embrace" category attend services at least once a month. They tend to be more conservative in their views on sex, sexual orientation, and abortion.[3] In 2019, the National Trust of Canada announced that one-third of the country's churches, nine thousand, would close in the next ten years. According to a report presented to the Anglican Church of Canada, if the current rate of decline continues, the church will run out of members in just over twenty years.

The majority of Catholics are not so much leaving the faith as not regularly practicing it. In the 1960s, 80 percent were present weekly at mass; today the number is 15 percent, and considerably less in Quebec. Most make their own decisions on ethical and moral questions, while large numbers disagree over issues like sexual behavior, abortion, sexual orientation, the role of women, and divorce. Thus, there is a split between most Catholics and the official church.

The sexual abuse scandal has also embarrassed the church in Canada. Most provinces report stories of sexual abuse. Many center in Newfoundland, which has a long and tragic history in First Nations schools, that is, schools for the children of indigenous peoples. In response to the scandal the Canadian Catholic bishops in 2018 published new national guidelines, pledging to welcome and support victims, reaffirming the policy of not returning offending priests to ministry—often called zero tolerance—and ending with a confidentiality clause regarding settlements, mandating full background checks, and cooperating with civil authorities. Father Federico Lombardi, coordinator of the February meeting of the heads of the world's episcopal conferences with Pope Francis, commended the Canadian guidelines shortly before the meeting opened.

Mexico

Catholicism in Mexico dates from the Spanish conquest of the Aztec Empire (1519–21) under Hernán Cortés. For several centuries the Catholic

---

[3] Angus Reid Institute, "Religion and Faith in Canada Today: Strong Belief, Ambivalence, and Rejection Define Our Views," March 26, 2015.

Church was the only church, and it played a significant role in Mexican life. However, after Mexico won independence from Spain in 1821, a long struggle followed to separate church and state. The church fought to preserve its religious freedom, while the state attempted to curtail the church's power. The enactment of a series of anticlerical laws nationalized church properties and took away basic civil and political rights from the clergy and religious communities, including the right to wear habits or clerical dress in public. Marriage became a civil, not a religious institution. Porfirio Diaz, who served as president for thirty-one years between 1877 and 1911, was friendlier to the church; he did not enforce the anticlerical laws, but he left them in place. The Constitution of 1917 further strengthened the state's power against the church.

Plutarco Elías Calles, who was elected president in 1924, sought to enforce the anticlerical laws with new energy. Imposing the registration of the clergy, he put them under the authority of the state rather than the bishops and denied foreign priests licenses, thus excluding them from Mexico. He closed churches, forced some priests to marry, and killed others. The church fought back by refusing to celebrate mass or the sacraments, bringing the conflict into the lives of the people. The result was the Cristero War (1926–29), which cost the lives of ninety thousand people. Calles's successor, Lázaro Cárdenas, was less confrontational, but he again left the anticlerical articles on the books; in 1935, his government nationalized all the churches, even private homes that had been used for religious services or schools. He also encouraged the few Protestant missionaries in the country. The long conflict finally ended with the election of Avila Camacho (1940–46).

The Second Vatican Council brought significant changes to Mexico's Catholic Church. Some, like the bishop of Cuernavaca, Sergio Méndez Arceo, whose episcopal ministry was reshaped by the council, sought a renewal that would benefit the poor. Often called a "Red" bishop, Dom Sergio supported the basic ecclesial communities. He also encouraged Ivan Illich, an Austrian philosopher who began the Intercultural Documentation Center (CIDOC), an "inverse mission" in Cuernavaca. With courses on language and culture its purpose was to sensitize missionaries from North America to the Latin American reality. Illich called it "de-Yankeefication." Another advocate of liberation theology was Bishop Samuel Ruiz of San Cristóbal in Chiapas, the state with the largest number of indigenous people. Training hundreds of catechists and ordaining indigenous deacons got him in trouble with Rome, which banned the ordinations, a rule Pope Francis later reversed.

Today, Mexico has the second highest number of Catholics in the world, and most have maintained their Catholic faith. However, the number of Protestants has also grown. In 2014, Catholics constituted 69 percent of the population, down from 90 percent in 1960. Nevertheless, a Pew Study Forum says that 81 percent of Mexican adults still identify as Catholics. The state of Chiapas has the highest percentage of Protestants, many of them evangelicals. In some Chiapas communities authorities have persecuted Protestants, cutting off their water supply and denying them burial in sites belonging to traditional churches for not contributing to funds for religious festivals.

The United States

For the Catholic Church in the United States, the offspring of the early English, French, and Spanish immigrant communities, polarities are nothing new. In the late nineteenth century tensions between the "Americanists" and more conservative traditionalists about how the Catholic Church in the United States should find its identity led ultimately to a Roman intervention. The Americanists saw American democracy as compatible with Catholicism, and many embraced the Protestant vision of America as the new Israel, God's chosen. They sought to incorporate American social and political values into the life of the Catholic Church in the United States, including the separation of church and state, lay participation in decision making, and a state-supported school system, with some provision for after-hours religious instruction. Some objected to the independence from episcopal control of the religious orders. Paulist founder, Isaac Hecker, in particular, was associated with Americanist ideas.

The Americanists included John Ireland, archbishop of St. Paul, Minnesota; Bishop John Keane, rector of the newly founded Catholic University of America; and Denis O'Connell, rector of the American College in Rome. Cardinal James Gibbons, archbishop of Baltimore, was generally sympathetic, as were magazines like the Paulist Fathers' *Catholic World* and Notre Dame's *Ave Maria*. The other side included Archbishop Michael Corrigan of New York; Bishop Bernard McQuaid of Rochester; the German American bishops of the Midwest, who favored ethnic parishes with

German-language instruction in the parish schools; and the Jesuits in the United States and in Rome, along with their Roman journal, *La Civiltà Cattolica*. Archbishop Ireland's efforts to Americanize the US Catholic Church led to conflicts with German American Catholics and especially with Byzantine or Eastern Rite Catholics, whose unique traditions he failed to appreciate. When the bishops imposed the discipline of celibacy on Byzantine Rite priests in the United States in 1893, twenty thousand left the Catholic Church and became Russian Orthodox, and many others followed later.

In 1891, Walter Elliott published his laudatory biography of Isaac Hecker, founder of the Paulist Fathers. Translated into French six years later, the book became immensely popular but also controversial. Hecker's enthusiasm for American values, freedom, individual rights, the Spirit working in the faithful, and democracy exacerbated tensions between progressives supporting the French Third Republic and others, conservative and royalists, who saw in such beliefs a heresy they called Americanism. They thought these beliefs smacked of liberalism. The result was Pope Leo XIII's 1899 encyclical, *Testem benevolentiae*, which cautioned against importing American ideas into Europe and rejecting, in particular, freedom of the press. The Roman intervention ended the controversy, though doubts remain as to whether such a heresy really existed. Many understood that the encyclical addressed issues in France more than in the United States.[4]

The Americanist controversy was only one of many. Controversy over the Second Vatican Council and its implementation left the Catholic Church highly polarized. In 1996, Cardinal Joseph Bernardin, archbishop of Chicago, launched the Common Ground Initiative with the assistance of Msgr. Philip J. Murnion, founder of the National Pastoral Life Center. The purpose of the initiative was to begin a respectful dialogue among US Catholics on some of the issues that divided them, with the hope of bringing about greater communion. However, not all members of the hierarchy supported the initiative; several leading cardinals—among them William Baum, formerly of Washington, DC; his successor, James Hickey; and Bernard Law of Boston—opposed it. Only Cardinal Roger Mahony of Los Angeles joined Bernardin in support.

---

[4] See James J. Hennesey, *American Catholics: A History of the Roman Catholic Community in the United States* (New York: Oxford University Press, 1981), 184–203.

The divisions were very real. And they are equally real today. As of 2017, there are 70,412,021 registered Catholics in the United States, 22 percent of the population. They represent the largest faith community, and they are highly diverse. In recent years immigration and other demographic changes have transformed their distribution. As parishes and Catholic schools in the Northeast and upper Midwest are forced to merge or close because of declining attendance, institutions in the South and West cannot keep up with their growth. When I studied in North Carolina in the early 1970s, there were fewer Catholics in that state than in any other, only 0.5 percent. Today, Charlotte has the largest parish in the country. In the Archdiocese of Atlanta, the Catholic population increased by 259 percent between 2000 and 2010.

Immigration is a driving force behind these changed demographics.

People of color—Latinos, African Americans, Asian Americans, Native Americans, and others—make up more than half of US Catholics born since Vatican II. Latinos alone account for 71 percent of the U.S. Catholic population's growth since 1960. Today, they compose about 38 percent of US Catholics, and well over half of Catholics under the age of forty.[5]

But Catholic diversity is more than ethnic. We have conservative and liberal Catholics, social-justice Catholics and members of Opus Dei, LGBTQ Catholics and Latin mass Catholics, members of the Catholic Worker Movement and of Legatus, Latino Catholics and Catholics less sympathetic to immigrants, culture warriors and social activists, and so on.

On the left, progressive or liberal Catholics advocate for a number of issues, including the ordination of married men and women, using inclusive language, sometimes including non-trinitarian blessings, and a greater acceptance of the LGBTQ community. Others see a significant division between academic theology and the pastoral life of the church, leading to a distrust of many of our best theologians by more conservative Catholics and their media. Still others are concerned about the theological illiteracy of so many students, who are unable to give a coherent account of what salvation means or summarize the gospel message.

---

[5] Susan Bigelow Reynolds, "Way Stations for a Pilgrim Church," *Commonweal* 147, no. 4 (April 2020): 25; see also Brett C. Hoover, "Joy and Strain in Shared Parish Life: Look Who's Here," *Commonweal* 147, no. 3 (March 2020): 32–37.

The Catholic Right

On the right, a conservative Catholic subculture has gained strength, driven by conservative writers, journalists, and bloggers, as well as by a group of neoconservative political writers that includes Michael Novak, Richard John Neuhaus, and George Weigel. While Neuhaus died in 2009 and Novak in 2017, the conservative subculture they helped shape has continued to grow, expanded by those opposed to the policies of Pope Francis.[6]

Right-wing media include magazines like *The Wanderer*, *The New Oxford Review*, and *Crisis Magazine*, and websites such as the Roman Catholic Faithful, Church Militant, LifeSiteNews, Catholics Online, and the Ruth Institute. Consistently criticizing theologians, bishops with whom they disagree, or the leadership of the church in the United States, these writers and magazines accuse each of modernism, caving in to contemporary culture, lack of courage, and even heresy. In the past some magazines like *The Wanderer* sought to exploit differences between the church in the United States and Rome, attacking bishops by name for policies it disagreed with or encouraging Catholics to write to the Congregation of the Doctrine of the Faith with their complaints.

Stephen Brady, president of the website Roman Catholic Faithful, ceased publishing his blog in July 2009, judging that the "conciliar church is corrupt from top to bottom." He advised his readers to give up on their "Novus Ordo" parishes and join Traditionalist Catholics in Latin mass communities, including the schismatic Society of St. Pius X, the Fraternity of Saint Peter, and the Institute of Christ the King Sovereign Priest.[7] Conservative commentators and magazines such as *The New Oxford Review* and *Crisis* have never been happy with Pope Francis's efforts at reform, and Raymond Arroyo at EWTN (Eternal Word Television Network) brings on guests who openly attack Pope Francis.

Others, like Deacon Keith Fournier's website Catholic Online, combine right-wing politics with a fundamentalist piety. Typical headlines include: "Traitorous liar Paul Ryan tries to deceive voters after supporting Obama's radical agenda," "Nancy Pelosi, boasting of her devout Catholic faith, is a

---

[6] See Mary Ellen Konieczny, Charles C. Camosy, and Tricia C. Bruce, eds., *Polarization in the US Catholic Church: Naming the Wounds, Beginning to Heal* (Collegeville, MN: Liturgical Press, 2016), xiii. See also James Davison Hunter, *Culture Wars: The Struggle to Define America* (New York: Basic Books, 1991).

[7] "A Message from Stephen Brady," July 2009, http://www.rcf.org/RCFgoodbye.pdf.

heretic," "Stunning photo shows soul leaving the body," "Statue of Virgin Mary weeping: Is this a warning?" Articles on the site have argued that Barak Obama is really a Muslim.

In 2017, Jesuit Father James Martin published *Building a Bridge: How the Catholic Church and the LGBT Community Can Enter into a Relationship of Respect, Compassion, and Trust*, a book praised by Cardinal Kevin Farrell, head of the Vatican office for the Laity, Family and Life. Nevertheless, the book inspired considerable criticism from the right wing. In September, the Catholic University of America's Theological College canceled a scheduled talk by Father Martin, claiming "increasingly negative feedback from various social media sites." The sites included Church Militant and a priest, John Zuhlsdorf, a conservative blogger who accused Martin of promoting a "homosexualist agenda."

In a commentary San Diego Bishop Robert McElroy called Martin's book a serious work fully consistent with Catholic teaching. He described the attacks on Martin as an example of a "cancer of vilification seeping into the institutional life of the church," in this case, part of a long history of bigotry driven by homophobia, a distortion of fundamental Catholic moral theology, and a veiled attack on Pope Francis and his campaign against judgmentalism in the church.[8] Pressure from the website Church Militant also led Madonna University to cancel a talk on Pope Francis's social agenda by Boston College theologian M. Shawn Copeland, a former president of the Catholic Theological Society of America and alumna of Madonna. In late September 2019, Pope Francis invited Martin to a private meeting, which was widely seen as a vote of confidence in his ministry.

The Neoconservatives

Neoconservatives Michael Novak, Richard John Neuhaus, and George Weigel were more intellectual in their criticism. Their goal was to forge a new Catholic identity that integrated Catholic social teaching with conservative politics.[9] Novak and Neuhaus were originally liberal in their politics; both were involved in the antiwar movement. Neuhaus, a Lutheran pastor, became a Catholic in 1990 and was reordained as a priest. He worked for civil rights, while Novak wrote on issues related to

---

[8] Robert W. McElroy, "Bishop McElroy: Attacks on Father James Martin Expose a Cancer within the US Catholic Church," *America*, September 18, 2017.

[9] See Todd Scribner, *A Partisan Church: American Catholicism and the Rise of Neoconservative Catholics* (Washington, DC: Catholic University of America Press, 2015).

the church and American political/economic life. However, both began moving toward the right during the 1970s and became associated with Reagan Republicanism, or, in Novak's words, "democratic capitalism." Neuhaus founded the conservative journal *First Things* in 1990 and with Charles Colson established an unofficial Catholic/evangelical dialogue called Evangelicals and Catholics Together.

George Weigel was a generation younger. He also moved from a liberal stance, working for peace with the World Without War Council, to embrace neoconservatism and the Reagan Revolution. He later became an unofficial advisor to George Bush, familiarizing him with Catholic social teaching and the language of a "culture of life." One of Pope John Paul II's biographers, he campaigned to gain him the title John Paul the Great.

In the 1980s, these neoconservative Catholics, convinced that the National Conference of Catholic Bishops, as it was then known, was dominated by the conference's liberal staffers, began to argue that what too often was presented as church teaching or policy more accurately represented the views of the elites in the universities and media. That is, they saw these views as quasi-socialist, supportive of liberation theology and other liberationist movements, and out of sympathy with mainstream Catholicism. As priests and even some bishops became radicalized and increasingly spoke out on social issues, the neoconservatives argued that a political Catholicism had begun to replace the church's transcendent concerns with leftist politics.

Jesuit theologian, and later cardinal, Avery Dulles shared some of their concerns; he lamented that "the politicization of the Gospel and the tendency to equate the Kingdom of God with the results of human efforts to build a just society" were substituting a social-justice agenda for the church's mission.[10] Part of the neoconservatives' objection was to what Novak described as a "confusion of roles," with the clergy taking over roles properly belonging to the laity, leading to subtle new forms of clericalism.[11]

The success of these neoconservative Catholic intellectuals in helping clothe the political initiatives of the Republican Party in the language of Catholic morality—while saying little about recent papal teachings on the death penalty, preemptive war, or justice for the poor—helped create the idea that Catholic faith committed Catholics to right-wing politics or the

---

[10] Avery Dulles, "The Gospel, The Church, and Politics," *Origins*, February 19, 1987.

[11] See Michael Novak, "What Can the Laity Teach the Church," in *Challenge to the Laity*, ed. Russell Barta (Huntington, IN: Our Sunday Visitor, 1980), 53.

Republican Party. Novak's caution about "reclericalizing" the church, not allowing the laity their proper place in the secular, seeking the kingdom of God by engaging in temporal affairs (cf. LG, no. 31) is an important one. However, too often the laity are not that familiar with the church's social teaching or reluctant to support it, evident when 51 percent of white Catholics voted for Donald Trump in 2016.

A New Generation of Catholic Conservatives

A new generation of Catholic conservatives emerged when Ross Douthat, a convert to Catholicism and op-ed columnist for the *New York Times*, delivered the 28th annual Erasmus Lecture, sponsored by *First Things* (October 2015). Entitled "A Crisis of Conservative Catholicism," he lamented that the conservative Catholicism that under Pope John Paul II and Pope Benedict XVI had seemed to leave liberal Catholicism behind was actually in a state of crisis. By way of explanation, he pointed to the sexual abuse crisis that had cast a shadow over John Paul II's final years and discredited a number of leaders of the conservative Catholic renewal. These leaders included Cardinal Bernard Law in Boston and Marcial Maciel, founder of the Legionaries of Christ, as well as those bishops who allowed the cover-up of offending priests to go on so long. Despite this undermining of conservative Catholic optimism, Douthat argued that there was no real alternative, given the waning of liberal Catholicism, aside from its survival in some theology departments and the pages of the *National Catholic Reporter*.

Then came Pope Francis. For Douthat, Francis is the villain in the story. While Francis is not a theological liberal, Douthat sees his "casual, prolix, and occasionally doctrinally ambiguous style," his sense that the church has talked too much about abortion and marriage as offering liberal Catholicism a second chance, opening the door to a mainline Protestantizing or Anglicizing of Catholicism.

Douthat is not a right-wing Catholic. While sympathetic to those who favor the Latin mass and homeschool their children, those are not his choices; nor is he comfortable with the separateness of neoconservative Catholic universities like Ave Maria. His issues are more those of the convert who fears that the church is moving in the direction of what he sees as the doctrinal vagueness of the Protestantism he once practiced. Indeed, in his article on the crisis of conservative Catholicism, he criticized Pope Francis's 2016 apostolic exhortation *Amoris Laetitia,* writing:

"I firmly believe that the proposals to admit remarried Catholics to Communion without an annulment strike at the heart of how the Church has traditionally understood the sacraments, and threaten to unravel (as for some supporters, they are intended to unravel) the Church's entire teaching on sexual ethics."[12]

In April 2019, a group of nineteen priests and academics published an open letter urging the bishops to denounce Pope Francis as a heretic. They object to the pope's approach to the divorced and remarried in his *Amoris laetitia*, his welcoming approach to homosexuals and religious pluralism, and his reaching out to Protestants and Muslims. They also accuse him of not speaking out enough against abortion. LifeSiteNews, a conservative Catholic website, published the letter. Thus, Douthat is not the only intellectual to oppose Pope Francis so openly. But opposition to Pope Francis flows from much more than disagreement over *Amoris laetitia*.

Opposition to Pope Francis

From the beginning of his papacy Francis has worked to reposition the church as a church that goes to the peripheries, a church that is poor and for the poor. This is evident in his apostolic letters, his foreign travel, and his appointment of cardinals, not from traditional cardinatial sees but from poorer nations in the developing world. He sees the cultural context in which the church now lives as a turning point in history, with great advances in science and technology but also with many of our contemporaries barely living, gripped by fear and desperation, even in wealthy countries.

The vision of a transformed church that he sets forth in his apostolic letter *Evangelii gaudium* is of a community of missionary disciples, a transformation that demands a pastoral conversion, not just of the faithful, but also of the papacy and the church's central structures. This was also the call of the Second Vatican Council (EG, nos. 20–33).

Particularly dear to his heart is what he calls the social dimensions of evangelization (EG, no. 176), challenging an economy of exclusion with its new idolatry of money; its ideologies that defend the absolute autonomy of

---

[12] Ross Douthat, "A Crisis of Conservative Catholicism," *First Things*, January 2016. See also Austen Ivereigh, *Wounded Shepherd: Pope Francis and His Struggle to Convert the Catholic Church* (New York: Henry Holt, 2019), 205–10, 277–81; Massimo Faggioli, *The Liminal Papacy of Pope Francis: Moving toward Global Catholicism* (Maryknoll, NY: Orbis Books, 2020), 1–22.

the marketplace and financial speculation; that steal from the poor; and that lead to injustice, exclusion, inequality, and violence (nos. 53–60). Francis wants to help fashion a welcoming church; to reach out to those of other religious traditions, particularly Muslims; to move beyond the culture wars, with their near exclusive focus on abortion and same-sex marriage; and to address the plight of migrants and the environment. All this has caused considerable pushback, especially from some in the United States.

Jesuit Father John O'Malley has referred to the "scandalous" anti-Francis sentiment among conservative American Catholics, including many bishops.[13] Archbishop Carlo Maria Viganò, former apostolic nuncio to the United States, has been particularly outspoken. Historian Massimo Faggioli sees the opposition as headquartered in the United States; he argues that the church is deeply divided, its internal communion already fractured.[14] Some conservative Catholics favor the traditionalist Catholicism of an earlier age. Favorite issues include the defense of religious liberty, traditional marriage, and the unborn, and, for some, the Latin liturgy.

Though the opposition represents only a minority within the United States church, it has been present since the beginning of Francis's papacy and has some powerful, well-funded representatives. Faggioli sees Archbishop Charles Chaput of Philadelphia as its episcopal leader, the journal *First Things* as its intellectual organ, and Cardinal Raymond Burke and Stephen Bannon as leaders of the movement. Burke is the cardinal who publicly opposed Pope Francis over his apostolic exhortation *Amoris laetitia*, charging him with changing Catholic doctrine in suggesting that in some cases, after careful discernment, some divorced and remarried Catholics might receive the sacraments. Burke has since dissociated himself from Bannon and questioned the Catholicism of his neo-populist program to "defend" the civilization of the Judeo-Christian West.

According to Faggioli, opposition to Francis "begins with a few moral issues (marriage and the family, homosexuality, the death penalty), but quickly expands to include critique of Francis's teaching on the economy, the environment, and immigration." One of the pope's critics is Steve Bannon, once chief strategist to President Donald Trump and a cofounder of Breitbart News, a far-right or "alt-right" conservative website. Since

---

[13] In Paul Baumann, "Stalemate: Why the Country and the Church Both Seem Stuck," *La Croix International*, April 13, 2919, first published in *Commonweal*, February 13, 2019.

[14] Céline Hoyeau, interview with Massimo Faggioli, "Communion in the American Church Is 'Already Fractured,'" *La Croix International*, September 13, 2019; see also Nicolas Senèze, *Comment l'Amerique veut changer de pape* (Paris: Bayard Publishing, 2019).

leaving the Trump administration, he has campaigned for various populist, nationalist movements in Europe, for reducing immigration, and defending what he sees as European culture from the threat of Islam.[15]

The Napa Institute, a network of affluent, conservative Catholics with access to likeminded bishops and cardinals, combines conservative theology with libertarian economics. It rarely if ever addresses issues dear to Pope Francis, including the environment, racial and financial inequality, and the plight of migrants in the United States and globally. A conference in July 2019 included Cardinal Burke and George Weigel.

A similar group is Legatus, an organization of affluent Catholic CEOs and business leaders founded by millionaire Tim Busch.[16] In 2015, several high-profile members canceled their membership in protest against what they saw as the organization's anti-gay rhetoric. Many academics are concerned about "advocacy funding" from such conservative philanthropic groups. For example, in 2016 Tim Busch and his wife, Steph, gave a fifteen million dollar gift to the Catholic University of America, which renamed its business school after them. Along with other gifts from the Koch Foundation, the school now stresses libertarian economics.

Thus, the opposition to Francis is not just theological; it is also social, economic, and political. Catholic social teaching rejects ethno-nationalism and the self-interest emerging not just in the United States, but with the right-wing Alternative für Deutschland (AfD) in Germany, Brexit in the United Kingdom, the anti-immigrant policies of Orbán in Hungary and Marine le Pen in France, and the policies of Putin in Russia and Erdogan in Turkey. Catholic social teaching has long been multicultural and internationalist. As a global church it urges multilateral cooperation through organizations such as the United Nations and UNESCO.

Others expressions of the conservative Catholic subculture include Catholics who attribute present problems in the church to the Second Vatican Council or who long for a simpler, less pluralistic, and more authoritative expression of the tradition. Among them, one could mention the Knights of Columbus under the leadership of Supreme Knight Carl Anderson. Early in his career Anderson worked for North Carolina Senator Jesse Helms, one of the most conservative members of Congress; Helms

---

[15] Massimo Faggioli, "Whose Rome? Burke, Bannon, and the Eternal City," *Commonweal*, October 18, 2018.

[16] See Michael Sean Winters, "Weigel Sustains Intellectual Whiplash under Francis," *National Catholic Reporter*, November 27, 2018.

opposed both civil rights legislation and arms control. The Knights have poured money into the support of conservative causes and organizations.

The Latin Mass

Some Catholics still favor the traditional Latin (or Tridentine) mass. Under the last two pontificates, it seemed to be making a comeback, leading some to speak about a reform of the reform, that is, undoing the liturgical renewal of the council. Pope John Paul II allowed bishops to give limited permission for the celebration of the Tridentine mass in 1984 and again in his *motu proprio Ecclesia Dei* in 1988. Pope Benedict XVI went a step further; in his apostolic letter *Summorum pontificum,* issued on July 7, 2007, he granted general permission for priests to celebrate what he called the "extraordinary form" of the Roman Rite using the 1962 edition of the Roman Missal promulgated by Pope John XXIII. Succeeding Pope John's missal was the missal of Paul VI, the Novus Ordo or new order of the mass incorporating the liturgical reforms of the Second Vatican Council, promulgated in 1969.

A number of conservative websites promote the Latin liturgy. They feature Latin chants, altars facing away from the congregation, pre–Vatican II "fiddleback" vestments, solemn pontifical or high masses with special ceremonies celebrated by a bishop or cardinal, assisted by a deacon and subdeacon, sometimes with the celebrant processing in wearing a *cappa magna* ("great cape"), some twenty-two feet of red watered silk carried by two clerics. Some argue for the use of traditional black chasubles at funeral masses rather than the current white ones. And only male servers. One of the more elegant websites is New Liturgical Movement, a beautifully produced website with multiple pictures or videos of solemn liturgies in the traditional form and chants on the audio. Nevertheless, its tastes are antiquarian rather than contemporary. Others are simply negative. Some *sedevacantists* (literally, "with the chair [of Saint Peter] vacant") dismiss popes after Pius XII as false or anti-popes, or refer to the contemporary church as the Novus Ordo Sect. Certain cardinals, bishops, and especially theologians are dismissed as heretics or modernists.

Some newly established religious communities are devoted to preserving the traditional Latin liturgy. The Priestly Fraternity of St. Peter, established in 1988, is a traditionalist society of priests and seminarians. Although originally part of Archbishop Marcel Lefebvre's Society of Saint Pius X, which broke communion with the Catholic Church after the

Second Vatican Council, the Priestly Fraternity is now in communion with the Holy See and runs two seminaries, one in Germany and another in Denton, Nebraska. Another is the Institute of Christ the King Sovereign Priest, a society of apostolic life founded in 1990 by Monsignor Gilles Wach and Father Philippe Mora in Gabon, Africa. Now centered at Gricigliano in the Archdiocese of Florence with a motherhouse and international seminary, the institute is dedicated to celebrating the liturgy according to the 1962 missal of Pope John XXIII.

There is some concern that the number of those attending traditional Latin masses may be declining. Msgr. Charles Pope, from the Archdiocese of Washington, DC, observes that while those few churches that offered the traditional Latin mass in the 1980s or 1990s often had standing room only crowds, today the number of those attending seems to have reached a ceiling. In the Archdiocese of Washington, with five parishes or communities offering the Latin mass, only about one thousand people attend, 0.5 percent of the total number of Catholics attending mass each Sunday.[17] Today, only 475 out of seventeen thousand parishes in the United States (one in every 250 parishes) celebrate the Latin mass. Pope Francis shows little interest in the Tridentine mass. As Allan Figueroa Deck, a keen observer of Francis, observes, "Pope Francis' lack of enthusiasm for the Latin Mass other than as a beautiful relic or 'museum piece' is the result of giving more importance to the pastoral challenges of reality than to restorationist ideologies."[18] It has strong appeal for some, but they probably will remain a small minority.

Cardinal Raymond Burke

One of the great patrons of the Latin mass is Cardinal Raymond Leo Burke. A canonist, he invited the Institute of Christ the King Sovereign Priest to St. Louis while he was the archbishop (2003–8), endowing it with the St. Francis de Sales Oratory, the second largest sanctuary in the archdiocese. He frequently presides at ordinations of its priests both in the United States and abroad. Earlier, while bishop of La Crosse, Wisconsin,

---

[17] Charles Pope, "An Urgent Warning about the Future of the Traditional Latin Mass," *National Catholic Register*, January 7, 2016.

[18] Allan Figueroa Deck, "Understanding Pope Francis: Roots and Horizons of Church Reform," in *New World of Pope Francis: Pope Francis and the Future of the Church*, ed. Michael L. Budde (Eugene, OR: Cascade Books, 2017), 41.

he helped found the Canons Regular of the New Jerusalem, a community of Augustinian canons dedicated to the traditional liturgy.

Burke is the leader of Catholicism's conservative wing and has frequently shown himself to be in opposition to Francis. In 2008, he was called to Rome to head the Apostolic Signatura, the church's highest judicial authority after the pope. In 2010, Pope Benedict XVI named him to the College of Cardinals. He was later appointed to the Congregation for Divine Worship and the powerful Congregation for Bishops, where he was responsible for a number of conservative episcopal appointments in the United States. However, his influence began to wane after the election of Pope Francis.

In 2014, Burke complained that under Francis, "there is a strong sense that the church is like a ship without a helm."[19] Francis later removed him from the Apostolic Signatura and made him patron of the Sovereign Military Order of Malta. The next year he was removed from the Congregation for Bishops, and a year later from the Congregation for Divine Worship. After the publication of *Amoris laetitia* (2016), responding to the synods on the family, Burke, with three other semi-retired cardinals, two of whom have since died, raised five *dubia* (doubts), official questions. They suggested that the apostolic letter's teaching on the possibility of divorced and remarried Catholics receiving communion after careful discernment was contrary to Catholic moral teaching and that the pope might be in need of formal correction. When Francis did not respond to their letter after two months, they released it to the press.

Liturgically, Burke wants the church to return to the traditional practice of celebrating the mass *ad orientem*, with the priest at the head of the people and both facing East. He likes to wear lace albs and the long *cappa magna*. He also has complained about the "feminization" of the church, using the introduction of altar girls as an example. He has long argued that Catholics should not vote for politicians who support abortion, though he later qualified his position somewhat, saying that they could so vote if another more significant moral issue was at stake, something he doubted was possible. He has repeatedly urged refusing communion to Catholic politicians who support legalized abortion and has spoken out frequently against changing attitudes toward gays and lesbians, describing homosexuality as an "ailment" that is not genetic but dependent on

---

[19] Cardinal Raymond Leo Burke, interview with Dario Menor Torres, *Vida Nueva*, October 31, 2014.

environment, a view few hold today. Moreover, he is less than comfortable with the church's efforts under Pope Francis to build bridges with Islam. He writes, "Islam is not just another religious practice that can coexist in harmony with other religions. Islam is a religion that, according to its own interpretation, must also become the State. The Qur'an, and the authentic interpretations of it given by various experts in qur'anic law, is destined to govern the world."[20] But Francis has not ignored Burke; in September 2017, he reappointed him to the Apostolic Signature, although this time simply as a member.

The Cardinal Newman Society

Though it has no official standing in the church, the Cardinal Newman Society is a nonprofit organization founded in 1993 by Fordham University alumnus Patrick Reilly, who was alarmed by Fordham's decision to recognize pro-choice and gay student organizations on campus. His organization's website describes its self-appointed mission as "promoting and defending faithful Catholic education." To do this, it monitors Catholic institutions of higher education, searching websites and statements by professors. Among its goals is to prevent any appearances by pro-choice speakers on Catholic campuses or productions of Eve Ensler's feminist play, *The Vagina Monologues*. He also demands that Catholic professors of theology have the mandatum from ecclesiastical authority, usually the local bishop, prescribed by Pope John Paul II's apostolic constitution *Ex cordae ecclesiae*. The Cardinal Newman Society's fundraising efforts brings in hundreds of thousands of dollars, mostly from small contributors.

The society's tactics include issuing "higher education alerts" and press releases, gathering signatures of protest online, and distributing free literature to Catholic families. It sponsors conferences and newsletters, targeting academics it considers dissidents. The annual *Newman Guide* identifies colleges in the United States and abroad where "students can reasonably expect a faithful Catholic education and a campus culture that generally upholds the values taught in their homes and parishes"[21] and notes which of them make available the Tridentine mass. In 2009, the society led conservative opposition to the University of Notre Dame's awarding

---

[20] Raymond Leo Burke, *Hope for the World: To Unite All Things in Christ, An Interview with Guillaume d'Alançon* (San Francisco: Ignatius Press, 2016), 54.

[21] *The Newman Guide to Choosing a Catholic College: What to Look for and Where to Find It,* ed. Joseph A. Esposito (Merrifield, VA: Cardinal Newman Society, 2007).

an honorary doctorate to President Barrack Obama and inviting him as commencement speaker. It also protested Sister Helen Prejean delivering the commencement address at Notre Dame de Namur in Belmont, California, in 2005, because it judged her a dissenter to Catholic doctrine because she is opposed to the death penalty.

Among others, Charles L. Currie, then president of the Association of Jesuit Colleges and Universities, challenged the society's tactics. He said their "attacks can no longer go unchallenged," adding that their recent activities "follow a long trail of distorted, inaccurate, and often untrue attacks on scholars addressing complex issues." John Beal, a canon law professor at Catholic University of America, calls their characterizing professors heretics as "red-baiting in ecclesiastical garb."[22]

However, some Catholic schools in fact have come close to giving up their Catholic identity. Georgetown University debated for over a year about whether or not to have crucifixes in classrooms, before finally deciding affirmatively in 1998. In 2017, San Dominico, the oldest Catholic school in California, formerly run by the Dominican Sisters of San Rafael, decided to remove its Catholic statues in an effort to be more "forward looking," justifying its action because 80 percent of its families no longer identified as Catholic.[23] So much for its Catholic identity.

Neoconservative Catholic Colleges

Another movement, beginning in the last quarter of the twentieth century, is the establishment of a number of neoconservative Catholic colleges with faculty and student bodies almost exclusively Catholic. Thomas Aquinas College in Santa Paula, California, established in 1971, sponsors a tutorial approach to higher education based on the Great Books. The Franciscan University of Steubenville, refounded by Father Michael Scanlon in 1974 to restore its Catholic heritage, is today 97 percent Catholic. All the professors at Christendom College in Front Royal, Virginia, founded in 1977, are Catholic. They annually make a profession of faith and take the "Oath of Fidelity" before the bishop of Arlington.

Similar institutions established since 2000, promising a "truly Catholic" education, include Ave Maria University in Ave Maria, Florida, founded

---

[22] Michael Kranish, "Group's Church Role Questioned: Organization's Tactics Generate Disputes, Cash," Boston.com News, August 28, 2005.

[23] Christopher White, "California's First Catholic School Removes Its Catholic Statues," *Crux*, August 27, 2017.

in 2003 by Domino's Pizza owner Tom Monaghan. Its student body is 90 percent Catholic, with 94 percent Catholic faculty. At John Paul the Great University in Escondido, California, founded in 2006, students take a course every quarter in some aspect of Catholic theology, philosophy, literature, or culture. The school offers undergraduate degrees in communications media and business as well as an MA in biblical theology and an MBA in film production. With 89 percent of the students and 59 percent of the faculty Catholic, the school is accredited by the Western Association of Schools and Colleges. Wyoming Catholic College, founded in 2007, is 98 percent Catholic, with a 100 percent Catholic faculty. Still small, its program emphasizes Catholic community, spiritual formation, a liberal arts education, an integrated curriculum, the Great Books, immersion in the outdoors, and excellent teaching. Some academic programs are offered online. The Anglicum Academy's Great Books Program, established in 2000 in Colorado Springs, Colorado, offers courses for high school or college credit. It combines a four-year Great Books program with four theology courses taught by Ignatius Press founder Jesuit Father Joseph Fessio. One might ask how these neoconservative colleges, with their virtually all-Catholic student bodies and faculties, can do the dialogue with culture so important to the Catholic mission today.[24]

In his address on the crisis of conservative Catholicism, Douthat observes that far more young American Catholics graduate from colleges and universities "in the Jesuit tradition" than from these more conservative institutions.[25] It is interesting to note that 10 percent of the 116th Congress (2018) are alumni of Jesuit colleges and universities, twelve senators and forty-three representatives.

A New Nationalism

In July 2017, Jesuit Father Antonio Spadaro, editor of the Vatican-vetted *La Civiltà Cattolica*, published an article with Argentine Presbyterian pastor Marcelo Figueroa describing a "surprising ecumenism" bringing together white evangelical fundamentalism and Catholic integralism. The two authors noted with alarm a fusion of religion and state, faith and politics, and religious values and the economy that too often results in an apocalyptic vision of a battle between good and evil.

---

[24] For detailed information on colleges, see "The Newman Guide," on the newman-society.org website.

[25] Douthat, "A Crisis of Conservative Catholicism."

What results is "a sort of 'anesthetic' with regard to ecological disasters and problems generated by climate change." Supported largely by whites in the American South, many of its positions are based on an evangelical fundamentalism that has moved from a Puritan pietism to the prosperity gospel (which promises financial success for following Jesus) proposed by millionaire pastors that has spread throughout the Global South. Evangelical fundamentalists and Catholic integralists have come together to make common cause around issues such as abortion, same-sex marriage, religious education in schools, and other issues important to conservatives. Rather than a traditional ecumenism, they pursue "an ecumenism of conflict that unites them in the nostalgic dream of a theocratic type of state."[26]

One example might be the initiative of Charles Colson and Richard John Neuhaus, Evangelicals and Catholics Together (ECT), an ad hoc dialogue rather than one sponsored by their churches that has frequently been described as an "ecumenism of the trenches," bringing Catholics and evangelicals together for "co-belligerency in the culture wars."[27] Naturally, the article was controversial. Philadelphia Archbishop Charles J. Chaput immediately joined in the debate, seemingly reducing the conflict between this new alliance of Catholics and evangelicals to a defense of religious liberty, an issue that the *La Civiltà Cattolica* authors also acknowledge as under threat. Nevertheless, the article was not simply about evangelicals and Catholics, as Chaput suggested; both belong to broad spectrums of opinion. The two authors were concerned with Catholic integralists—an anti-Enlightenment, ultramontane movement that sought a Catholic foundation for all social or political action, rejecting liberalism, secular humanism, and the historical-critical method in theology—and evangelical fundamentalists. The symbiosis between evangelical Christianity and right-wing white Americanism is of long standing.[28] In the 1970s it emerged as an identifiable movement, the Christian Right, fused with the Republican Party, particularly in the South. It played a significant part in Donald Trump's 2016 election to the presidency, with 81 percent white evangelical support, but also with 52 percent of white Catholics.

---

[26] Antonio Spadaro and Marcelo Figueroa, "Evangelical Fundamentalism and Catholic Integralism in the USA: A Surprising Ecumenism," *La Civiltà Cattolica*, July 2017.

[27] Timothy George, "Charles Colson's 'Ecumenism of the Trenches,'" *National Catholic Register*, April 25, 2012.

[28] See Susan L. Trollinger and William Vance Trollinger, Jr., *Righting America at the Creation Museum* (Baltimore: Johns Hopkins Press, 2016).

On July 10, 2017, a group of evangelical pastors gathered in the Oval Office to lay hands on Trump. Jerry Falwell, Jr., called him a "dream president" for evangelicals, and Franklin Graham said that God had had a hand in his election. Among those invited to pray at his inauguration was Florida megachurch pastor Paula White, a prosperity-gospel advocate. Another early proponent was Norman Vincent Peale, pastor of New York's Marble Collegiate Church, which Trump once attended. Peale presided at Trump's first wedding.[29]

Conservative politicians today deny the evidence for climate change or dismiss it as a Chinese invention. Vice President Pence said recently that since God had a hand in creating Israel, his support for that country is rooted in faith.[30] When President Trump, responding to threats from North Korea's Kim Jong Un in August 2017, threatened Pyongyang with "fire and fury like the world has never seen," Robert Jeffress, one of his evangelical advisers, released a statement saying that "God has given Trump authority to take out Kim Jong Un."[31] In a later interview with Religious News Service Jeffress said, "The Bible has given government the authority to use whatever force necessary, including assassination or war, to topple an evil dictator like Kim Jong Un."[32]

Some of the episcopal culture warriors as well as much of the conservative Catholic press virtually endorsed Trump's campaign, focusing on his conversion, relatively recent, to an anti-abortion stance. Archbishop Chaput wrote that both Donald Trump and Hillary Clinton had "astonishing flaws." But while he argued that Hilary should be under indictment, John Gehring notes that he "somehow manages to never mention that Trump has demonized Mexican immigrants as 'rapists,' branded all Muslims as suspicious, boasts that he doesn't ask God for forgiveness, embraces torture, intimates violence against his opponent, and clashed with Pope Francis over immigration."[33] Many of those bishops who silently supported Trump were distressed when he began

---

[29] Gwenda Blair, "How Norman Vincent Peale Taught Donald Trump to Worship Himself," *Politicomagazine*, October 6, 2015.

[30] Lauren Markoe, "Pence Roots Administration's Support for Israel in Faith," *National Catholic Reporter*, July 18, 2017.

[31] Sarah Pulliam Bailey, "'God Has Given Trump Authority to Take Out Kin Jong Un,' Evangelical Adviser Says," *Washington Post*, August 9, 2017.

[32] In Bobby Ross, Jr., "A Pastor Explains His Politics after Saying That Trump Has Authority to Attack North Korea," Religious News Service, August 15, 2017.

[33] John Gehring, "A False Equivalency: Archbishop Chaput's Dangerous Political Analysis," *Commonweal*, August 16, 2016.

enforcing his anti-immigrant policies, though his views on immigrants had been clear throughout his campaign.

Unfortunately, many young Catholics have concluded that being a Christian means being right wing. As Robert Putnam and David Campbell reported in writing about the dissociation of so many young Americans from religion, by the early twenty-first century many had come to view religion "as judgmental, homophobic, hypocritical, and too political."[34]

More balanced in its public statements is the United States Conference of Catholic Bishops (USCCB). As Father Tom Reese's research indicates, "the number of press releases and the rhetoric used in the releases does not support the contention that the bishops only care about abortion, gay marriage and religious freedom, but the choice of spokespersons does give a higher focus to these issues. Sadly, the strong language of the bishops on immigration, refugees and health care for the poor does not get the attention it deserves."[35] Nationalist voices are also being heard increasingly in Europe.

The Catholic Left

If there is an active conservative Catholic subculture, the Catholic left is also alive and well. It is well populated with groups such as Call to Action, the Catholic Worker Movement, Corpus, Dignity, the Leadership Conference of Women Religious (LCWR), New Ways Ministry, Voice of the Faithful, We Are the Church, and the Women's Ordination Conference, all working for reform within the church's structures. Others, like Catholics for Choice and Roman Catholic Womenpriests, are more marginal to the official church. Here we can only consider some of them.

Call to Action

Call to Action (CTA) grew out of a conference sponsored by the American bishops in Detroit, Michigan, in 1976, though the 1,340 delegates moved considerably beyond where the bishops themselves wanted to go. At this first meeting the delegates recommended that the church should "reevaluate its positions on issues like celibacy for priests, the male-only

---

[34] Robert D. Putnam and David E. Campbell, *American Grace: How Religion Divides and Unites Us* (New York: Simon and Schuster, 2010), 121.

[35] Thomas Reese, "Political Priorities of US Bishops May Surprise You," *National Catholic Reporter*, July 28, 2017.

clergy, homosexuality, [and] birth control" with "the involvement of every level of the church in important decisions."[36] After the conference, approximately four hundred people gathered in Chicago in 1978 to establish Call to Action as a local movement for change, keeping the original name. Dan Daley, one of its founders, describes its dual focus: "One eye was on church institutions which needed reform and renewal, and the other eye was on the larger society and issues of justice and peace that ought to have church involvement. The emphasis has shifted from time to time."[37] After a 1990 Call for Reform in the Catholic Church, developed by the movement's leaders and printed as a full-page ad in the *New York Times* on Ash Wednesday, it became a national organization.

Today, with over twenty-five thousand members and fifty chapters nationally, the CTA embraces a multitude of Catholic organizations working for change. It advocates for women's ordination, an end to clerical celibacy, and the full inclusion of gays and lesbians as well as changes in the church's sexual teaching and governance. While Bishop Thomas Gumbleton, an auxiliary bishop of Detroit, supported CTA, most bishops did not, finding some of its positions contrary to church teaching. Bishop Fabian Bruskewitz of Lincoln, Nebraska, issued an edict leading to automatic excommunication for any member of his diocese who was a CTA member. His successor lifted those excommunications.

Voice of the Faithful

One of the unanticipated results of the sexual abuse scandal that has so convulsed the Catholic Church in the United States is the realization on the part of the laity of how little real say it has in the government of the church. This was first brought home when many who were aware of situations of abuse went to the church authorities and found that nothing was done. But as Catholics began talking to one another about their frustration, they began to realize that while this was the most serious case of not being heard, it was not the only one.

What was becoming evident to many lay people was that there were no institutional checks and balances that allowed them some say about how authority is exercised in the church, whether at the parish, the diocesan, or the universal level. They had no way to address the problem of

---

[36] Mary R. Sawyer, *The Church on the Margins: Living Christian Community* (Harrisburg, PA: Trinity Press International, 2001), 249.

[37] See the cta-usa.org website.

an incompetent pastor or an authoritarian bishop (save for their financial contributions), no say over their appointment, and no way to bring their own concerns and experience to the decision-making processes of the universal church. There were no structures of accountability. Without them, many felt that the church was treating them as children. Moreover, they increasingly saw the sexual abuse crisis as calling them to adult status in the church. This was clearly the intention of the Second Vatican Council in its concern to articulate a theology of the laity.

Though the council rediscovered the dignity of the vocation of the baptized, the church is still struggling to find ways to express fully the laity's share in the church's mission. The idea of the autonomous, monarchical bishop, accountable only to Rome, has more to do with developments in the Late Middle Ages than with anything intrinsic to the office. Donald Cozzens's expression, a "still feudal church,"[38] is too often accurate. Finding effective ways to give laity and clergy some participation in the church's decision-making processes is clearly one of the crucial issues the church faces today.

As a result of the sexual abuse crisis, a new initiative for greater lay involvement has emerged, Voice of the Faithful (VOTF). A lay organization, VOTF has rapidly spread throughout the United States and now comprises more than thirty thousand members and 181 parish affiliates. Its website describes it as a group of Catholics who love and support the Roman Catholic Church; accept its teaching authority, including the role of the bishops and the preeminent role of the pope as the primary teachers and leaders of the church; and believe what the Catholic Church believes. The VOTF mission is "to provide a prayerful voice, attentive to the Spirit, through which the Faithful can actively participate in the governance and guidance of the Catholic Church," while its stated goals include: (1) to support those who have been abused, (2) support priests of integrity; and (3) shape structural change within church.[39] Since July 2002, a Structural Change Working Group has been seeking ways to renew church structures in light of Vatican II, with canon lawyer Jesuit Father Ladislas Orsy as an outside consultant.

The US Catholic bishops have not exactly welcomed the appearance of VOTF. At a 2003 meeting, only ten bishops were willing to meet with the group. Eight bishops, all but one on the East Coast, ordered their pastors

---

[38] Donald Cozzens, *Sacred Silence: Denial and Crisis in the Church* (Collegeville, MN: Liturgical Press, 2002), 6.

[39] Voice of the Faithful, "Who We Are," votf.org.

to refuse VOTF permission to use church facilities for their meetings, though Bishop Thomas Daily of Brooklyn later reversed himself, acknowledging after a dialogue with VOTF leaders that many of those involved were "good and dedicated members of our diocese."[40] Cardinal Francis George of Chicago later expressed some cautions about the movement, but he also pointed out that the VOTF agenda is still in formation and so it should not be dismissed as an expression of dissent.

Leadership Conference of Women Religious

Founded in 1956 as the Conference of Major Superiors of Women as a canonically approved organization designed to represent the congregations of women religious in the United States, the conference changed its name in 1971 to the Leadership Conference of Women Religious (LCWR). Today its fifteen hundred members represent 80 percent of the 48,500 women religious in the United States. More conservative congregations are represented by the Congregations for Institutes of Consecrated Life and Societies of Apostolic Life. The LCWR website describes its mission as follows:

- Assisting its members personally and communally to carry out more collaboratively their service of leadership in order to accomplish further the mission of Christ in today's world.
- Fostering dialogue and collaboration among religious congregations within the church and in the larger society.
- Developing models for initiating and strengthening relationships with groups concerned with the needs of society, thereby maximizing the potential of the conference for effecting change.

However, its work has not been without controversy. In April 2008, Cardinal William Levada, prefect of the Congregation for the Doctrine of the Faith (CDF), announced that his congregation would begin a doctrinal assessment of the LCWR. The assessment would cover three areas: addresses at LCWR assemblies that were theologically or doctrinally problematic; taking positions that dissented from church teaching on the ordination of women; and the prevalence of certain radical feminist themes incompatible

---

[40] Bishop Thomas Daily, "Brooklyn Diocese to Allow Voice of the Faithful Meetings in Church-related Facilities," *Origins* 33, no. 1 (May 15, 2003): 3.

with Catholic faith. In April 2012, the CDF gave its report, calling for a major reform of the LCWR's programs and activities, particularly in the areas of abortion, euthanasia, and homosexuality, and delegating Archbishop J. Peter Sartain of Seattle to work with the conference.

From the beginning the assessment generated negative publicity. Many Catholics saw it as an inquisition, punishing the sisters, who were widely admired for their work running schools, hospitals, and charitable works and for their progressive views. The sisters charged that the accusations were unjust, unsubstantiated, and the process lacking transparency. The LCWR leadership called for further dialogue with the Holy See in a respectful and prayerful spirit of careful listening. They expressed the wish to remain a canonically approved conference, but not at the expense of their mission.

The investigation came to a sudden and unexpected conclusion on April 16, 2015, with a meeting of the LCWR leadership, Archbishop Sartain, and representatives of the CDF. Stating that the goal of oversight had been accomplished, the Vatican press release said that the process had ended in a "spirit of cooperation." Later that day the LCWR leaders had an unprecedented fifty-minute meeting with Pope Francis. Eileen Burke-Sullivan, a theologian at Creighton University, said, "It's about as close to an apology, I would think, as the Catholic Church is officially going to render."[41]

New Ways Ministry

In 1977, Sister Jeannine Gramick and Father Robert Nugent established New Ways Ministry in an effort to gain greater acceptance of the gay and lesbian community (now the LGBTQ community) within the Catholic Church. Its website describes the mission of New Ways Ministry as follows: "Through research, publication and education about homosexuality, we foster dialogue among groups and individuals, identify and combat personal and structural homophobia, work for changes in attitudes and promote the acceptance of LGBT people as full and equal members of church and society."

From the beginning the movement has been controversial. In 1984, Cardinal James Hickey banned it from the Archdiocese of Washington

---

[41] Cited in Laurie Goodstein, "Vatican Ends Battle with US Nuns Group," *The New York Times*, April 16, 2015. See also Joseph J. McElwee, "Vatican Ends Controversial Three-Year Oversight of US Sisters' Leaders," *National Catholic Reporter*, April 16, 2015.

for its failure to support church teaching, while the Vatican ordered Gramick and Nugent to cease working with the organization. In 1999, the Vatican Congregation for the Doctrine of the Faith under Cardinal Joseph Ratzinger condemned its position on homosexuality and ordered Gramick and Nugent to cease their ministry. Nugent complied, returning to parish ministry; he died in 2014. Gramick refused, saying that, for her, it was a question of conscience. She left her community, joining the Sisters of Loretto, who continued to support her ministry. In 2010, Cardinal Francis George, Archbishop of Chicago and president of the United States Conference of Catholic Bishops, stated that the organization's ministry did not present an authentic view of Catholic teaching, a position reaffirmed a year later by the USCCB.

Few bishops extended sympathy by name to the gay and lesbian community after the terrible shooting at a gay nightclub in Orlando, Florida, in June 2016, killing forty-nine, but gays and lesbians continue to experience a greater acceptance from the Catholic community. Some call it the Francis effect. Father James Martin, an editor-at-large of the Jesuit magazine *America*, published a book calling for greater understanding between the LGBT community and the Catholic Church.[42] Cardinal Joseph Tobin, Archbishop of Newark, New Jersey, welcomed one hundred gay and lesbian Catholics to his cathedral in June 2017, saying, "I am Joseph your brother . . . a sinner who finds mercy in the Lord." Such a welcome from a cardinal would have been unthinkable five years earlier. Other bishops have also spoken out in support.

Catholics for Choice

Catholics for Choice (CFC) was established in 1973 (originally called Catholics for a Free Choice) to advocate for women's access to contraception and abortion. In an early effort to publicize its agenda, one of the group's founders, Patricia Fogarty McQuillan, had herself crowned as pope on the steps of St. Patrick's Cathedral in 1974. Another early member was Joseph O'Rourke, then a Jesuit priest, who against his superior's orders baptized a baby before three hundred people on the steps of a church in Marlboro, Massachusetts, after the mother of the child's public advocacy for abortion had led to her parish priest and then Cardinal

---

[42] James Martin, *Building a Bridge: How the Catholic Church and the LGBT Community Can Enter into a Relationship of Respect, Compassion, and Sensitivity* (New York: HarperCollins, 2017).

Humberto Medeiros refusing to allow the baptism. Dismissed from the Jesuits, O'Rourke served briefly as the CFC's president. So the group has long been controversial.

In 1978, Frances Kissling, a former abortion clinic operator and one of the founders of the National Abortion Federation, joined CFC; she became its president in 1982, an office she held until 2007. When Archbishop John Joseph O'Connor objected to Geraldine Ferraro's vice-presidential candidacy in the 1984 presidential election, Kissling placed an advertisement in the *New York Times*, signed by ninety-seven prominent Catholics, among them twenty-four nuns, two brothers, and two priests.[43] The ad included "A Catholic Statement on Pluralism and Abortion," stating that direct abortion can sometimes be a moral choice. The Vatican required most of the nuns who signed the statement to withdraw their names; two refused and later left their communities. CFC has long excelled at getting its name in print. For example, in 1999, it began a highly publicized campaign to have the Holy See's United Nations membership downgraded from Permanent Observer to NGO status, a ploy to deny it a vote.

CFC is an advocacy group with paid employees and some selected volunteers, not a membership organization. Much of its funding comes from secular foundations such as the Ford Foundation, the John D. and Catherine T. MacArthur Foundation, the Rockefeller Foundation, and the Playboy Foundation. The USCCB has long objected that Catholics for a Free Choice and its successor are not authentic Catholic organizations. In 2000, it stated that "CFFC is, practically speaking, an arm of the abortion lobby."[44]

One criticism frequently raised is that CFC claims a Catholicism not practiced by those who represent it. Marjorie Reiley Maguire, a disillusioned former member of the group, was quoted as saying that it was "an anti-woman organization" whose agenda is "the promotion of abortion, the defense of every abortion decision as a good, moral choice and the related agenda of persuading society to cast off any moral constraints about sexual behavior." She added that during her involvement with the group she was never aware that any of its leaders ever attended mass.[45]

---

[43] See Tom Davis, *Sacred Work: Planned Parenthood and Its Clergy Alliance* (New Brunswick, NJ: Rutgers University Press, 2005), 146–47.

[44] Bishop Joseph A. Fiorenza, "NCCB/USCC President Issues Statement on Catholics for a Free Choice," United States Conference of Catholic Bishops, May 10, 2000.

[45] Quoted in Donald DeMarco, "'Catholics for Choice' Is Neither," *National Catholic Register*, January 15, 2008.

Roman Catholic Womenpriests

Some Catholic women, who argue that they have been called to the priesthood, have moved beyond the communion of the church, though they still claim to be Roman Catholics. In June 2002, seven women from Austria, Germany, and the United States took part in an ordination ceremony on a ship in the Danube River, performed by Rómulo Antonio Braschi and two other bishops. From this has come a movement known as Roman Catholic Womenpriests (RCWP). According to its website, it is an international movement to prepare, ordain, and support women called to the priesthood in an inclusive church.

The movement, which as of 2017 included six bishops and over one hundred priests, claims apostolic succession for its ordinations. Braschi is a schismatic bishop; he was ordained by two bishops not in communion with the Roman Catholic Church. RCWP has not released the names of the two ordaining bishops. Another group, the Association of Roman Catholic Women Priests, claims succession from a Roman Catholic bishop in communion with the pope. The two groups cooperate with each other and share resources but are separately administered. The Roman Catholic Church does not recognize the ordinations of either group as valid.

Conclusion

Catholics constitute the largest churches in Canada, Mexico, and the United States. The social ministries of the Catholic Church are exceptional. According to the *Economist,* "of all the organizations that serve America's poor, few do more good work than the Catholic church; its schools and hospitals provide a lifeline for millions."[46] Catholic Charities is the fifth largest charitable organization in the United States, serving one out of five Americans living in poverty. The Catholic Church has resettled nearly one-third of all refugees received by the United States since 1980,[47] while US-based Catholic Relief Service serves nearly 100 million people in need in ninety-three countries.

But the church, once so dominant, continues to lose members and influence. In the United States the situation is critical. In 2018,

---

[46]"The Catholic Church in America: Earthly Concerns," *Economist,* August 18, 2012.

[47] Courtney Grogan, "The Catholic Church's Long History of Resettling Refugees in the U.S.," *Crux,* July 23, 2018.

there were 143,000 Catholic marriages in the United States compared with more than 426,000 in 1970. Infant baptisms numbered 615,000 as against 1.089 million back then. The percentage of Catholics attending Mass weekly fell from 54.9% in 1970 to 21.1% in 2018. Half the Catholics age 30 and younger have left the church, while, as Auxiliary Bishop Robert E. Barron of Los Angeles points out, for every person who joins the church today, six leave.[48]

Nor is it just the youth. A 2012 study by W. Bradford Wilcox at the University of Virginia reports that church attendance by whites between twenty-five and forty-five years of age without a college degree has declined at twice the rate of their college-educated peers since the 1970s.[49] Some bishops have suggested the need for a national or regional synod to address the sexual abuse crisis.

In both Canada and the United States, losses to the church would be much worse if it were not for immigrants, especially—for the United States—those from Mexico and Central America and today increasingly from Asia.[50] This will probably change under the anti-immigrant policies of the Trump administration.

Still, Hispanic immigrants have changed the face of US Catholicism. Today they represent about 40 percent of US Catholics and nearly 60 percent of Catholic millennials. Canada, with an aging population, has been particularly welcoming to immigrants, pledging in 2017 to admit one million over the next three years. While they come from all over the world, a majority come from India, China, the Philippines, and the United Kingdom.

We have only surveyed here some of the more obvious polarities in American Catholicism today. Many focus on sexual issues such as marriage and divorce, abortion, homosexuality, and same-sex marriage, often grouped under the term *culture wars*. And there are others polarities.

The first expression of American Catholic social radicalism is due to Dorothy Day and Peter Maurin. Together they established the Catholic Worker Movement, which formed a generation of advocates for social

---

[48] Russell Shaw, "Is It Time for the US Church to Hold a Regional Synod to Address the Abuse Crisis," *America*, August 20, 2019.

[49] David Clay, "White Working-Class Adults Are Leaving the Church. What Can We Do to Keep Them?" *America*, August 28, 2019.

[50] See Simon C. Kim, *A World Church in Our Background* (Collegeville, MN: Liturgical Press, 2016).

change, among them Ed Marciniak, James O'Gara, John Cogley, Michael Harrington, James Forest, and Robert Ellsberg.

Dignity is an organization that seeks to bring together gay, lesbian, bisexual, and transgender persons and advocates for their right to express their sexuality in ways that are life giving and life affirming. Courage is a more traditional ministry for those with same-sex attraction who seek to live in chastity according to church teaching, in communion with God and others.

Corpus, an organization for resigned priests, describes itself as one of the oldest reform groups in the Catholic Church committed to a renewed priesthood of married or single men and women. CITI Ministries is a free referral service of ordained, married Roman Catholic priests who are willing to celebrate the sacraments and officiate at weddings in different venues for Catholic, Jewish, or interfaith couples.

The polarities within the Roman Catholic Church raise the question of how to preserve unity and communion. Some on the right are united in their opposition to Pope Francis's efforts at reform, his emphasis on immigrants, and his critique of an "economy of exclusion." Yet he is popular with most Catholics who welcome his efforts to renew the church and his social concern. The pope clearly has favored more open discussion in the church than his predecessors. As Tom Reese writes:

> Disagreeing with the pope was not welcomed during the papacies of John Paul and Benedict. Bishops, priests, theologians, and Catholic publications were expected to unreservedly cheer any statement that came out of Rome. Priests were silenced, seminary professors were removed, and magazine editors were fired if they strayed from the party line. The open debate that occurred during the Second Vatican Council was closed down. Candidates for the episcopacy were chosen based on loyalty to Rome rather than on intelligence or pastoral abilities.[51]

But the Roman Catholic Church is a big tent. Its genius is precisely its ability to maintain unity in diversity, with diversities in theologies, spiritualities, liturgical styles, lay and religious communities and movements.

---

[51]Thomas Reese, "More Catholic Than the Pope," *National Catholic Reporter*, October 3, 2017. For Francis's efforts to change the character of the hierarchy, see Ivereigh, *Wounded Shepherd*, 174–90.

And there are diverse churches within global Catholicism, as in the twenty-three Eastern Rite churches that are part of the universal Catholic communion but differ in terms of their liturgical traditions, spiritualities, canon law, even the discipline of celibacy for priests. In today's pluralistic, individualistic culture, preserving unity will remain a challenge.

3

Africa

Christian communities flourished in Africa in the early centuries of the faith, producing both saints and martyrs, including Tertullian from Carthage; Cyprian, a Carthaginian bishop; Clement of Alexandria; Athanasius, bishop of Alexandria; Augustine, bishop of Hippo; and the martyrs Felicity and Perpetua. An ancient tradition attributed the evangelization of Alexandria to Saint Mark. Christian monasticism also flourished in North Africa. However, the spread of Islam into North Africa in the seventh century, when Africa had over four hundred bishoprics, greatly reduced the churches; only the Coptic Church in Egypt, the Ethiopian Church, and some scattered Catholic communities have survived into modern times. Others are the heirs of European colonialism.

For example, Morocco, a country 99.9 percent Muslim, has approximately thirty-five thousand Catholics—0.08 percent of the total population. Before independence in 1956, there were more than two hundred Catholic churches; today only forty-four remain. Most Catholics in Morocco are foreign workers, while some come as students from Sub-Saharan countries. The majority are young. Much of the church's ministry is caring for migrants, who arrive in Morocco from the South, fleeing poverty, unemployment, or war, and then find European countries closed to them. The Moroccan constitution enshrines religious freedom, but it is very limited for non-Muslims. Those who convert must keep their Christianity a secret, for it is a criminal offense to attempt to evangelize or convert another. When Pope Francis visited Morocco in late March 2019, he called for religious freedom, not just "freedom of worship," as well as for progress beyond mere tolerance "to respect and esteem for others."[1] A staffer acknowledged the many obstacles but emphasized the pope's awareness that dialogue was the only way to be true to Christ.

In Sub-Saharan Africa modern missionary work began in the fifteenth century with the arrival of priests accompanying the Portuguese. The Dutch Reformed came to the south of Africa in 1652, some Protestant groups in the eighteenth century, and various missionary groups in the nineteenth, including the French in North Africa. The work of the missionaries remains controversial. Some were highly motivated to bring the gospel and Christian faith. In translating the scriptures into African languages, they developed a vernacular alphabet as well as dictionaries and grammars for societies that were still illiterate, thus helping to preserve their indigenous languages. Lamin Sanneh writes, "Christian growth has been slightest in areas where vernacular languages are weak—that is, where a *lingua franca* such as English, French, Portuguese, Arabic or Swahili has succeeded in suppressing mother tongues."[2]

The missionaries also established schools, healthcare clinics, and hospitals. African Christians recognize the debt they owe to the schools established by the missionaries. Nelson Mandela, in addressing the Eight General Assembly of the World Council of Churches (WCC) in Harare in 1998, said: "My generation is the product of missionary education. Without [that] I would not be here today. I will never have sufficient words to thank the missionaries for what they did for us."[3]

However, with the missionaries came traders, military forces, and administrators—in a word, colonialism—as European nations, eager for the continent's rich resources, established colonies. The worst was the exploitation of the Congo, a late effort of King Leopold II to establish a colony for Belgium. From 1885 to 1908, he privately controlled a vast area of central Africa, virtually enslaving the people to gather first ivory and later rubber to enrich himself and his supporters. Leopold's agents used violence, floggings, the imprisonment of wives and children, terror—cutting off the hands and feet of reluctant workers or their children—and murder to control the people.

---

[1] Nicolas Senèze, "Pope Francis Launches Dialogue by Word and Action in Morocco," *La Croix International*, April 1, 2019.

[2] Lamin Sanneh, "Christian Missions and the Western Guilt Complex," *The Christian Century*, April 8, 1987.

[3] Cited in Paul Gifford, *Christianity, Development, and Modernity in Africa* (New York: Oxford University Press, 2016), 85; see also Elizabeth A. Foster, *African Catholic: Decolonialization and the Transformation of the Church* (Cambridge, MA: Harvard University Press, 2019).

Growing international condemnation, especially after George Washington Williams, an African American Civil War veteran, pastor, and historian, published the first full exposure of Leopold's crimes in an open letter to the king, led to the transfer of the Congo to the Belgian government in 1908. Real changes, however, were very slow in coming. Historians estimate the death toll of the Congo's inhabitants at between ten and thirteen million.[4] Emmanuel Katongole sees *King Leopold's Ghost* as a story, not just about the rapacious Belgian king's plundering of the Congo, but as a metaphor for Africa itself, with the story of greed, dispossession, and state brutality continuing under so many of Africa's postcolonial rulers.[5]

Africa Today

While the growth of Christianity in Africa in modern times was initially slow, in the later part of the twentieth century it was extraordinary. The Pew Research Center says that the future of Christianity lies in Africa, or more precisely Sub-Saharan Africa, often called Black Africa.[6] In this part of the world Christians are relatively young and have more children than Christians elsewhere.[7] George Weigel notes that the 542 million African Christians may perhaps reach 1.2 billion by 2050, making Africa's Christian population twice that of Latin America and Europe combined.[8] Northern Africa is mostly Arab and Muslim.

The current population of Africa is about 900 million, with 100 million identifying with indigenous religions. Christians represent about 45 percent of the population and Muslims about 40 percent, though Muslims are growing rapidly, as are evangelical and Pentecostal Christians. The Catholic population increased by 33 percent between 2000 and 2010.[9]

---

[4] See Adam Hochschild, *King Leopold's Ghost: A Story of Greed, Terror, and Heroism in Colonial Africa* (London: Pan Books, 2012), 315.

[5] Emmanuel Katongole, *The Sacrifice of Africa: A Political Theology for Africa* (Grand Rapids, MI: Eerdmans, 2011), 15–18. Katongole tells wonderful stories of Africans working against hatred, violence, and tribalism.

[6] Much of the material in this chapter is representative of Sub-Saharan Africa, which comprises forty-six of Africa's fifty-four countries. For simplicity I will use the term *Africa* in a more general sense.

[7] David McClendon, "Sub-Saharan Africa Will Be Home to Growing Shares of the World's Christians and Muslims," Pew Research Center, April 19, 2017.

[8] George Weigel, "World Christianity by the Numbers," *First Things*, February 25, 2015.

[9] Pew Research Center, "Global Christianity—A Report on the Size and Distribution of the World's Christian Population," December 19, 2011.

According to the *Annuarium Statisticum Ecclesiae 2016*, the number of African Catholics rose from 185 million in 2010 to 228 million in 2016; that means 17.6 percent of the world's Catholics live in Africa. It is Catholicism's fastest-growing church.[10]

The following African countries have more than 25 percent Catholics among their population: Angola (38%), Benin (26.6%), Burundi (62.1%), Cameroon (25.6%), Central African Republic (25%), Republic of Congo (33.1%), Democratic Republic of Congo (36.8%), Gabonese Republic (50%), Lesotho (45.7%), Madagascar (29.5%), Malawi (28.4%), Mozambique (28.4%), Rwanda (43.7%), South Sudan (30%), Tanzania (27.2%), Togo (26.4%), and Uganda (41.9%). Estimates place Catholics in Nigeria at twenty million.

Nigeria is Africa's most populous country, with a population of two hundred million. The country is almost equally divided between Muslims, mostly Sunni, and Christians, with Muslims slightly in the majority. The majority of Christians are Protestants, mostly evangelicals and Pentecostals, as well as those belonging to the African Instituted Churches (AICs). There is also a sizable Anglican Church. Catholics constitute about one-quarter of the population, 24.8 percent. Pentecostalism today attracts an increasing number of Nigerian Catholic students, with its emphasis on spiritual gifts and the direct experience of God's presence and the fact that non-Catholics often accuse Catholics of an unbiblical faith, worshiping Mary, or not believing in the Spirit. Some students leave the Catholic Church to join a Pentecostal congregation; others attend both churches, which some Catholics see as helpful ecumenically, breaking down rigid barriers between traditions.[11] This loss of Catholics to the "new" churches—evangelical, Pentecostal, and AIC—is not a problem only in Nigeria. There has also been considerable conflict in Nigeria between Christians and Muslims, driven by Boko Haram terrorists, and bloody conflict between Fulani tribesmen and mostly Christian farmers over grazing rights.

An African Christianity

The growth of Christianity in Africa has not been without challenges. These include moving beyond the church's colonial and missionary history to

---

[10] Cited in James Roberts, "Increase of Number of Catholics Worldwide, according to Vatican Stats," *Tablet*, June 14, 2018.

[11] Linus Unah, "Young Nigerians Are Connecting with Pentecostal Churches: Will They Return to Catholicism?" *America*, November 16, 2017.

develop a genuinely African expression of Christian faith, leaving behind a residual tribalism, helping the local churches become self-sufficient, and addressing the continent's social and political problems. The Nigerian Jesuit theologian Agbonkhianmeghe E. Orobator cautions about reducing Christianity's growth in Africa to numbers. Referencing Katongole's work, he argues that Christianity in Africa has not lived up to its promise if it is not "promoting human flourishing, social transformation, economic development, and a transformative political imagination."[12]

While some missionaries did their best to learn from and value African culture, many were unable to appreciate the customs and religious practices of the people or their genuine religious impulses. Formed in an Enlightenment culture, the missionaries often looked down on African customs as primitive or unsophisticated; they condemned them as heathen or barbaric, leading to a superiority complex that was ultimately racial. The result was that Christianity became a "second home" alongside the traditional spirituality of the people.

In *African Christianity* Joseph Galgalo argues that because Africans are still largely shaped by their distinct ethnic and family ties and cultures, Christianity's potential as a religion of peace and brotherhood has "remained elusive," with Africans' first loyalty remaining "first and foremost to the tribe."[13] Katongole also points to tribalism as an ongoing problem in Africa. In *The Sacrifice of Africa* he analyzes what he calls the founding story of Africa's modernity, "tribalism, violence, poverty, desperation, the lies of identity, and the wastage and sacrificing of Africa."[14] He argues that, despite the claim of protecting the peoples from tribalism, Africa's nation-state politics actually reproduce it in order to provide its own self-justification as the pacifier of regions overrun by tribal conflicts.

Tribalism can affect Catholics as well. One example was the terrible genocide in Rwanda from April 7 to mid July 1994, in which eight hundred thousand Tutsis, perhaps as many as 70 percent of the Tutsi population, were slaughtered by their Hutu neighbors. Most of the victims were murdered with machetes, while rape was widely used as a weapon against Tutsi women and those Hutu women who tried to protect them. Rwanda is 43.7 percent Catholic. While some priests and nuns tried to

---

[12] Agbonkhianmeghe E. Orobator, *Religion and Faith in Africa: Confession of an Animist* (Maryknoll, NY: Orbis Books, 2018), 47.

[13] Joseph D. Galgalo, *African Christianity: The Stranger within* (Limuru, Kenya: Zapf Chancery, 2012), 19; see also Katongole, *The Sacrifice of Africa*, 48.

[14] Katongole, *The Sacrifice of Africa*, 24.

protect their Tutsi neighbors, others participated in the murders. In a statement in March 2017, Pope Francis asked God's forgiveness for the church's failures during the genocide. Another example was the refusal of many of the priests and laity of the diocese of Ahiara in Nigeria to accept Bishop Peter Ebere Okpaleke, appointed by Benedict XVI in 2012 as their bishop. They objected that Okpaleke was an outsider, not a member of the Mbaise ethnic group that dominates the diocese.

But there are other, more positive examples. Katongole tells the story of Bishop Paride Taban in the Sudan; after helping to bring about a peace agreement between the Southern rebels and the Khartoum government in 2005, he gave up his see to found the Holy Trinity Peace Village in Kuron. There, he welcomed people from all communities and faiths as one small step toward overcoming tribalism.[15] The Peace Village has gained international recognition.

Inculturation

Crucial to the church's spiritual mission is the question of inculturation, developing a theology, spirituality, and church that is not an import but truly African. The Catholic Church's long commitment to missionary work has been more sensitive to the values of indigenous cultures than is usually acknowledged. For example, a 1659 Instruction of the Vatican congregation Propaganda Fide (now called the Congregation for the Evangelization of Peoples) addressed all the vicariates apostolic in China and Indochina. It included "an explicit commitment to inculturation, a prohibition against combating the local customs and traditions of a given country, except when they stood in opposition to faith or morals."[16] In other words, it rejected the idea of simply implanting the home cultures of the missionaries in China.

Laurenti Magesa, a diocesan priest from Tanzania and one of Africa's premier theologians, comments by pointing to the work of Matteo Ricci (d. 1610) in China and Roberto de Nobili (d. 1656) in India. They serve as classic examples of an approach to mission or evangelization that stresses inculturation; it includes learning the languages and respecting the cultural symbols and religious customs of the countries where they are working.

---

[15] Katongole, *The Sacrifice of Africa*, 139–42; the book is rich in such stories.

[16] See the Vatican document "The Congregation for the Evangelization of Peoples," no. 2.

While the wisdom of this instruction was not always honored in the subsequent tradition, Magesa shows how Pius XII, Vatican II's *Gaudium et spes*, Paul VI, and John Paul II all affirmed it.[17]

The issue of developing a genuinely African Christianity is an important one. Because the missionaries worked within the context of European colonialism, the church often took root in a climate of suspicion and mistrust. Missionaries planted churches on the model of those at home, and in the process they imposed on their converts their own brand of denominational Christianity, dividing African communities along denominational lines. At the same time African theologians reject the idea that the missionaries "brought God to Africa," a prejudice that ignores the religious sensibility so deeply embedded in African culture as well as in contemporary Catholicism's recognition that God is present and at work in the histories and cultures of all peoples.

In *Anatomy of Inculturation* Magesa explores questions of inculturation in depth. He asks if polygamy is useful and especially if it is respectful of the dignity of women, given the different socioeconomic situations of Africa today. He also questions the tradition of levirate unions, where a male relative "inherits" the wife of a deceased member of the family. Both can contribute to the spread of HIV/AIDS. African religion, for Magesa, has a more comprehensive view of spirituality. He sees it as encompassing all dimensions of the human—body, mind, will, and emotion. The key is whether these faculties lead a person toward or away from greater communion with God.

Mainline Protestant worship still has a European flavor in prayer and melody, while evangelical and especially Pentecostal services have almost entirely imported the American style of "concert" services. Jacob Olupona, a professor of African religious traditions at Harvard Divinity School, sees the Pentecostals reliance on English and French bibles and a globalized Christian identity as eroding indigenous languages and the values of extended families; the result is "the movement having imbibed a new form of ethics that supports autonomous individualism and global capitalism at the expense of the communal life-affirming ethos."[18]

Catholics lack greater participation by the faithful. While Catholic liturgy is generally more adaptable, it still suffers from a rigid formalism.

---

[17] Laurenti Magesa, *What Is Not Sacred? African Spirituality* (Maryknoll, NY: Orbis Books, 2013), 7–9.

[18] Jacob K. Olupona, "World Christianity: The African Experience," *Ecumenical Trends* 48, no. 7 (July/August 2019): 4.

The challenge is to adapt Western forms to better express the African search for the divine and to bring out the African character of the church. Because African religion is deeply aware of the unity between the human and the rest of the universe, both visible and invisible, Magesa urges the promotion of ritual gestures, especially in liturgy, that are expressive of this unity.

Other gestures, like kissing or striking the breast as a sign of repentance, more appropriate in the West, may not be appropriate in Africa. Magesa makes a number of bold suggestions, including the incorporation of music and dance. Dancing does not require performers; it involves all and entails providing space for movement in church buildings. Regarding music, drums hold pride of place. Preaching, always a solemn activity, should be morally instructive and rooted concretely in the life of the community. Magesa supports the idea that the eucharistic elements do not necessarily have to be wheat bread and grape wine, avoiding the idea that God is not willing to be identified with the fruits of the people's own soil.[19]

Magesa also offers some suggestions for developing more innovative African liturgies that are more in touch with African spirituality than classical Roman Catholic liturgical forms. Among them he mentions adapting some of the traditional African initiation rituals, such as seclusion; using more concrete language, with a strong concern for human life in eucharistic liturgies; including penitential and reconciliation rites; recognizing the importance of repentance; invoking the ancestors, so important in African culture; and practicing eucharistic hospitality so as not to exclude others from the meal. Finally, he suggests developing liturgies to consecrate those making religious professions or being ordained priests.[20]

Similarly, in writing about inculturation, Agbonkhianmeghe Orobator remarks that the word *inculturation* is a new term in African theology. He suggests some similar terms such as *adaptation, accommodation, indigenization,* and *contextualization*. Such terms recognize and suggest how Christian faith and worship can embrace elements or aspects of African religion or of local cultural customs and practices. Thus, inculturation means far more

---

[19] Laurenti Magesa, *Anatomy of Inculturation: Transforming the Church in Africa* (Maryknoll, NY: Orbis Books, 2004), 202–24. In contrast, Joseph Ratzinger states that dancing is not a form of expression for Christian liturgy (Joseph Ratzinger, *The Spirit of the Liturgy* [San Francisco: Ignatius Press, 2000], 198–99).

[20] Magesa, *Anatomy of Inculturation*, 237–46.

than song, dance, and African musical instruments; it means developing an authentically African Christianity, something Pope Paul VI spoke of as a right when he visited Uganda in 1969.[21]

Tensions between the challenge of inculturation and a more traditional Catholicism continue to divide some African Catholics. Many of the older bishops, Roman trained, seem more Roman than African. There are still many "who have an orthodox, traditional, and cautious style."[22] Cardinals Francis Arinze and Robert Sarah, both of whom served as prefects of the Congregation for Divine Worship and the Discipline of the Sacraments, were supporters of the so-called reform of the reform. Its supporters were in favor of initiatives such as a revision of the Vatican II liturgy, including using only one eucharistic prayer, with priest and people facing *ad orientem* or to the East, as well as returning to Latin or even the Tridentine liturgy. Pope Francis has publicly corrected Cardinal Sarah three times for giving an alternative interpretation to his instructions on the liturgy.

Sarah has continued to advocate the use of the *ad orientem* posture, not just for the traditional extraordinary form of the mass, but also in the ordinary form, as well as for more silence in the liturgy. Such an approach to liturgy leaves little room for inculturation; its perspective is backward, not forward. After an article attributed to Sarah said that the pope's motu proprio *Magnum principium* did not really change the rules for the translation of liturgical texts, the pope wrote that the article "attributed to Sarah" was not a faithful and correct interpretation of the papal decree. Sarah has also criticized Jesuit Father James Martin's book, *Building a Bridge: How the Catholic Church and the LGBT Community Can Enter into a Relationship of Respect, Compassion, and Trust.* Sarah's concern is to reiterate church teaching about abstention from sex for the unmarried; Martin says his book is not about moral theology but an invitation to dialogue and prayer.[23]

---

[21] Agbonkhianmeghe E. Orobator, *Theology Brewed in an African Pot* (Maryknoll, NY: Orbis Books, 2008), 127–31.

[22] Joseph G. Healey, "Beyond Vatican II: Imagining the Catholic Church of Nairobi I," in *The Church We Want: African Catholics Look to Vatican III,* ed. Agbonkhianmeghe E. Orobator (Maryknoll, NY: Orbis Books, 2016), 206.

[23] Christopher White, "Vatican Cardinal Critiques Jesuit Martin on Homosexuality," *Crux,* September 1, 2017. James Martin, *Building a Bridge: How the Catholic Church and the LGBT Community Can Enter into a Relationship of Respect, Compassion, and Trust* (New York: HarperCollins, 2017).

An African Spirituality

A related issue is that of developing a genuinely African spirituality. Magesa objects to the term *African traditional religion* as both inaccurate and anachronistic; he prefers the term *African religion,* as it refers to the beliefs and way of life of so many of the African people. Not respecting these values has impaired the church's evangelical efforts. A better expression might be *African spirituality.* While some missionaries—for example, Daniel Camboni of the Verona Fathers—recognize the need to learn from the culture, most continued to dismiss African customs and sensibilities as pagan. Not so Magesa. He has become an outspoken advocate for a genuinely African spirituality.

He argues that despite the fact that those who have received a Western education tend to ignore or forget the values of their inherited African spirituality, spirituality is still present in the wells of their memories. To illustrate this, he shows how those who are sick, when the doctor's treatment brings no cure, will consult a diviner or attribute the malady to the power of witchcraft. Rather than reject this African spirituality or way of perceiving the world, he suggests that it may have something to teach not just Africans but the wider world. It represents an alternative ethic, one different from the technological approach to life that is unable to recognize that there is more to life, to the survival of humankind, and to the good of the universe than modern science and technology. The technological paradigm has led to the domination of the earth, excessive materialism, consumerism, and neglect of the weak.

African spirituality can offer an alternative wisdom, one that stresses the wholeness of existence, the connectedness of all things, the living with the dead, and the cosmic order with its force of life or spirit in every creature that grounds a respect for nature and for all human beings. In village life each river, forest, lake, and well has its own spirit, ancestral or natural, that watches over or protects it.[24]

Death plays a central role in African spirituality, connecting the African imagination with invisible powers. Each death affects not just the individual but also the community and is surrounded by elaborate rituals, usually performed even when the church tries to proscribe them. These rituals symbolize the connectedness of all things, allowing the living to live in peace and making it possible for the dead one day to return to

---

[24] Magesa, *What Is Not Sacred?,* 90.

the realm of the living.[25] Thus, the African approach to life is personalist rather than materialist as in the West.

Because ritual plays such an important role in African spirituality, Magesa suggests that liturgy might be an ideal meeting place for a "ritualistic" approach to spirituality that engages the world and creation in a positive way. In addition, he argues that there is a need to adopt a language that goes beyond ordinary, conceptual systems of thought, a language that uses symbols with their power to touch the heart, the use of dance and song that can express both body and spirit, and the exchanges of gifts, so important in Africa. The obligation to marry and have children links the living with the departed; for this reason, he finds the church's inflex-ibility toward polygamy and celibacy as a condition for ordained ministry indicative of an insensitivity toward these symbols. The power of spiritual beings in African spirituality can find expression in the popular Christian belief in the power of Satan, the Evil Spirit, even if Christian theology has lessened belief in Satan's power.[26]

Orobator is also concerned to develop an authentic African theol-ogy and spirituality. A convert to Christianity at the age of sixteen, he writes that he cherishes his religious and cultural background as an African, born and raised in the ancient kingdom of Benin. He argues that African religion is not a competitor to Christianity or Islam, but rather is something deeply rooted in the consciousness of the African peoples, "the *bedrock* on which Islam and Christianity are planted." It is what secures the foundation of either in the soul of the people.[27] He sees Africans as a deeply religious people who take God's existence for granted. Traditionally stressing the immanence of God, the African imagination is sacramental; it sees the divine disclosed in nature and art, symbol, story, and persons. Life, present in human beings, animals, and plants is sacred, and therefore creation itself is sacred. This grounds the African respect for nature.

> Some animals are considered sacred and may not be killed or eaten for food; some natural elements (rocks, groves, streams, mountains, and so on) are considered sacred and because they are the abode of the gods, goddesses, spirits, deities, and ancestors; some plants are

---

[25] Magesa, 81–85.
[26] Magesa, 114–21.
[27] Orobator, *Religion and Faith in Africa*, 67.

revered (sacred trees, shrubs, and so on) and may be used only for medicinal/curative purposes. Based on this awareness of their affinity with the rest of creation or nature, one of the primary concerns of Africans is *harmony with nature*, a balanced relationship with the entire universe. A breach of this harmony can result in nefarious consequences, hence, the constant preoccupation . . . with taming, controlling, placating, or neutralizing potentially harmful elements in our relationship with nature.[28]

Is this so different form the vision of Pope Francis, who in his encyclical on the care for the earth, *Laudato Si'*, repeats numerous times that all things are connected and dependent on one another (LS, nos. 16, 42, 70, 89). Further,

time and space are not independent of one another, and not even atoms or subatomic particles can be considered in isolation. Just as the different aspects of the planet—physical, chemical, and biological—are interrelated, so too, living species are part of a network which we will never fully explore and understand. A good part of our genetic code is shared by many living beings. (no. 138)

At the same time, inculturation cannot be an uncritical process. At a March 2017 conference in the United States at the University of Notre Dame on the future of African Catholicism, speakers cautioned against simply imitating Pentecostal styles of worship and embracing the African spirit world. One speaker reported that some Catholic parishes are uncritically expanding the use of popular music and dancing to keep pace with the exuberant Pentecostal style of worship. Another speaker said that some African priests and lay leaders involved in the charismatic movement openly embrace witchcraft and appeals to local spirits. "Bishop Godfrey Onah of Nsukka, Nigeria, openly lamented that in the early centuries of ecclesiastical history, Africa produced doctors of the church, and even great heretics, but today 'what we seem to produce are faith healers and miracle centers.'"[29]

---

[28] Orobator, *Theology Brewed in an African Pot*, 48.

[29] John L. Allen, "Pentecostal, Evangelical Boom Forces African Church to 'Wake Up,'" *Crux*, March 25, 2017.

Internal Tensions

As traditional African spirituality becomes intertwined with Christianity, not all cultural values are positive. Paul Gifford, a student of African Christianity, sees African Christianity as having two distinct religious visions: Pentecostal and Catholic. An "enchanted Christianity" is particularly strong among African Pentecostals, although found also among some Catholics. It stresses the pervasiveness of supernatural forces, particularly evil forces responsible for ills such as the failure to find a spouse, infertility, personal failures, and damaged offspring. The Catholic vision, with its emphasis on development and social ministry, risks an internal secularizing of the church's mission.

Enchanted Christianity

In August 2006, the Catholic bishops of Southern Africa, including South Africa, Swaziland, and Botswana, issued a pastoral letter warning their priests not to moonlight as witchdoctors and fortunetellers. Nevertheless, for many Africans witchcraft is deeply embedded in their culture; they will consult traditional healers to ward off illness, drive off evil spirits, even to improve their sex lives. The Catholic University of East Africa in Nairobi, Kenya, sponsored a three-day conference in February 2007 on the pastoral challenges of witchcraft: "Experts warned that witchcraft was 'destroying' the Catholic Church in Africa, in part because skeptical, Western-educated clergy are not responding adequately to people's spiritual needs."[30]

Gifford profiles Daniel Olukoya's Mountain of Fire and Miracles Ministries in Lagos, one of the largest congregations in Africa, as an extreme example of the enchanted religious imagination. It sees evil working through witchcraft, spirit possession, and spirit wives, manifested through physical signs like dreams, crying or screaming in the night, or vomiting small objects or animals. Olukoya's movement focuses on spiritual warfare, deliverance, and especially prayer to combat the evil forces, with Olukoya himself often playing the leading role.[31]

---

[30] John L. Allen, Jr., "Focus on Witchcraft at Exorcists' Summit Signifies a Paradigm Shift," *Crux*, April 18, 2018.

[31] Gifford, *Christianity, Development, and Modernity in Africa*, 18–28.

This cultural interpenetration of the spiritual and physical worlds is widespread in Africa. It gives power to spiritual healers, witchdoctors and medicine men who use prayer, exorcisms, anointings, and religious objects as well as rituals that sometimes involve human sacrifice and the use of body parts, particularly from albinos. Gifford cites a World Council of Churches document descriptive of this enchanted religious imagination:

> The issue of witchcraft goes to the heart of the African psyche. African societies, like the biblical-Semitic world, have a religious and spiritual understanding of reality. We are surrounded by a host of spirit beings—some good, some bad—which are considered able to influence the course of human lives. For that reason calamities are attributed to personal forces of evil. In such a setting it is an important role of religion to help free humanity from the tyranny of those forces of evil. *It is useless to debate the reality of such spirit beings* (emphasis added).[32]

The Prosperity Gospel

To profile another prominent subgroup, this time emphasizing the so-called prosperity gospel or gospel of health and wealth, Gifford discusses the Living Faith Church Worldwide, more commonly known as Winners' Chapel, founded in Lagos in 1983 by David O. Oyedepo. By 2013, Oyedepo's church had six thousand branches in Nigeria and seven hundred in other African countries. In Ota, a suburb of Lagos, the Winner's Chapel has the largest church auditorium in the world, seating 50,400; in 2013, it opened the biggest church in East and Central Africa. For Oyedepo, Christianity's message about salvation and the kingdom of God means victory for believers over all the forces of darkness, including poverty, sickness, disease, family disintegration, and ill health; thus Christianity brings health and material prosperity. Believers, taught to have absolute faith, proclaim loudly their belief in these blessings, releasing the supernatural through the production of sound.

Oyedepo acknowledges his indebtedness to American Pentecostals, particularly prosperity-gospel preachers such as Kenneth Copeland and

---

[32] Gifford, 157–58. See also John S. Pobee and Gabriel Ositelu II, *African Initiatives in Christianity: The Growth, Gifts, and Diversities of Indigenous African Churches: A Challenge to the Ecumenical Movement* (Geneva: WCC, 1998), 29.

Kenneth Hagin. Rather than stressing evil forces, like Olukoya, he places more emphasis on understanding the truth of scripture as he interprets it. He counsels obedience, particularly tithing—giving to God, which means giving to the church—with the expectation that it brings the covenant blessings of financial prosperity. Oyedepo claims to be a prophet, able to heal by his touch, with even the touch of his garments curative. His rituals include the oil of anointing, foot washing, and the blood of Jesus, made such by proclaiming a blessing over ordinary fluids including bath water or breast milk.[33]

Gifford argues that all Africa's Pentecostal churches share the idea that a Christian is destined for victory in every aspect of life, including material prosperity. Nor is prosperity-gospel preaching confined to Africa. Its roots are traceable to the United States and preachers such as E. W. Kenyon, Norman Vincent Peale, and Oral Roberts.[34] It is also prominent in Asia and Latin America. Some prosperity-gospel preachers have become billionaires. They flaunt their wealth as a way of demonizing poverty as the work of Satan. The net worth of Brazil's Edir Macedo is US$1.1 billion, while that of Chris Oyakhilome, known as Pastor Chris of Nigeria, is reported to be US$30–50 million.

Resolving the Differences

Developing a genuinely African spirituality that is also Christian should not have to juxtapose Christianity and African religion as polar opposites, a choice between the enchanted religious imagination that Gifford sees as typical of African Pentecostals and what he describes as a disenchanted, internally secularized Christianity.

Magesa calls for a dialogue between Western Christian and African spiritualities in order to develop a credible African Christian spirituality, one that incorporates indigenous African perspectives while still respecting the uniqueness of the gospel. His intention is not to add new beliefs on top of the old, but rather to develop new sensitivities and horizons for the meeting of these different spiritual experiences. Thus, he brings

---

[33] Gifford, *Christianity, Development, and Modernity in Africa*, 29–44. See also Simon Coleman, *The Globalization of Charismatic Christianity: Spreading the Gospel of Prosperity* (New York: Cambridge University Press, 2000).

[34] See Brian Stanley, *Christianity in the Twentieth Century: A World History* (Princeton, NJ: Princeton University Press, 2018), 296–304.

together two different approaches to God, like two parents who together produce a child.[35]

Gifford warns that Catholicism's refusal to embrace any form of enchanted Christianity—a tendency toward a rationalism that overlooks the divine presence—may actually result in a secularization of the church's mission. Shaped by a post–Vatican II emphasis on engagement with modernity and its commitment to development in terms of schools, hospitals, and healthcare services, the Catholic Church has become "the biggest single development agency on the continent." All this is to its credit. However, Gifford worries that these commitments together with a broader sense of development embracing human rights, justice, and peace means that the church is actually becoming more secular. Because it draws considerable support from major donors, it risks making African Catholicism an "NGO-ization," or as he humorously suggests, an "Oxfam with Incense."[36]

Development and Social Ministry

Is Gifford correct in seeing the Catholic Church's commitment to development and social ministry as risking a secularization of the church's religious mission? The Second Vatican Council broke with an earlier defensive Catholicism that saw the world as evil, placing the church at its service. The *Pastoral Constitution on the Church in the Modern World* (*Gaudium et spes*) begins by declaring that "the joys and the hopes, the griefs and the anxieties of the men of this age, especially those who are poor or in any way afflicted, these are the joys and hopes, the griefs and anxieties of the followers of Christ. Indeed, nothing genuinely human fails to raise an echo in their hearts" (GS, no. 1). In responding to this message and conscious of the many needs of the African people, the Catholic Church in Africa has invested heavily in development in the areas of education, healthcare, and reconciliation.

Although this was not always the case, of all the churches, the Catholic Church is the most committed to education. It sponsors both grant-aided schools (with government subsidies) and private schools. For example, in Zambia, roughly 15 percent of all education is under Catholic sponsorship. At the University of Zambia, 68 percent of all students have done

---

[35] Magesa, *What Is Not Sacred?*, 107.
[36] Gifford, *Christianity, Development and Modernity in Africa*, 151.

part or all of their preparation in Catholic schools. These schools have experienced the challenges faced by Catholic education elsewhere: increasing government regulation at the expense of the schools' religious mission; increasing expenses and diminishing funds; and fewer religious priests, sisters, and brothers. Moreover, as postcolonial Africa continues to develop, many students are far less interested in the faith dimension of their schools.

Healthcare is another area in which the church is heavily invested. In 2010, 178 healthcare centers—including 1,074 hospitals, 5,373 out-patient clinics, 186 leper colonies, 753 homes for the elderly and physically and mentally disabled, 979 orphanages, and 2,947 educational and rehabilitation centers—were operated by the Catholic Church. Though these institutions sometimes join wider Christian agencies, the Catholic Church is the most significant member. "Anecdotal evidence suggests that half of all AIDS-related services in Africa are provided by Catholic organizations; the proportion is even higher in rural areas."[37]

How are all these works supported? Gifford argues that the Protestant churches have long stressed the self-sufficiency of their local churches. Like the churches in China, they follow the "three-self" mantra: self-governing, self-propagating, and self-funding. He says that self-reliance is becoming a mantra for Catholics also, but nobody really means it: "Many bishops simply don't pay their dues to regional Catholic structures, or to the continent-wide symposium of Episcopal Conferences of Africa and Madagascar (SECAM), knowing that the necessary money will be found elsewhere."[38]

The Vatican's Congregation for the Evangelization of Peoples contributes an annual subsidy to most dioceses, though the amount is small. Catholic funding agencies such as Missio, Adveniat, and Aid to the Church in Need are able to contribute larger amounts. Catholic religious orders also generously subsidize their ministries in Africa. They frequently raise funds for new facilities, train religious personnel, and support publishing houses and magazines. They also bring the resources of their benefactors. For example, Conrad Hilton established a Fund for Sisters that in 2009 received 23.7 million dollars. The Porticus Foundation, based in the Netherlands, also provides generous funds.[39] However, as funding sources for specifically religious purposes diminish, secular sources have become

---

[37] Gifford, 95.
[38] Gifford, 94.
[39] Gifford, 94.

more active in supporting development activities. They are often reluctant to contribute to governments seen as corrupt. As a result, many church development offices have dual sources: one, Catholic charitable organizations: the other, governments and international agencies.

Still, as central to the gospel as the church's social message is, there is the danger of reducing the good news of the gospel to a purely social or political message. Some theologians describe the concentration on the social as a *regnocentric* or kingdom-centered approach as opposed to one that is Christocentric or ecclesiocentric.[40] Some proponents of liberation theology in Latin America made that mistake, where, as has often been said, the church chose the poor, but the poor chose the Pentecostals. In other words, the social needs of the people should not ignore their religious needs.

The Catholic Church's social engagement has drawn criticism, not just from government officials but also from some other churches, who object that the church's mission is primarily spiritual. Based on scripture texts, such as Romans 13:1–3, they object that the church should not challenge civil authority. Even worse, preaching the prosperity gospel, so common among Africa's neo-Pentecostal and African Instituted Churches, results in an over-spiritualization or fundamentalist interpretation of the gospel, ignoring the Paschal Mystery.

Reconciliation, Justice, and Peace

The two Special Assemblies of the African Synod of Bishops addressed some of these issues. The first, in 1994, developed the idea of the church as the family of God; the second, in 2009, focused on the mission of the church. Commenting on the second synod, Jesuit Father Peter Henriot, long engaged in the social apostolate, acknowledges that addressing issues of economic development and the needs of the poor as well as governance, corruption, and constitutional reform is always political, but it is not necessarily partisan. The real question, he says, is how to avoid the extremes of either an over-politicization or an over-spiritualization. The church's social teaching, found in scripture and articulated in statements of popes, councils, synods, and bishops, is the foundation for addressing social issues. Henriot reminds his readers of Pope Benedict's warning

---

[40] Peter Phan, *In Our Own Tongues: Perspectives from Asia on Mission and Inculturation* (Maryknoll, NY: Orbis Books, 2003), 61.

that this ministry must begin with the profound conversion that comes from an encounter with God. Remaining faithful to the church's social teaching safeguards it from falling into the purely political realm. Henriot calls it a balancing act, trying to implement two contrasting views of the mission of the church. One challenges the church to be more active in politics to promote reconciliation, justice, and peace; the second sees the church's contribution to these goals by building up the spiritual life of the people.[41] The church has to continue to grapple with these two dangers.

Nevertheless, reconciliation, justice, and peace are gospel values. Henriot cites Ghanaian Cardinal Peter Turkson, president of the Pontifical Council for Justice and Peace, on the "inseparable" link between the two African synods:

> For it is in its theological content and character as family of God that the church-family becomes an image of and a foreshadowing of the kingdom of God on earth and in history, animating the African society and the world with values of the kingdom of God, namely, reconciliation, justice, truth, and peace.[42]

The contributors to Orobator's book on the second synod suggest ways that the church might more effectively take on a new mission, working toward the reconciliation, justice, and peace that witness to God's reign, an emphasis that seems to have eluded many in Africa.[43] Thus, they urge African theologians to use African languages for their theological reflection; encourage the development of small Christian communities (SCCs) as local embodiments of the church; and engage secular society in a wide range of issues dealing with justice as well as promoting sustainable development, healthcare, higher education, and good governance.

For example, in the Democratic Republic of the Congo (formerly Zaire), the National Episcopal Conference helped mediate the transfer of power in December 2018. Earlier, the bishops played a key role in helping mediate the 2016 New Year's Eve Agreement between the government

---

[41] Peter Henriot, "Epilogue: A Balancing Act: Facing the Challenge of Implementing the Direction of the Second African Synod," in *Reconciliation, Justice, and Peace: The Second African Synod,*" ed. Agbonkhianmeghe E. Orobator (Maryknoll, NY: Orbis Books, 2011), 238.

[42] Henriot, "Epilogue: A Balancing Act," 243. For Cardinal Peter Turkson's text see "A New Pentecost for the Church in Africa," *Post Synodal Consultation on the Second Special Assembly for Africa of the Synod of Bishops,* Maputo, Mozambique, May 24, 2010.

[43] Orobator, *Reconciliation, Justice, and Peace,* 6–10.

and the political opposition, allowing President Joseph Kabila to remain in office for two more years and to step down after an election in 2018. After the election, disputed because of numerous charges of irregularity, the bishops called on the country's electoral commission to release the results. They claimed to be in possession of data from polling stations that designated the selection of one candidate as president. Despite the concerns about voting irregularities, with perhaps one million people prevented from voting, Félix Tshisekedi, not Kabila's candidate, was sworn in as president on January 24, 2019, marking the first peaceful transfer of power since the Congo gained independence in 1960.[44]

In Zimbabwe, at the beginning of 2019, the bishops' justice and peace commission collected information on violence and human rights abuses due to the government's brutal handling of dissent, accusing President Mugabe's successor of mishandling the economy. Unemployment in the country after Mugabe's misrule stands at over 80 percent. Other issues included sociopolitical unrest in Northern Uganda and the Ivory Coast; economic injustice endemic in the mining industries in Congo and Nigeria; sexual, gender-based violence in South Africa and South Sudan; and ethnic, religious, and sectarian violence in Kenya and Egypt.

A renewed mission must also address the question of the church's leadership, its inability to recognize the gifts of women and hear their voices, and its need to find ways to involve a critical mass of lay Christians. Nor can the church afford to ignore the theological and ethical issues related to ecology and the continent's natural resources. A final section of Orobator's book examines a number of ethical issues, such as the HIV/AIDS pandemic, which seems to be less urgent today thanks to antiretroviral treatments, although these still remain beyond the reach of many because of ignorance or poverty. The ongoing debate about the use of condoms to prevent the transmission of HIV also needs to be addressed.

Ecumenism

In spite of the spectacular growth of Christianity in Africa, there is little movement toward reconciliation and Christian unity. As Jerry Pillay,

---

[44] Rose Gamble, "DRC Bishops Say They Know Election Result and Urge Government to Publish Result," *Tablet*, January 4, 2019.

president of the World Alliance of Reformed Churches (WARC) and a professor of church history at the University of Pretoria, writes:

> Africa is so full of vitality and charisma, such that the numerous new theologies of life and the varied interpretations of the gospel can hardly define it. It is no small wonder that it is said that Africa is going to be the centre of Christianity by the year 2040. Churches are mushrooming in most parts of Africa, especially with the growth of Pentecostalism and the charismatic movement. However, attempts at Christian unity are weak. If anything, we continue to perpetuate denominationalism and separation, often encouraging a spirit of competition rather than cooperation and unity.[45]

The churches continue to be divided over the ordination and role of women, sexuality, and worship. Some African churches do not believe in ecumenism. Some "spiritualize" the gospel, overlooking its social dimension, while many preach the prosperity gospel. They need to embrace a preferential option for the poor.[46]

There are some new initiatives in Africa aimed toward engaging with evangelicals. In Nairobi, the Jesuit Historical Institute in Africa (JHIA), directed by Festo Mkenda, SJ, has organized two conferences on encounters between Jesuits and Protestants in Africa. While the 2016 conference was largely historical and limited in attendance, the 2017 conference drew more participants from the evangelical side. Several papers explored the spiritual, theological, and practical linkages between Catholicism and evangelicalism. The JHIA has also begun working ecumenically with other institutions to establish the African Theological Network Press, an ecumenical press with three partner institutions, the Akrofi-Christeller Institute in Ghana, largely Presbyterian; SPCK in England, Anglican; and the Missio Africanus, mostly evangelical.

Dialogue with Islam

Vatican II's *Declaration on the Relation of the Church to the Non-Christian Religions* (*Nostra aetate*) called for dialogue, making possible a more

---

[45] Jerry Pillay, "Ecumenism in Africa: Theological, Contextual, and Institutional Challenges," *The Ecumenical Review* 67, no. 4 (December 2015): 637–38.

[46] Pillay, 638–42.

sympathetic engagement with African religions, though the council did not link dialogue explicitly with justice. Magesa argues that the African synod did just that. Just as the Old Testament was hostile toward other religions, and the New Testament demanded conversion to Christianity, so the story of the Christian missions from the sixteenth century on—despite its achievements—called for destroying the altars, temples, and sacred images of the indigenous religions. With some exceptions this was the church's practice. In his 1994 *Tertio millennio adveniente* (*On the Threshold of the Third Millennium*) Pope John Paul II called for repentance for the "acquiescence given, especially in certain centuries, to *intolerance and even the use of violence* in the service of truth" (no. 35). Magesa sees the need for a similar apology today for the violence done by missionaries to African religion; he also sees a need for a dialogue characterized by mutuality and respect with Islam and African religion if the church is to discover God's presence in each.[47]

Especially important today is a dialogue with Islamic communities, although it remains a challenge. The Pew Forum estimates that 24.3 percent of all Muslims will live in Sub-Saharan Africa by 2050. While Christians and Muslims often live side by side in many African countries, in recent years relations between the two communities have deteriorated. This is especially true of Nigeria, a country with large Muslim and Christian populations. Tension between the two religions continues to lead to bloodshed. In 2015, there were 2,484 killings of Christians and 108 church attacks in northern Nigeria; in 2016, the number increased by 62 percent, to 4,028 killings and 198 church attacks.[48]

Boko Haram, a radical Islamic group whose goal is a strict Islamic state in northern Nigeria, has killed more than 27,000 since 2009 and more than 130,000 have been displaced from their homes.[49] In a petition presented to the Nigerian President Buhari on February 8, 2018, the International Society for Civil Liberty and the Rule of Law claimed that 21,800 Christians have been killed in northern Nigeria since June

---

[47] See Laurenti Magesa, "On Speaking Terms: African Religion and Christianity in Dialogue," in Orobator, *Reconciliation, Justice, and Peace*, 25–36.

[48] Janelle P., "Killings of Christians in Nigeria Has Increased by 62%," Open Doors, March 1, 2016.

[49] "Boko Haram Kills 27,000 in Nigeria in Decade-Long Militancy: UN," Xinhua, August 1, 2019.

2015.[50] Others claim an equal or greater number of Muslim victims. Jack McCaslin, a research associate for Africa policy studies at the Council on Foreign Relations in Washington, DC, argues that "despite Boko Haram's murderous hostility to Christians, most of its victims have always been Muslim, not least because the insurgency takes place in a predominantly Muslim part of the country."[51]

Disputes between Muslim Fulani herders and Christian farmers have also been deadly, with over 2,000 Christians killed in 2018 alone. The political elites that dominate the government in northern Nigeria have done little to stop the violence. The country's Catholic bishops have several times suggested that the president should "consider stepping aside." Christians in northern Nigeria find it difficult to join the civil service, police, military, or other security agencies because of anti-Christian prejudice.[52]

The Central African Republic has also seen considerable religious violence since 2012, when Séléka, an Islamic terror group supported by foreign fighters from Chad and the Sudan, began to take over towns in the north. Since 2018, the violence on both sides has escalated, resulting in thousands of deaths and more than 450,000 refugees. Kenya and Uganda have also experienced considerable sectarian violence, much of it from the Somali militant group al-Shabaab. Under these circumstances, dialogue, while difficult, is even more important. Pope Francis visited the Central African Republic, Kenya, and Uganda in 2015, and his visit to the United Arab Emirates in February 2019 was one more attempt to build bridges with the Islamic world.

Some interreligious tensions in Africa spring from foreign influences. They include conflicting values and laws regarding marriage; the drive by some Muslims to impose Sharia law, if not for all, at least for Muslims in some countries; and the rejection of tolerance by some evangelicals who seem to find nothing of value in Islam or African religion. With its mixed population, Catholic and Islamic, Nigeria should play a key role in the dialogue with Islam.

---

[50] Leo Sobechi, "Group Petitions Buhari over Killing of 21,800 Northern Christians," *Guardian/Nigeria*, February 11, 2018. The 2018 United States Commission on International Religious Freedom (USCIRF) gives similar numbers, but from 2009.

[51] John Campbell, "Conflict in Nigeria Is More Complicated than 'Christians vs. Muslims'," Council on Foreign Relations, May 1, 2019.

[52] "Reflection on Christians and Discrimination in Northern Nigeria," Zenit, May 4, 2016; "USCIRF 2018 Annual Report," 55.

Sexual Abuse

The sexual abuse of young people that has surfaced in the church is a sensitive topic in Africa, where there is a cultural reluctance to speak about sexual matters. A Tanzanian priest acknowledged that while it is a universal problem in the church, it is rarely covered by the media or discussed in Africa. According to the 2019 Ratzinger Prize winner, Jesuit Father Paul Béré from Burkinabe, who teaches at Rome's Pontifical Biblical Institute: "Our local culture is sometimes a culture of shame. If there are subjects we are not sure about, we do not know how to talk about them."[53] Since 2015, bishops' conferences in Southern Africa (including Botswana, South Africa, and Swaziland) as well as Nigeria have introduced policies to safeguard children.

After Pope Francis's *Vos estis lux mundi* (May 9, 2019), his motu proprio establishing universal procedures to combat sexual abuse, Kenya, the Central African Republic, Togo, the Ivory Coast, and the Democratic Republic of the Congo announced they will launch consultations to establish their own procedures for reporting abuse.[54] The Gregorian University in Rome offers a course on child protection by German Jesuit Hans Zollner, president of the Gregorian's Center for Child Protection. The Vatican's Congregation for the Evangelization of Peoples offers scholarships, most of which have gone to students from Africa.

Celibacy

Also sensitive is the topic of celibacy. In 2019 reports surfaced about the abuse of religious women by priests and even bishops. It was widely reported that the Vatican had received reports as far back as the 1990s about priests sexually abusing nuns in Africa because they were considered "safe" during the HIV crisis. A Ugandan priest said in March 2018 that many bishops and priests in his country had "failed the celibacy test."

Some priests are leaving the Catholic Church over celibacy to join other churches. The Renewed Universal Catholic Church, a schismatic movement founded by a former priest, Peter Njogu, associated with former

---

[53] Lucie Sarr, "Sexual Abuse: The Challenge Facing the African Church," *La Croix International*, November 18, 2019.

[54] Lucie Sarr, "Several Bishops' Conferences in Africa Announce Sex Abuse Protocols," *La Croix International*, June 27, 2019.

Zambian Archbishop Emmanuel Milingo, now has churches in a number of African countries and some thirty thousand members. It includes over eighty former priests, including eight from Kenya now considered bishops. Estimates put Milingo's movement at 300,000 members across Africa, and it appears to be growing.[55]

Some women are leaving the church, believing their gifts are not recognized. Orobator makes the point that patriarchal interpretations of scripture and a clerical approach to theology place women in subordinate and secondary roles: "Anecdotal evidence suggests that to counter this trend some African women have joined or founded new religious movements, where they find outlets for their ministerial charisms by exercising liturgical leadership and ecclesial authority, especially in the ministry of healing."[56] Thus, the church in Africa is in danger of losing the ministries of many talented women. They are an unrecognized resource.

Conclusion

Although the vital African churches of Christianity's first centuries largely disappeared after the rise of Islam, the growth of Christianity in Africa today is breaking all records. In 1900, Africa had nine million Christians, but by the year 2000, there were an estimated 380 million, approximately 45 percent of the African population. The Catholic population between 2000 and 2010 increased by 33 percent, numbering today some 228 million.

Nevertheless, the Catholic Church in Africa continues to face many challenges. One of the most significant as the churches leave their colonial past behind is developing an authentic African Christianity while maintaining communion with global Catholicism. Related to this is the development of a genuine African spirituality that incorporates the religious sensibility so deep in the African spirit, a close identification with nature, and the importance of ancestors and family. These values should find a place within the church's wealth of spiritual traditions. An African spirituality should also find expression in African liturgy, beyond the stereotypical emphasis on dance and drums.

African Catholicism has many values to bring to a spirituality, without falling prey to the prosperity gospel and premodern emphasis on spiri-

---

[55] "African Married Priests Want African Pope: Schismatic Clergy Creates New Church," Religion News Service, August 14, 2013.

[56] Orobator, *Religion and Faith in Africa*, 133.

tual warfare so common to the neo-Pentecostal and African Instituted Churches. A 2019 working paper of the Episcopal Conferences of Africa and Madagascar's theological committee warned against those churches promising access to material goods and freedom from suffering. The tribalism and "scourge of corruption" that still plague the continent constitute other challenges.

In Africa, where religious and ethnic differences frequently lead to violence, the Catholic Church's dialogue with Islam becomes all the more important, but it is still in its early stages. Not always welcome by representatives of Islam or by all the churches, it is a difficult project. The Catholic Church also needs to join with other churches and Christian communities to continue working for the reconciliation, justice, and peace that symbolize God's reign, as the contributors to Orobator's book on the two African synods insist.[57] Finally, new tensions are emerging around issues of human sexuality: contraception, abortion, and homosexuality.

While older African bishops trained in Rome remain deeply conservative, another generation of young men and woman is emerging, many educated in Europe or the United States. These young church professionals, theologians, priests, and sisters, as well as a new generation of bishops appointed by Pope Francis, are reshaping the African church. Half of them are women, both lay and religious. These women are unaccustomed to more traditional, subservient roles in either church or society. Indeed, the Second Synod of Bishops for Africa, held in 2009, recommended advanced theological training for women. The synod called women "the 'back bone' of the local church" ("Message of the Synod," no. 25). At conferences or workshops dominated by males, they speak out of their experience with passion and confidence.

At a conference on Catholic theological ethics held in Nairobi, Kenya, in August 2012, church leaders—such as Archbishop (now Cardinal) John Onaiyekan of Abuja, Nigeria; Archbishop John Baptist Odama of Gulu of Uganda; and Bishop Eduardo Hiiboro Kussala of Tombura-Yambio, South Sudan—attended not primarily as speakers but as conversation partners. Women participants included Alison Munro, the South African nun who leads the HIV/AIDS Office of the Southern African Catholic Bishops' Conference; the Nigerian-American scholar Anne Arabome; and some younger women still doing their theological studies.

---

[57] Orobator, *Reconciliation, Justice, and Peace.*

This new generation of theologians is concerned not just with inner ecclesial issues—clericalism, patriarchy, ecclesiastical status—but also with "the trauma of ethnic division, economic mismanagement, human rights abuses, political bigotry, and civil and sectarian violence," crises that affect the lives of all Africans. Thus, Orobator notes, there is far more to African Catholicism than the erroneous stereotype of "the dancing church." Echoing Pliny the Elder, he adds, "There is always something new out of Africa!"[58]

---

[58] Agbonkhianmeghe E. Orobator, "Out of Africa: How a New Generation of Theologians Is Reshaping the Church," *America,* November 5, 2012; see also Orobator, *The Church We Want.*

4

Latin America

Catholicism came to Latin America with the explorers and colonists from Portugal and Spain in the sixteenth century. The Franciscan, Dominican, and Jesuit missionaries who came with them did much to shape Latin American culture. Arriving as early as the second voyage of Columbus, Franciscans established missions where they catechized and taught children, including girls, to read. Franciscan bishop Juan de Zumárraga established the first printing press in the Americas in Mexico City, in 1539. There were some three hundred Franciscan missionaries in New Spain (Mexico) as early as 1569. At least 129 friars died as martyrs during native uprisings in Peru and the region north of the Amazon.

Dominican friars arrived at Santo Domingo as early as 1510. Dominicans Antonio de Montesinos, murdered in 1540 by a Spanish officer, and Bartolomé de las Casas both campaigned against the enslavement of the native peoples. The missionary work of the Dominicans in Peru produced two saints, Saint Rose of Lima, a member of the Dominican third order, and Blessed Martin de Porres, a lay brother. Both were of mixed race.

The Jesuits organized city states called reductions (*reducciones*) for the native peoples in Brazil, Paraguay, Argentina, and Bolivia. Sometimes described as "socialist utopias," these places were economically self-sufficient, autonomous communities governed by the Indians themselves under the careful guidance of the Jesuit fathers. They also served to protect the native peoples from the efforts of colonial slave traders, ultimately forming native militias to defend them—one of the causes that led to the expulsion of the Jesuits from their missions and ultimately to the suppression of the order in 1773. A recent study of thirty of these Jesuit reductions done at the University of British Columbia suggests that they had a greater long-term effect than anyone could have expected. In his dissertation Felipe Valencia Caicedo writes:

> In everything from literacy and skills training to overall levels of education, the areas around the former Jesuit missions continue to show significantly higher levels of achievement than equivalent communities without missions—with median years of schooling and literacy levels 10 to 15 percent higher, and modern per-capita incomes nearly 10 percent higher. These areas also show the persistence of skills that can be quite specific.

Valencia offers the example of embroidery, introduced by Jesuit missionaries mostly from the Low Countries.[1]

For several centuries most Latin Americans were Catholic, though in their own way. In many parts of the continent a syncretic Catholicism blended Catholic faith with traditional religious practices and beliefs including shamanism and *curanderismo,* while from colonial times regular sacramental practice and attendance at mass were rare, especially among the poor. At the same time, as the modern Latin American nation states emerged from Spanish and Portuguese colonialism, Catholicism remained the established religion, supported by the alliance of church and state, especially with conservative governments that privileged the church at the expense of the late-arriving Protestant and still later Pentecostal churches. Catholic institutions and schools were often subsidized or granted tax-exempt status, while Protestant institutions paid taxes; in some countries, public schools taught Catholic doctrine and morals or offered Catholic religion classes. In Argentina and Chile, Catholic bishops sought to have the state require legal registration requirements on all non-Catholic churches because of the growth of Pentecostal churches.

Catholicism's privileged place changed significantly as the old alliance of church and state began to break down in the final decades of the twentieth century. First, the movement known as Catholic Action, with its method of "see-judge-act," was influential in mobilizing a more engaged laity in countries like Brazil, Chile, Peru, and Central America before and after the Second World War, though it remained a movement under the firm control of the hierarchy. In the 1950s and 1960s it began to move

---

[1] Jim McDermott, "Centuries Later, Jesuit Missions in South America Are Still Strengthening Communities," *America*, December 11, 2018.

increasingly into the political arena, alarming the bishops. Some of the students and young people involved began to move beyond the church itself in their commitment to social action. As Todd Hartch writes, "Although Catholic Action gradually lost momentum across Latin America because of its internal contradictions, by the 1960s it had trained two generations of Catholic laity, mobilizing them for various projects, and giving them the expectation of involvement in social, political, and religious affairs."[2]

Latin American Catholicism after the Council

The Second Vatican Council was to bring new life to the church in Latin America. Newly energized by the council's turn to the poor and the emergence of liberation theology, the church began to embrace a more critical position over against society and the state. Perhaps most significant, toward the end of the council, on November 16, 1965, about forty bishops gathered in the ancient Catacombs of Saint Domitilla to celebrate the Eucharist. Most of them were from Latin America, though some came from Europe, Asia, and Africa. They were led by Dom Hélder Câmara of Recife in Brazil, famous for his remark: "When I feed the poor, they call me a saint; when I ask why they are poor, they call me a communist." The gathered bishops signed an agreement, the Pact of the Catacombs, pledging themselves to a simple lifestyle, without privilege, embracing a certain austerity and poverty as well as solidarity with the poor and the promotion of justice and liberation. Though significant for Latin America, the Pact of the Catacombs was to have influence far beyond its borders. And it continues to influence some bishops today; toward the end of the October 2019 Synod on the Amazon around forty bishops gathered again to renew the Pact of the Catacombs, pledging themselves to defend the Amazon rainforests, a major concern of the synod.

When the bishops returned from Vatican II, they began working to bring its reforms to life in their churches. First on their agenda was their scheduled assembly of the Latin America Episcopal Conference (CELAM), at Medellín, Colombia, in 1968. Bishops and theologians were already well aware of the crushing poverty, political oppression, and government-sponsored violence that maintained the status quo.

---

[2]Todd Hartch, *The Rebirth of Latin American Christianity* (New York: Oxford University Press, 2014), 134.

At Medellín the bishops began to use the new language of liberation theology emerging in the works of theologians like Juan Luis Segundo of Uruguay, Gustavo Gutiérrez of Peru, and Lucia Gera of Argentina, one of Jorge Mario Bergoglio's teachers. They spoke of structural evil, a church of the poor committed to liberation, and forming disciples committed to the example of Jesus. They hoped for a poor church that "denounces the unjust lack of this world's goods and the sin that it begets; preaches and lives in spiritual poverty, as an attitude of spiritual childhood and openness to the Lord; is herself bound to material poverty."[3] Another meeting of CELAM at Puebla in 1979 encouraged a preferential option for the poor and the formation of comunidades eclesiales de base or base Christian communities (CEBs), small gatherings of neighbors to reflect on the words of scripture and to apply them in the concrete context of their lives. The Fifth CELAM meeting at Aparecida, Brazil, in 2007, reaffirmed many of these themes, with Jorge Mario Bergoglio playing a major role.

Many Latin American Catholic churches took up the challenge set before them by CELAM; they began to speak out on behalf of the poor and to oppose oppressive military governments in Central America, Argentina, Brazil, Bolivia, Chile, and elsewhere. The conflicts that followed resulted in many martyrs, including catechists and lay leaders, clergy, nuns, even bishops.[4] Bishop Enrique Angelelli was killed in 1976 in La Rioja, Argentina, when his car was run off the road. Two senior military officers were later convicted for their involvement. Archbishop Oscar Romero of San Salvador was shot while saying mass in 1980. Pope Francis canonized him on October 14, 2018, overruling opposition from some in the Curia. Bishop Juan José Gerardi of Guatemala was beaten to death in 1998 after he submitted a report on government atrocities in its counterinsurgency campaign. Three military officers were convicted for his death.

The Second Vatican Council revitalized the Catholic Church in Latin America, with its concern for social justice, its preferential option for the poor, and the evangelical challenge of its CEBs. Many pastoral leaders saw the CEBs as forming the church of the future, a church from the base rather than from the top down, energized by lay leaders. By 1979, there

---

[3] See Hosffman Ospino and Rafael Luciana, "How Latin America Influenced the Entire Catholic Church," *America*, August 21, 2018.

[4] See Penny Lernoux, *Cry of the People: United States Involvement in the Rise of Fascism, Torture, and Murder and the Persecution of the Catholic Church in Latin America* (Garden City, NY: Doubleday and Co., 1980).

may have been as many as eighty thousand CEBs in Brazil.[5] However, by the late 1980s the energy of the movement had been considerably diminished. What had happened?

Movements, Challenges, and Changes

One factor was the explosive growth of evangelical Protestantism, particularly the Pentecostal and neo-Pentecostal communities. Along with evangelical Protestantism was the Catholic charismatic renewal (CCR), a Catholic version of Pentecostalism that has been a positive movement contributing to considerable renewal. A second factor was the inability of liberation theology, with its postmodern, European roots, to speak to the hearts of the poor of Latin America, as well as opposition to liberation theology from Rome. A third factor was a growing secularization, leading to a new opposition to Catholic teaching on feminist and LGBTQ issues—abortion, gay rights, same-sex marriage, and gender identity, as well as the loss of many to religion in general. Finally, a fourth factor was the problem of the sexual abuse of minors.

The Pentecostal Explosion

The loss of tens of millions of Latin American Catholics to the "new" churches, the rapidly expanding evangelical and Pentecostal communities, has changed the continent's religious demographics. Scholars often speak of three waves of Pentecostals. The first wave consists of classical Pentecostals such as the Assemblies of God and the Church of God in Christ. They stress conversion, baptism in the Holy Spirit, and the charismatic gifts, especially tongues, often seen as a sign of the Spirit's presence. The second wave is represented mostly by Christians in the mainline churches involved in the charismatic renewal, including a very large number of Hispanic Catholics. The third wave consists of the "new" churches, often referred to as neo-Pentecostal or neo-charismatics. It includes evangelicals and other Christians from independent or indigenous churches; they are concerned with spiritual warfare against evil spirits and the devil,

---

[5] James C. Cavendish, "Christian Base Communities and the Building of Democracy: Brazil and Chile," *Sociology of Religion* 55, no. 2 (Summer 1994): 191.

exorcisms, and miraculous cures. Many preach the prosperity gospel, asking parishioners to offer sacrifices, tithing, or making "pacts" with God in order to receive divine blessings.[6]

Even as late as 1970, 92 percent of Latin America was Catholic; since then, there has been rapid change. A 2014 Pew Forum survey found that the region was only 69 percent Catholic, while another survey by the respected Chilean polling firm Latinobarómetro put the number of Catholics at 59 percent.[7] Even under Pope Francis the numbers have continued to drop. According to Andrew Chesnut, the Latinobarómetro survey shows Catholics are no longer the majority in six Latin American countries. Uruguay, the most secularized in the region, is only 38 percent Catholic; Chile, 45 percent; Guatemala, 43 percent; El Salvador, 40 percent; Honduras, 37 percent; and Nicaragua 40 percent. Brazil is still 54 percent Catholic, but Chesnut predicts the country will no longer have a Catholic majority after 2025.[8] Nor are losses to the church confined to Catholics. The number of religiously unaffiliated in Latin America, the "nones," has risen from 8 percent in 2014 to 17 percent in 2017.[9]

When asked why they left the Catholic Church, a Pew Research Center report said that the most common explanation was that they were seeking a more personal connection with God. For many, Pentecostalism speaks to their thirst in a secular culture for an ongoing encounter with the supernatural and the transcendent. Others said that they were looking for a different style of worship or a church that was more helpful to its members. In addition, evangelizing efforts by Protestant churches have seemed to pay off. Of the more than half of those who joined Protestant congregations, 58 percent said that their new church reached out to them. The survey also found that Protestants were much more likely than Catholics to report sharing their faith with people outside their

---

[6] See Thomas P. Rausch, "Catholics and Pentecostals: Troubled History, New Initiatives," *Theological Studies* 71, no. 4 (2010): 926–50; see also R. Andrew Chesnut, *Born Again in Brazil: The Pentecostal Boom and the Pathogens of Poverty* (New Brunswick, NJ: Rutgers University Press, 1997), 80–84.

[7] Juan Marco Vaggione and José Morán Faúdes, eds., "Introduction: *Laicidad* and Religious Diversity: Themes in the Debates on the Regulation of Religion in Latin America," in *Laicidad and Religious Diversity in Latin America* (Cham, Switzerland: Springer, 2017), 10.

[8] Andrew Chesnut, "Is Latin America Still Catholic?" *Catholic Herald* (UK), January 25, 2018; see also Pedro Lopez-Gallo, "The Decline of Catholicism in Latin America," *The BC Catholic* (April 25, 2018).

[9] Lopez-Gallo, "The Decline of Catholicism in Latin America."

own religious groups.[10] Another scholar said that Pentecostalism attracts because it locates everyday life experience in a plausible story of salvation, is preached by neighbors, and is validated in direct spiritual experience.[11]

Furthermore, a class distinction often separates Catholic pastors from their congregations. Pentecostal preachers tend to look and sound more like their flocks. They are often unlettered. In Guatemala, many are Mayan, and in Brazil, they are Afro-Brazilian. "By contrast, in the Catholic Church, most priests are part of the elite. They are either white or *mestizo* and many are actually from Europe."[12]

Some attribute the success of Pentecostalism and especially neo-Pentecostalism to its ability to take on a Latin American expression, its emphasis on healing and promoting healthy lifestyles, and men joining giving up alcohol and substance abuse, gambling, and womanizing.[13] I have heard this from some of my Latin American colleagues, while others disagree. For example, Edward Cleary argues that not all evangelicals and Pentecostals are that fervent, neither going to church every week nor following the perfectionist admonitions of their pastors.[14] Many of these are in neo-Pentecostal communities, which are less identified with classical Pentecostalism.

In *Christianity in the Twentieth Century* Brian Stanley writes that the global Pentecostal movement in the first three-quarters of the twentieth century drew most of its adherents from the poor, offering the impoverished of Africa and Latin America the blessings of healing and a democratic voice through the charismata of speaking in tongues and prophecies. However, from the 1980s on, the neo-Pentecostal churches, now appealing to the upwardly mobile, began to stress spiritual warfare and the prosperity gospel. "For many—though not for all—in these churches Pentecostal Christianity was in danger of becoming a form of theology of liberation

---

[10] Pew Research Center, "Religion in Latin America: Widespread Change in a Historically Catholic Region," November 13, 2014.

[11] Rowan Ireland, "A Pentecostal Latin America?" *The Way* 38, no. 3 (July 1998): 217.

[12] Pew Research Center, "Why Has Pentecostalism Grown So Dramatically in Latin America?" November 14, 2014.

[13] Pew Research Center, "Why Has Pentecostalism Grown So Dramatically in Latin America?" See also R. Andrew Chesnut, *Born Again in Brazil: The Pentecostal Boom and the Pathogens of Poverty* (New Brunswick, NJ: Rutgers University Press, 1997), 108–13; Allan Figueroa Deck, "Pentecostalism and Catholic Identity," *Ecumenical Trends* 40, no. 5 (May 2011): 6.

[14] Edward L. Cleary, *How Latin America Saved the Soul of the Catholic Church* (New York: Paulist Press, 2009), 11. Cleary says that a survey of Chilean evangelicals, most of them Pentecostals, found the majority nonobservant, 52 percent did not attend church weekly, and almost 38 percent seldom or never attended.

focused almost entirely on the individual and unashamedly yoked to the ideology of capitalism."[15]

Despite the losses in recent years, Latin America is home to more than 450 million Catholics, nearly 40 percent of the world's total Catholic population. Mexico has the world's second-largest Catholic population (96 million). Only Brazil has more Catholics, over 120 million, accounting, over 50 percent of the country's population. But even as the "nones" rise and the Catholic percentage continues to decline, there are some signs of hope. Pentecostalism is also leaving its mark on Latin American Catholics, often with positive results.

The Catholic Charismatic Renewal

Todd Johnson says that the Catholic charismatic renewal (CCR), the largest charismatic renewal today, is found in significant numbers across Latin America.[16] As even more Hispanics become involved in the charismatic renewal, they have contributed to the revitalization of their church. Unlike Protestant Christians, who often leave their traditional churches when they become Pentecostals, Catholic charismatics remain Catholics. Many have found a revitalized religious life in the Renewal, which in many ways represents a Catholic expression of Pentecostalism.

Credit for the beginnings of the CCR generally goes to the Duquesne Weekend, a retreat in the spring of 1967 when a group of university professors and students from Duquesne University in Pittsburg experienced an outpouring or "baptism" of the Spirit, including the gift of tongues. From this small beginning the movement spread rapidly, forming charismatic prayer groups, communities gathered around universities and parishes, and soon covenant communities. By 1987, there were 10,500 prayer groups in the United States. For many Catholics it brought a new, more affective experience of their faith, making them comfortable with spontaneous prayer and more bodily expression. But the movement in the United States went into a decline in the 1990s; participation in prayer groups fell off, covenant communities broke up, and many moved on to

---

[15] Brian Stanley, *Christianity in the Twentieth Century: A World History* (Princeton, NJ: Princeton University Press, 2018), 311.

[16] Todd Johnson, *World Christian Encyclopedia*, 3rd ed. (Edinburgh University Press, 2019); see also Todd M. Johnson, "Pentecostal/Charismatic Christianity," Gordon Conwell Theological Seminary (May 27, 2020).

greater involvement in works of social justice. Nevertheless, the CCR has had a continuing effect on how Catholics pray.

The CCR has been much more fruitful in Latin America. In Brazil, Catholics were slow to use the mass media, in contrast to the Pentecostals, but they expanded rapidly into a radio ministry in the 1980s. In 1979, an American Jesuit, Edward Dougherty, established a production company in a garage in Campinas; before long he was producing television programs for his network, Século 21, and exporting them to other countries. By 2003, television efforts sponsored largely by charismatic Catholics had grown enormously, with several wide-reaching networks. The CCR claimed thirty-three million Catholics in Brazil by 2008.[17] In Colombia, the renewal has been concerned with social justice since its emergence in the early 1970s.

A Pew Forum 2007 report noted that more than half of Brazilian Catholics had adopted elements of spirit-filled or renewalist Christianity, including speaking in tongues and healing. This phenomenon continues to grow, nor is it confined to Brazil. Thorsen has observed it in Guatemala and elsewhere.[18] In Guatemala, 34 percent of the country are Catholic charismatics. While the number of Catholics continues to decline, scholars like Chesnut argue that "those losses would have been much more acute if it hadn't been for this renewal movement in the Latin American Catholic Church."[19] Todd Hartch submits that the CCR "might even be more significant than the rise of Pentecostalism. But it is less visible."[20] He cites Pentecostal historian Donald Dayton who says that while Pentecostalism was born in the United States, "it is discovering its destiny in Latin America," in both its Protestant and Catholic versions.[21]

Thorsen argues that the renewal has influenced far more Catholics in Latin America than liberation theology and the CEB movement. Sixteen percent have participated to some extent in the charismatic renewal, as compared to 2–5 percent in the CEBs.[22] No one has been more aware

---

[17] Hartch, *The Rebirth of Latin American Christianity*, 118.

[18] Luis Lugo, "Pope to Visit 'Pentecostalized' Brazil," Pew Research Center, May 9, 2007; Jacob Egeris Thorsen, *Charismatic Practice and Catholic Parish Life: The Incipient Pentecostalization of the Church in Guatemala and Latin America* (Leiden: Brill, 2015).

[19] David Masci, "Why Has Pentecostalization Grown So Dramatically in Latin America."

[20] Hartch, *The Rebirth of Latin American Christianity*, 113; for an overview of the movement in Latin America, see chapter 6, "The Heartland of Charismatic Catholicism," 114–26.

[21] Hartch, *The Rebirth of Latin American Christianity,* 124.

[22] See Jacob Egeris Thorsen, "Charismatic Catholicism in Latin America," in the *Cambridge History of Religions in Latin America*, ed. Virginia Garrard-Burnett, Paul Freston, and

of this gap between liberation theology as a European import and popular religion than Pope Francis, who himself has charismatic tendencies. Catholics who have become Pentecostals speak of the lively, affective Pentecostal worship services in contrast to the more formal rituals of Catholicism, of an emphasis on healing and lay ministry, and of the ability of Pentecostalism to help them change the disordered aspects of their lives. Many have stories of being set free from depression, alcoholism, drug addiction, or marital infidelity.

The CCR and Protestant Pentecostalism have much in common, including a more biblically focused faith; a commitment to the historic doctrines of Christianity; and an emphasis on life in the Spirit, healing, and conversion. They find more agreement on issues of sexuality and marriage than they do with many historic Protestant denominations. However, there are also significant differences. Catholics place less emphasis on speaking in tongues, which for Pentecostals is usually evidence for baptism in the Spirit. Neo-Pentecostals place far more emphasis on miracles, spiritual warfare, and the prosperity gospel.

Catholic charismatics have been able to keep their renewal movement within the life of their church; baptism in the Spirit does not replace the other sacraments but represents a new outpouring of grace in their lives. Their understanding of the charismatic gifts is more inclusive, and they see conversion as an ongoing, lifelong process, not a single event, as is typical of many evangelical Protestants. They retain their basic identities, with lifestyles and habits frowned on by Pentecostals, for example, smoking and the use of alcohol. The Eucharist remains central, though often with an emphasis on healing during the liturgy, and their devotion to Mary remains strong. Some Catholic theologians have been involved in the movement since the beginning and have served as mediators with church authorities. Cleary calls attention to the way the CCR has led to an empowerment of the laity in the Catholic Church in Latin America, something largely ignored by other commentators.[23]

Commentators often overlook the vitality and growth of the CCR. While the mainline Protestant churches did not generally welcome the Pentecostal movement, Catholic leaders did, if at first somewhat hesitantly. Cardinal Suenens and Pope John Paul II supported the movement from early on. In 1993, the Vatican officially recognized the renewal, renaming

---

Stephen C. Dove (Cambridge: Cambridge University Press, 2016), 466.

[23] Edward L. Cleary, *The Rise of Charismatic Catholicism in Latin America* (Gainesville: University Press of Florida, 2011), 15–16.

the central coordinating commission the International Catholic Charismatic Renewal Service. Thanks to structures linking the renewal and the Latin American episcopal conferences, most of the bishops support the renewal; they appreciate its efforts for evangelization and the sense of community it provides. The movement has touched millions. In 2003, Gastón Espinosa reported that there were more Latino Catholic charismatics than Protestant Pentecostals in Latin America and the United States.[24] Methodist pastor and theologian William Payne affirmed that in 2016 in regard to Latin America, but he also argued that in the long run Catholicism will continue to lose ground as Latino Pentecostalism continues to grow.[25]

Still, as Cleary and Hartch argue, the CCR has done much to revitalize Latin American Catholicism. Lay movements are strong, and many of the laity are engaged in evangelization. In 2007, vocations to the priesthood increased dramatically in many Latin American countries, most of them native born.[26] Uruguay was the only country, aside from Cuba, to experience a decrease in clergy (30 percent from 1957 to 2008).[27]

But a shortage of priests remains a problem, particularly in the vast Amazon basin. In 2019 the Vatican acknowledged that the number of priests worldwide had declined for the first time in a decade. The Amazon region is affected critically by the decline, where some communities can have mass only a few times a year. For example, the diocese of Caxias do Maranhao in Brazil has only twenty-five priests for 825,000 Catholics.

Ecumenism

With tensions between Catholics and the new evangelical and Pentecostal churches, ecumenical relations should be particularly important, but for the most part they have yet to develop. Tensions between Catholic and evangelicals go back to the sixteenth century, exacerbated by the Black Legend, a collection of myths demonizing Spanish colonialism and Catholicism. Latin American Protestants have not forgotten the persecution they suffered at the hands of the Inquisition, which used torture and the

---

[24] Gastón Espinosa, "The Impact of Pluralism on Trends in Latin American and US Latino Religions and Society," in *Perspectivas: Hispanic Theological Initiative Occasional Paper Series* 7 (Fall 2003): 16; see also Cleary, *The Rise of Charismatic Catholicism in Latin America*, 1.

[25] William P. Payne, "Folk Religion and the Pentecostalism Surge in Latin America," *The Asbury Journal* 71 (2016): 161–62.

[26] Cleary, *The Rise of Charismatic Catholicism in Latin America*, 53.

[27] Cleary, *The Rise of Charismatic Catholicism in Latin America*, 214.

death penalty in the attempt to force the conversion of those who fell into its hands. In Lima, Peru, there is a Museum of the Inquisition exhibiting the underground dungeons and instruments of torture used to punish heretics. It is also true that Latin American countries privileged an established Catholicism at the expense of Protestant communities, adding to the tensions. Today, much of that is gone; the region's growing religious pluralism has led to an increasing emphasis on the separation of church and state. Still, it was only in April 2019 that Bolivian evangelicals were granted the same rights as Catholics.

Nonetheless, there are few examples of developing ecumenical relations. Some Catholic bishops have reached out to evangelicals and Pentecostals in Argentina. The first meeting between Catholics and Pentecostals in Brazil did not take place until 2008, with the Pentecostals coming on their own initiative, not as representatives of their churches.

Ecumenism has a better record in El Salvador. According to a poll by Latinobarómetro 2017, Catholics in El Salvador make up 39 percent of the population and Protestants 28 percent. Roughly half the Protestants are Pentecostal, but Lutherans in El Salvador share certain liberationist perspectives with Catholics. Lutheran Bishop Medardo Gómez was among other church leaders who were present for the celebration of the beatification of Archbishop Oscar Romero in 2015 in San Salvador.[28]

As early as 1989, the Chilean episcopal conference invited Chilean Pentecostal Juan Sepúlveda to take part in a conference. Out of it came a commitment from the bishops to respect what Pentecostals emphasize, to refrain from derogatory comments, and to begin to work toward solidarity with these "separated brethren," all in hopes of better relationships. In 1997, Sepúlveda attended the CELAM Synod for America as a Pentecostal observer, and in 2007, he gave a plenary address at the CELAM Conference at Aparecida in the presence of Pope Benedict. Two evangelicals were invited to the 2019 Synod on the Amazon as "fraternal delegates," one of whom addressed the assembly. However, working with the many and diverse neo-Pentecostal communities remains a challenge.

Liberation Theology

Despite the enthusiasm for liberation theology in the years following the Second Vatican Council, under Popes John Paul II and Benedict XVI the

---

[28]The Lutheran World Federation, "Salvadoran Catholic Archbishop: A Great Friend and a Great Ecumenist," San Salvador, May 28, 2015.

church in Latin American moved in a more conservative direction. Coming from Communist East Europe, John Paul remained deeply suspicious of the Marxist strains in liberation theology and sought to reverse course by appointing conservative bishops, many from Opus Dei. Joseph Ratzinger, John Paul's head of the Congregation for the Doctrine of the Faith, had long been "allergic" to political theology. Under his prefecture the congregation issued two documents critical of liberation theology: *Instruction on Certain Aspects of the "Theology of Liberation"* (1984) and *Instruction on Christian Freedom and Liberation* (1986).

It is also true that liberation theology remained foreign to the religious sensibilities of many of the faithful. Though it provided the theological foundation for the CEBs in the 1970s and early 1980s, it remained a European import. Its Latin American advocates were for the most part educated in Germany or Belgium, and the "contextual" theologies they sought to develop failed to make room for the popular religion so deeply a part of the religious imagination of Latin American Catholics. These theologies failed to speak to the people's hearts, with their affective faith and openness to the supernatural. As one hears frequently today, "The Catholic Church opted for the poor, while the poor opted for the Pentecostals."

Phillip Berryman notes a gap between the religious sensitivity of the people and many of their priests who, with their post–Vatican II education, no longer shared the people's faith in miracles, promises made to God, novenas, and rituals with holy water.[29] Pope Francis has attempted to address this with his emphasis on *religiosidad popular*, with its emphasis on feeling or sentiment. It was this affective side of faith that Francis found missing in what to him was a more ideological liberation theology, with its elements of Enlightenment rationalism and Marxism. There is some evidence today that the tension between the renewal and liberation theology may be diminishing. A project in 2020 notes a "warming" of Brazilian liberation theologians to the movement's emphasis on faith, citing Leonardo Boff as an example.[30]

Secularization

A second significant cultural shift is a growing secularization across the Latin American continent. Secularization has diminished the influence

---

[29] Phillip Berryman, *Religion in the Megacity: Catholic and Protestant Portraits from Latin America* (Maryknoll, NY: Orbis Books, 1996), 151.

[30] Samir Knego, "The Catholic Spirit: Music, Media, Miracles, and the Brazilian Catholic Charismatic Renewal," Religious Studies Honors Projects 16, Macalester College, 2020.

of the church in favor of autonomy in the areas of social and political life. The Catholic Church had long opposed liberal attitudes toward issues of sexuality, marriage, and divorce, and even sex education; in the twenty-first century its efforts refocused on abortion, homosexuality, and same-sex marriage.

However, sexual mores were changing. Same-sex marriage has been legalized in Mexico (2007), Argentina (2010), Brazil and Uruguay (2013), and Colombia (2016). While abortion under any circumstances is illegal in six countries, in the majority, including Argentina, Bolivia, Colombia, Ecuador, Venezuela, and Chile, it is legal if for rape or maternal health. The number of abortions continues to increase. The Guttmacher Institute reported in 2018 that the proportion of pregnancies in Latin America and the Caribbean ending in abortion increased between 1990–94 and 2010–14 from 23 percent to 32 percent. A presidential effort to legalize abortion in Argentina in 2018 failed to clear the senate but led to a "protest of colors" in Buenos Aires, the pro-choice side using green while pro-lifers there and in other cities wore light-blue handkerchiefs.

Along with the loss of so many Catholics to Pentecostalism and the new religious pluralism, secularization has led to the privatization of religion. The result is what some have described as the disestablishment of the Catholic Church.[31] Other churches are also experiencing significant losses. Many in Latin America are leaving religious practice all together, joining those who no longer identify with any faith tradition. In 2014, the Pew Center reported that the religiously unaffiliated in Latin America had risen from 4 percent to 8 percent.[32] Yet three years later, the number had increased to 17 percent.[33] This aslo may affect the future of Pentecostalism. As early as 1998, Rowan Ireland noted signs, documented in the case of Chile, "that the Pentecostal churches, under changing socio-economic conditions, do not retain their numbers well and do not attract the better-educated young or the x-generation global consumers."[34] Ten years later Andrew Chesnut reported that though

---

[31] See Julieta Lemaitre, "The Problem of the Plaza: Religious Freedom, Disestablishment, and the Catholic Church in Latin America's Public Square," in *Laicidad and Religious Diversity in Latin America*, ed. Juan Marco Vaggione and José Morán Faúdes (Cham, Switzerland: Springer, 2017), 36–39.

[32] Pew Research Center, "Religion in Latin America: Widespread Change in a Historically Catholic Region," November 13, 2014.

[33] Lopez-Gallo, "The Decline of Catholicism in Latin America."

[34] Ireland, "A Pentecostal Latin America?" 218.

Pentecostalism has continued to expand over the past decade, it does so today at a slower rate.[35]

There is also growing evidence that many of those who convert to Pentecostalism later leave and end up not practicing any religion at all. According to Kurt Bowen's study on evangelism and apostasy in Mexico, 43 percent of adults in the second generation were no longer part of the evangelical world; while some returned to Catholicism or took up another faith, the majority (41 percent) were simply "nones" (nothing). The dropouts were highest among Pentecostals.[36] Cleary argues from interviews with Charismatic leaders that "most dropouts remain Catholic and continue to attend church with a bit more fervor and a greatly enhanced musical repertoire. Many dropouts from Pentecostalism fall into the category of 'no religion,' a growing cohort in Latin America. This does not seem to be the case with Catholic Charismatics."[37] Hartch notes, "Protestants proved much better at conversion than at retention."[38]

Though more research is needed on this question, if it is true that many of those who join Pentecostal communities eventually end up practicing no Christian faith at all, it might make more sense both ecumenically and from an evangelical perspective for Catholics and Pentecostals to try to support one another rather than working in competition.

Sexual Abuse

The scandal of the sexual abuse of minors by priests was slow to emerge in Latin America, but when it surfaced in Chile, it embarrassed even Pope Francis. In January 2015, Francis had named Juan Barros the bishop of Osorno, though several Chilean bishops questioned the appointment because of his close ties to Father Fernando Karadima, a popular priest the Vatican had forced into retirement in 2011 for sexually abusing minors. Even though most of the bishops of Chile did not attend Barros's

---

[35] Chesnut, "Is Latin America Still Catholic?"

[36] Kurt Bowen, *Evangelism and Apostasy: The Evolution and Impact of Evangelicals in Modern Mexico* (Buffalo, NY: McGill-Queen's University Press, 1996), 70–71. The most important factor in these "defections" was mixed marriages with Catholics (72). See also Espinosa, "The Impact of Pluralism on Trends in Latin American and US Latino Religions and Society," 14, 23.

[37] Cleary, *The Rise of Charismatic Catholicism in Latin America*, 26; see also Bowen, *Evangelism and Apostasy*, 70–71.

[38] Hartch, *The Rebirth of Latin American Christianity*, 55.

installation, a ceremony that drew furious protests, the Vatican continued to defend Barros. When Francis visited Chile in January 2018, he apologized for the "irreparable damage" done to those who had been abused, though he continued to defend Barros, saying that he had received no evidence against him and that the continuing opposition was slander. The next day Cardinal Sean O'Malley acknowledged the pope's concern for those who had so suffered, but added that his words seemed to abandon and discredit them.[39]

After returning to Rome, Francis sent Archbishop Charles Scicluna of Malta, the Vatican's specialist on sexual abuse, and Father Jordi Bertomeu to examine the charges against Barros. After the two submitted a twenty-three-hundred-page report uncovering a long history of sexual abuse and cover-ups, Francis publicly apologized to the Chilean church in a letter to the country's bishops.[40] He summoned the country's thirty-four bishops to meet with him in Rome to address charges of "grave negligence" and invited the three victims of Karadima to meet with him to share their stories. After a three-day summit with the pope (May 17–21), the bishops submitted their resignations in writing, asking pardon of the victims, the pope, and the people of their country for their errors and abuse of power.

Francis has since accepted at least eight episcopal resignations and expelled from the priesthood two retired bishops accused of abusing children. In March 2019, he accepted the resignation of Cardinal Ricardo Ezzati, archbishop of Santiago, accused by the prosecutor's office of covering up cases of abuse. The Chilean national prosecutor's office has identified 266 victims, including 178 who were children or teenagers at the time of the abuses. The investigations are looking at reports filed since 2000, though some of the cases date as far back as 1960. Bishops kept silence, and some apostolic nuncios protected accused priests. Italian Cardinal Angelo Sodano, who as Vatican secretary of state under Pope Benedict backed Marcial Maciel, had long supported Karadima.

Similar cases have surfaced in other Latin American countries. More than 150 priests have been suspended for abuse in Mexico since 2019, though the first conviction of a priest did not take place until 2018. The first priest in Brazil was convicted in 2010, and a second in 2018. One source cited by *Crux* news said that 40 percent of the cases currently under investigation by

---

[39] "Pope Apologises to Sex Abuse Victims, Defends Accused Chilean Bishop," *Tablet*, January 22, 2018.

[40] Inés San Martín, "Pope Francis Tells Sex Abuse Survivors, 'I Was Part of the Problem,'" *Crux*, May 2, 2018.

the Congregation for the Doctrine of the Faith are from Latin America.[41] NGOs and government sources report numerous cases occurring every day in Brazil. Bishops conferences in Latin America are just beginning to take the steps necessary to develop systems to protect minors.[42]

Snapshots

Many countries in Latin America have faced crises in their economic, cultural, or political life, and political violence is common. Thousands have become refugees. Since becoming bishop of Rome, Francis has made five trips to the continent; he has spoken out against threats to indigenous communities and on behalf of efforts to protect the environment. Let us now examine briefly some of those countries and regions.

Brazil

No country has more Catholics than Brazil, but in recent years the church has lost thousands to evangelical and especially Pentecostal congregations. A Datafolha study in 2013 reported that Catholics amounted to 57 percent of the Brazilian population, and evangelicals 28 percent. A 2020 study puts Brazilian Catholics at 51 percent and evangelicals at 31 percent. Some estimate that evangelicalism will surpass Catholicism in Brazil by 2032. While many of those who profess to be Catholic do not participate in the church, those who do are growing in their commitment, and the number of diocesan priests ordained each year is increasing.[43]

Venezuela

Both Venezuela and Nicaragua have experienced political turmoil and violence, with people fleeing their country and repressive governments. In Venezuela, President Hugo Chávez's fourteen years of mismanagement left the country in chaos, and protests have racked the country under his

[41] Inés San Martín, "Latin American Cardinals Add Their Voices to Press for Abuse Reform," *Crux*, February 19, 2019.

[42] Marie Malzac, "Awareness Rising over Scale of Abuse in Latin America," *La Croix International*, February 18, 2019.

[43] Eduardo Campus Limes, "As Evangelicals Gain, Catholics on Verge of Losing Majority in Brazil," *National Catholic Reporter*, February 5, 2020.

successor, Nicholas Maduro. In July 2017, the country's bishops accused Maduro of trying to impose a dictatorship by changing the constitution and have continued to speak out against the damaging policies of his administration.

On April 25, 2018, the bishops released a statement saying that the country is living a "history of death." "The State is every day more compromised in its role of ensuring basic goods for the subsistence of the people,"[44] a failure that translates into more hunger and unemployment. There is a basic lack of public services. "Day after day, we continue to descend into a spiral of conflicts, which have their roots in the widespread lack of food, medicine, water, electricity, transport, and in increasing insecurity and inflation."[45] Nearly three million of the country's eight million schoolchildren are missing some or all of their classes. The health of the people is suffering.

According to the World Health Organization, cases of malaria in Venezuela increased by 69 percent, rising from 240,613 in 2016 to 406,000 in 2017. The Center for Strategic and International Studies stated that the average Venezuelan lost about twenty-four pounds in 2017, in a population where almost 90 percent live below the poverty line. The reelection of Nicholas Maduro on May 20, 2018, was widely seen as fraudulent, with the government giving out sacks of food to those who voted for Maduro. In total, at least three million Venezuelans have left their country for Colombia, Argentina, Chile, Brazil, and other nations, seeing no future for themselves and their families at home. Ecuador and Peru have closed their borders to those without passports, which the government of Venezuela is reluctant to issue. Colombia, hitherto quite generous, has also begun requiring a valid passport and refugee status to enter the country in an effort to diminish the number of refugees.

Colombia

Colombia faces its own problems. The Catholic Church in Colombia has sought to welcome and aid the refugees coming across the border, but the long war between the government and the FARC, a leftist guerrilla movement, has left the country with 7 million internally displaced persons. The church helped to broker a peace accord between the government and the

---

[44] Inés San Martín, "Bishops Warn Venezuela Is Headed for a 'Humanitarian Catastrophe,'" *Crux,* April 25, 2018.

[45] Claire Lesegretain, "Catholic Church at the Forefront of Opposition to Maduro," *La Croix International,* May 24, 2018.

FARC, and Jesuit Refugee Services, engaged in the country since the early 1980s, is trying to respond to the one million refugees from Venezuela.

Chile

During his visit to Chile in January 2018, Pope Francis reached out to the Mapuche people, who constitute 9 percent of the country's population and have the highest unemployment. He spoke of the "injustice of centuries" as subsequent generations of colonizers and great companies deprived them of their lands. Nevertheless, he also warned them against resorting to violence themselves "which can turn a just cause into a lie." He also extended his greeting "in a special way" to "the other indigenous peoples who dwell in these southern lands: the Rapanui (from Easter Island), the Aymara, the Quechua and the Atacameños, and many others."[46]

In a letter to "the Pilgrim People of God in Chile" released on May 31, 2018, Francis called on each member of the church to become involved to help eliminate "the culture of abuse" that has so damaged the church. In his eight-page letter he publicly thanked the victims of sexual abuse "for their courage and perseverance," and he thanked those who had assisted them. The pope acknowledged that "one of our main failures and omissions" has consisted in "not knowing how to listen to the victims." Since there are not different categories of Christians, all Christians, all members of the people of God must work together. Finally, he told them "with you the necessary steps can be taken for a renewal and an ecclesial conversion that is healthy and long term; with you the necessary transformation of that which is needed can be generated; but without you nothing can be done!"[47]

Argentina

As of 2014, estimates put Argentina at 92 percent Catholic, but fewer than 20 percent regularly practice. The country has seven Catholic universities and hundreds of primary and secondary schools run by religious orders. An ambivalent attitude to the military dictatorship during the "Dirty War" (1974–83), when perhaps thirty thousand people "disappeared," many of

---

[46] Gerald O'Connell, "In the Land of the Mapuche, Pope Francis Calls on Indigenous Peoples to Say 'No' to Violence," *America*, January 17, 2018.

[47] Gerald O'Connell, "In a Letter to Chilean Catholics, Pope Francis Calls Them to Help Eliminate the Culture of Abuse," *America*, May 31, 2018.

them dropped into the ocean out of helicopters, considerably damaged the church's reputation. A few bishops spoke out against the violence, while a few others openly supported the military. Jorge Mario Bergoglio, now Pope Francis, lived through those days as provincial of the Argentine Jesuit province and worked quietly behind the scenes. Adolfo Perez Esquivel, awarded the Nobel Peace Prize for the defense of human rights in Argentina, said of him: "There were bishops that were accomplices to the dictatorship, but Bergoglio was not one of them [though] I think he lacked the courage to accompany our struggle for human rights in the most difficult times."[48]

The country's government took a secular turn with the election of Néstor Kirchner in 2003 and under his wife, Christina Fernández, who succeeded him in 2007. The government clashed with the church over contraception, abortion, sex education, and same-sex marriage. As archbishop of Buenos Aires, Bergoglio argued in 2010 that what was at stake in approving same-sex marriage was "the lives of many children who will be discriminated against in advance, and deprived of their human development given by a father and a mother and willed by God. At stake is the total rejection of God's law engraved in our hearts." His view has broadened since becoming pope.[49] The 2010 bill approving same-sex marriage brought about protests that united Catholics with Protestant and evangelical Christians, rare for Latin America, though Bergoglio himself enjoyed excellent relations with evangelicals and Pentecostals in Buenos Aires. However, since the Argentine senate banned all abortions, more than thirty-seven hundred Catholics have submitted apostasy applications to the Argentinian synod, an act both symbolic and political of formally withdrawing from the church.

Bolivia

Bolivia, one of the poorest countries in Latin America, is about 70 percent Catholic and 17 percent Protestant. Catholicism lost its status as the official religion of the country in 2009; in 2019, evangelicals were granted equal rights with Catholics. Many of the indigenous people in Bolivia still speak their native languages, Aymara or Quechua. The Catholicism

---

[48] Cited in Paul A. Vallely, *Pope Francis: Untying the Knots* (London: Bloomsbury, 2013), 91.

[49] See Christopher Hale, "Pope Francis's Public Transformation on LGBT Rights," *New Republic,* October 3, 2015.

of the Indian communities of the Altiplano incorporates elements of their pre-Columbia religion into their Catholic faith, honoring especially Pachamama, the Earth Mother.

When Pope Francis visited Bolivia in 2015, he apologized for the church's part in the oppression of Latin Americans during the colonial era. "Many grave sins were committed against the native people of America in the name of God." This statement drew rare praise from Bolivia's socialist president, Evo Morales, who said, "For the first time, I feel like I have a pope." Though unpopular with the Bolivian bishops, Morales is an old friend of Cardinal Toribio Ticona Porco. Both are from the country's indigenous people. Morales grew up speaking Aymara; Ticona speaks Quechua. Known for his simple lifestyle and closeness to the poor, Ticona has frequently been the target of criticism from traditionalist Catholics, who dismiss him as an indigenist and accuse him, without evidence, of having a wife and children. Pope Francis named him cardinal in 2018.[50]

The church waged a long battle over what the government called the decolonizing of education, emphasizing productive skills, indigenous languages, community involvement, and culture. Students no longer study Catholicism as the official religion. The adult literacy rate is over 90 percent, and the government has invested in universal healthcare and some retirement benefits.

Several schismatic groups, called parallel churches, threaten Catholic unity in Latin America. Originating in Brazil in 1945, when former bishop Carlos Duarte Costa broke with Rome and established the Brazilian Catholic Apostolic Church, other schismatic churches trace their origins to former priests or seminarians. Recently, some of these parallel churches have appeared in Bolivia; while at first they had little success, more recently they have gained adherents, alarming the Bolivian bishops.

Central America

Massive social inequality, corrupt politicians and social structures, and gang violence continue to mark the countries of Central America. Thousands of migrants have fled crushing poverty and gang violence in El Salvador, Guatemala, and Honduras, many attempting to enter the United States.[51]

---

[50] Jerry Ryan, "Privilege Masked as Orthodoxy: What the Slander of Cardinal Ticona Reveals," *Commonweal*, March 2, 2019.

[51] See Linda Dakin-Grimm, *Dignity and Justice: Welcoming the Stranger at Our Border* (Maryknoll, NY: Orbis Books, 2020).

The churches of Central America have a long history of standing with the poor of their countries, a stance that has resulted in many martyrs.

In El Salvador, Archbishop Oscar Romero was murdered in 1980; Dorothy Kazel, Ita Ford, and Maura Clarke, three religious women, and Jean Donovan, a lay missionary, were raped and murdered in 1980 by national guard troops. Six Jesuits at Universidad Centroamericana José Simeón Canãs (the UCA) were taken from their residence in 1989 and executed by the Salvadoran military. The soldiers also shot their housekeeper along with her sixteen-year-old daughter in the room in which they were hiding. The murder of the Jesuits led to the end of US support for the Salvadoran government and military; today the country has a democratic political process, but the violence continues now with the scourge of gangs, much of it fueled by narcotics.

Protests have also exploded in Nicaragua over government-imposed changes to social security affecting especially the elderly and low-income workers. Some see former Sandinista Daniel Ortega as a new Somoza, whose dictatorial regime he helped overthrow. The country's major cities have seen hundreds of thousands of citizens filling the streets, many of them closed by barricades set up by the protesters or by police and paramilitary forces. Perhaps as many as five hundred have been killed, many of them students, and hundreds have been "disappeared" or are in prison. In July 2018, a mob of government supporters attacked a number of bishops, including Cardinal Leopoldo Brenes of Managua. After the government prevented public health centers from treating the wounded, Catholic churches began functioning as hospitals. Some thirty thousand have fled to Costa Rica.

The bishops have long sought to establish a dialogue between President Daniel Ortega and those who continue to protest against his rule. SEDAC, the Secretariat or episcopal conference for the bishops of Central America and Panama, would like to see a federation of Central American countries to address common issues. When Pope Francis addressed SEDAC from Panama City during World Youth Day on January 24, 2019, he encouraged the bishops to follow the example of the martyr and now saint Archbishop Oscar Romero of San Salvador by listening to the needs of their people and embracing a church of the poor:

> Our continent is experiencing a plague . . . armed gangs and criminals, drug trafficking, the sexual exploitation of minors and young people, and so on. It is painful to observe that at the root of many of

these situations is the experience of being "orphaned," the fruit of a culture and a society run amok. Often families have been broken by an economic system that did not prioritize persons and the common good, but made speculation its "paradise," without worrying about who would end up paying the price.[52]

The pope called attention to the special needs of migrants, many of them with young faces. However, the violence continued. In April 2019, Francis called Auxiliary Bishop Silvio Baez to Rome after the bishop received death threats for his criticism of Ortega.

The Caribbean

The more than seven hundred islands of the Caribbean Sea are home to Cuba, Haiti, the Dominican Republic, Puerto Rico, Jamaica, the Cayman Islands, the Bahamas, and Bermuda. Most of the people are Christians, though other religious groups are present, including Islam, Judaism, Rastafarianism, and various Afro-American religions that combine elements of Christianity with traditional African religions. The Vatican's 2009 statistical yearbook lists the Caribbean as 65 percent Catholic, but that represents a significant drop from 78 percent Catholic in previous years. Numbers of Catholics range from 88 percent in the Dominican Republic to 4 percent in Barbados and Jamaica. Challenges to Catholicism in the Caribbean include a lack of native clergy and the growth of evangelical communities, many of them focused on social issues like poverty.

Haiti, one of the world's most impoverished nations, is approximately 55 percent Catholic, while estimates place the number of Protestants at roughly 28 percent, with growth occurring especially among evangelical and Pentecostal congregations. Good Friday services in Haiti frequently mix in elements of voodoo (more commonly referred to as vodou in Haiti). The country seems to have a sufficient number of priests, with four hundred diocesan priests, three hundred seminarians, and over thirteen hundred religious priests. The 2010 earthquake and the cholera outbreak that followed it are said to have killed between 220,000 and 300,000 Haitians, including the archbishop of Port-au-Prince, and left 1.6 million

---

[52] Pope Francis, "Pope's Address to Bishops of Central America," *Zenit*, January 24, 2019.

homeless. Many moved to Brazil, which initially welcomed them but after an economic downturn became less accepting.

Haiti's neighbor, the Dominican Republic, has 7.6 million Catholics, 78 percent of the population, though their faith is often mixed with a spiritualism whose roots lie in Africa.

Relations between the two countries remain tense. The Dominican Republic has been hostile to refugees or migrants from Haiti, much of the hostility based on race. Human Rights Watch reported a 2013 Dominican court decision that stripped citizenship from tens of thousands of Dominican migrants and their families, mostly of Haitian origin. In the summer of 2015, some sixty-six thousand returned to Haiti, some of them forcibly removed. Others left the Dominican Republic on their own, fearing mob violence. On the Haitian side of the border, Jesuit Refugee Services, several congregations of women religious, and other nongovernmental agencies like Catholic Relief Services and UNICEF have struggled to meet the needs of refugees with little help from the Haitian government.[53]

In Cuba prior to Fidel Castro's revolution, about 90 percent of Cubans identified as Catholic. Today the number is much less, about 60 percent, but only about 5 percent of them attend mass with some regularity. As elsewhere in the Caribbean, Catholic faith often embraces elements of Afro-American religion, in this case Santería, with its roots in Africa. Protestants are estimated to make up about 5 percent, with the rapid growth of evangelical churches. After the revolution, the government seized Catholic Church properties throughout Cuba, closed Catholic schools, and deported 130 priests to Spain. Over the next years several thousand priests and nuns left the island.

The 1998 visit of Pope John Paul II to Cuba led to new, more positive relations with the state. The church is free to build and open new churches, but financing remains difficult. Some Cuban congregations partner with Catholic congregations in the United States. Other congregations still meet in private homes. According to Jason Barry, bishops, priests, nuns, and lay workers operate Cuba's de facto social safety net with financial help from Catholic charitable organizations like Catholic Relief Services and Caritas. This is a safety net that the cash-strapped government is unable to provide. The country has the highest literacy rate in Latin America and a free healthcare system, but its economy is a failure. Since Raúl

---

[53] Chris Herlinger, "At the Haitian-Dominican Border, a Ministry to Help the Displaced Who 'Fight to Survive,'" *Global Sisters Report*, October 3, 2016.

Castro succeeded his brother in 2006, he has brought about changes in his country's top-down Marxist economy and made major concessions to the church. On a visit to Rome he thanked Pope Francis for helping to bring about a new relationship with the United States,[54] though relations have suffered under the Trump administration.

Puerto Rico's Catholics number about 56 percent of the population, according to a 2014 Pew Research Center report, down from an earlier 85 percent.[55] Protestants number 33 percent. Some report a religious revival with more people going to church and greater respect for religious leaders. Public concern over the United States using the adjacent island of Vieques, home to ten thousand people, for live bombing exercises—especially after April 1999, when a bomb from an F/A-18 Hornet jet accidently missed its target and killed a civilian security guard. The incident has united Catholics, Protestants, and evangelicals for the first time, including Jorgé Raschke, an ultraconservative preacher famous for his denunciation of Catholic faith and practice.[56]

Also influential have been Franciscan Archbishop Roberto González Nieves's emphasis on social justice, and Jesuit Bishop Alvaro Corrada del Río's championship of the church's social engagement. Sociologist José Casanova in a 1994 book traces this militancy to the churches' ability to provide a "religious critique" when governments are not able to resolve an issue.[57] Catholic sources in the United States were also active in providing financial assistance after hurricane Maria devastated the island in 2017.

Conclusion

In many ways the Second Vatican Council brought new energy and a new vision to the Catholic Church in Latin American, and since the council, the church has experienced considerable change rooted in demographics, culture, political life, and the failures of the church itself. On a continent once securely Catholic, millions of the faithful have departed for evangelical and Pentecostal churches, whose growth has been explosive. At the

---

[54] Jason Barry, "How the Catholic Church Survived in Cuba," *The Atlantic*, September 18, 2015.

[55] Pew Research Center, "Religion in Latin America."

[56] Anthony M. Stevens-Arroyo, "Catholicism's Emerging Role in Puerto Rico," *America*, April 15, 2000.

[57] José Casanova, *Public Religions in the Modern World* (1994), cited in Anthony M. Stevens-Arroyo, "Catholicism's Emerging Role in Puerto Rico, *America*, April 15, 2000.

same time, the growth of the CCR has led to considerable renewal in many Catholic churches and in some cases new vocations to the priesthood. Most important, according to Todd Hartch, "the CCR restored the confidence of Catholics."[58]

Moreover, as Hispanics from the Dominican Republic, Colombia, El Salvador, and especially Mexico—countries especially influenced by the charismatic renewal—flooded into the United States, they began to change that country's religious landscape. According to the Pew Research Center, more than half of US Hispanic Catholics identify as charismatics. Most remain committed to the Catholic Church and its traditional teachings, but with a faith strongly influenced by the Pentecostal and charismatic renewal movements.[59]

The council's postconciliar efforts to engage with "those who are poor or in any way afflicted" (*Gaudium et spes*, no. 1) brought new life to the church. Many of its bishops and theologians embraced a contextual theology of liberation and a preferential option for the poor. Thus the church found itself in conflict with many of the continent's repressive governments, bringing persecution and a new generation of martyrs. Liberation theology was an effort to renew the church from the base up, bringing the concrete words of scripture into the daily lives of ordinary Catholics and giving a new sense of sharing in the church's mission to many of the laity. Pope Francis named two cardinals from Latin America in 2019, Archbishop Juan de la Caridad García Rodríguez of Havana, Cuba, and Bishop Álvaro Leonel Ramazzini Imeri of Huehuetenango, Guatemala, both known for their social justice concerns.

Churches outside of Latin America began to model their own pastoral reflections on the Southern churches' reflections on social justice, evangelization, and concern to develop a mature, internalized faith. The *Encuentros* developed for the growing US Hispanic population adopted their "see-judge-act" methodology. Other movements for liberation expanded in the church, perhaps inspired by the Latin American example, for black, Hispanic, Asian, feminine, and LGBTQ groups.

But for many liberation theology remained more European than truly Latin American, alien to the religious sensibilities of many of the people who often turn to evangelical or Pentecostal communities for a more af-

---

[58] Hartch, *The Rebirth of Latin American Christianity*, 124.

[59] See Pew Research Center, "Changing Faiths: Latinos and the Transformation of American Religion," April 25, 2007; see also Cleary, "Mexico: Number One Exporter to the United States," in *The Rise of Charismatic Catholicism in Latin America*.

fective faith. Pope Francis has attempted to address this with his emphasis on *religiosidad popular*, with its emphasis on feeling or sentiment. That does that take away from his concern for the poor in a world where, in 2019, 1 percent of the world's population owns 44 percent of the world's wealth.[60]

At the same time, a growing secularism has resulted in the disestablishment of the Catholic Church in many countries and a loss of privilege that has been welcomed by other churches. Furthermore, the early twenty-first century has witnessed new conflicts between church and state over questions of marriage and divorce, abortion, homosexuality, and same-sex marriage. These cultural shifts have also resulted in a loss of religious faith by many, a privatization of religion, and for many others, a departure from the Catholic Church. Some see Pentecostalism as the last stop before dropping out of organized religion entirely.

The recognition of the sexual abuse of young people by clergy, a global problem, only recently emerged in Latin America. In 2018, in Chile, Pope Francis apologized publicly for the damage done to those who had been abused. Since then, scandals have emerged in other Hispanic countries. In January 2019, Francis summoned the heads of the world's episcopal conferences to Rome to deal with the crisis.

Ecumenical relations remain an area yet to be developed. Though Pentecostalism has left its mark on many Latin American churches, both Pentecostals and Catholics need to remain more open to the Spirit, the source of unity. With both Protestants and Catholics losing parishioners, partly influenced by an increasingly secular culture, it would make sense for them to move beyond their differences and try to work together. The ecumenical movement is not primarily for peace between and among the churches, but for the church's evangelical mission. All the churches of Latin America need to find ways to begin moving toward one another.

---

[60] Credit Suisse, *Research Institute: Global Wealth Report 2019,* October 2019.

5

Asia

Asia includes five regions: Central Asia (mainly the Republics of Ka-
zakhstan, Kyrgyzstan, Tajikistan, Turkmenistan, and Uzbekistan); East Asia
(mainly China, Japan, Korea, and Taiwan); South Asia (Bangladesh, India,
Myanmar, Nepal, Pakistan, and Sri Lanka); Southeast Asia (Cambodia,
Indonesia, Laos, the Philippines, Singapore, Thailand, and Vietnam); and
Southwest Asia (the countries of the Middle East, Near East, or West
Asia).[1] As Peter Phan notes, the immense seize of the Asian continent
makes it difficult to talk simply of Asian Christianity. Given the diversity
of Christian ecclesiastical traditions, rites, and denominations, Phan says
it is more accurate to use "Christianities" in the plural.[2]

While Christianity was born in the Middle East, which is part of
Southwest Asia, many Asians even today regard it as a foreign religion,
brought to Asia by Spanish and Portuguese missionaries and colonists
in the sixteenth century. In most Asian countries today Christianity is
a minority religion, except for the Philippines and East Timor, where
Christians constitute 92.5 and 96 percent of the population respectively.
South Korea (29.2 percent) and Vietnam (7 percent) also have significant
Christian populations, and Christianity is growing rapidly in China, which
by some estimates may have the world's largest Christian population by
2030. However, except for the Middle East, where the Christian population continues to diminish, Christians amount to little over 9 percent of
the Asian population.

---

[1] Peter C. Phan, "Reception of and Trajectories for Vatican II in Asia," *Theological Studies* 74 (2013): 305; see also *Christianities in Asia*, ed. Peter C. Phan (Malden, MA: Wiley-
Blackwell, 2011).
[2] Phan, 308.

Despite its minority status Asian Catholicism displays a surprising vitality. At their 1970 meeting in Manila, the Asian bishops decided to form the Federation of Asian Bishops Conferences (FABC). The FABC has eighteen conferences as full members and nine associate members, coming from all five Asian regions. Unfortunately, the bishops of China have not been able to attend, though after the agreement signed between China and the Vatican in 2018, two bishops from China attended the 2018 Synod on Young People, the Faith, and Vocational Discernment.

The FABC's mission shows a commitment to "episcopal collegiality, ecclesial communion, and dialogue as the mode of being church."[3] The formation of the FABC has helped the Asian churches to find their voice. At its Fifth General Assembly meeting at Bandung, Indonesia, in July 1990, the bishops described a renewed sense of mission for their churches, centered on a threefold dialogue "with Asia's poor, with its local cultures, and with other religions" (FABC V, 3.1.2.). At the 1998 Synod of Bishops for Asia, held in Rome, the bishops criticized the Roman-drafted outline document (*lineamenta*) for being too Eurocentric and insufficiently concerned with the development of a church with a genuinely Asian faith—in other words, with the inculturation of their churches.[4]

They found the document's emphasis on the uniqueness and universality of Jesus Christ as savior problematic in an Asian context. The real question was how to proclaim Christ in Asia. The curial emphasis on the uniqueness of Christ was not a good starting point for interreligious dialogue, as it seemed to deny that the non-Christian religions of Asia could play a salvific role or that grace could be accessible through their teachings and rituals. The FABC bishops continued to stress the importance of the threefold dialogue: with other religions, with the poor, and with culture. Their bishops' conferences have asked repeatedly for the right to develop their own liturgical translations and pastoral strategies without Roman interference, and they have lamented a lack of dialogue.

Thus, the Indian bishops argued for the right of their local churches to develop their own ways of preaching the gospel. The Japanese and Vietnamese bishops found the Christology of the *lineamenta* too defensive, with the Japanese calling for a certain independence in determining the agenda: "The decision concerning the global direction of the synod should not be made by the Roman secretariat, but should be left to the

---

[3] Phan, 312.

[4] See Thomas C. Fox, *Pentecost in Asia: A New Way of Being Church* (Maryknoll, NY: Orbis Books, 2002).

bishops from Asia."[5] The bishops of Indonesia called for the development of non-Latin liturgical rites for Asia and stressed that Christians could learn from dialogue with other religious traditions, holding up the courage of Muslims, who recite their daily prayers in public.[6] Some bishops objected to curial instructions to avoid the word *subsidiarity* on the questionable grounds that it was not a theological term. The relations with Rome have improved considerably under Pope Francis.

Nevertheless, the Asian churches face many challenges, among them outright persecution in some countries. A report prepared by Aid to the Church in Need surveyed 13 countries where persecution is most serious. It revealed "evidence of the most serious persecution against Christians in terms of violations of fundamental human rights: violence, including rape, unlawful detention, unfair trial, prevention of religious assembly and peaceful (religious) expression."[7]

In India, Christians frequently face false charges of coercive practices to gain new converts, in violation of the anti-conversion laws now in place in some states. They struggle for religious liberty against the Hindu nationalist approach of the dominant Bharatiya Janata Party (BJP), which seems to tolerate frequent outbreaks of violence against Christians or their churches. In 2016, there was an escalation of attacks on Christians, usually led by Hindu nationalists acting with impunity. The All India Christian Council records an increase of almost 20 percent in attacks against Christians in 2016. It claims that physical violence against Christians is up 40 percent and murders have doubled. Churches are vandalized or burned, and many Dalit Christians have been forced to "reconvert" to Hinduism. Always concerned about alienating his Hindu nationalist base, Prime Minister Narendra Modi has done little to stem the violence, and his cabinet includes no Christian ministers, leaving them without representation at the highest level. Just over 2 percent of India's population is Christian; nearly 80 percent is Hindu.

In China, under President Xi Jinping, Christian churches and the Islamic community have experienced increasing government restriction

---

[5] Cited in Fox, 152.

[6] See Peter C. Phan, *The Asian Synods: Texts and Commentaries* (Maryknoll, NY: Orbis Books, 2002), 13–51.

[7] *Persecuted and Forgotten? A Report on Christians Oppressed for Their Faith 2015–17 Executive Summary* (Brooklyn, NY: Aid to the Church in Need–US), 10; see also Hubert van Beek and Larry Miller, eds., *Discrimination, Persecution, Martyrdom: Following Christ Together* (Bonn: Verlag für Kultur und Wissenschaft, 2018; Eugene, OR: Wipf and Stock, 2018).

with its efforts to "Sinicize" religions, which means putting them under the control of the Communist Party. In Vietnam, the Catholic Church is growing, despite occasional conflicts with the government. And today, Christians often face persecution in Muslim-dominated countries.

The Middle East

The largely Muslim countries in the Middle East include Afghanistan, Pakistan, Syria, Iraq, and Iran.[8] Christians had generally been able to live peacefully under Saddam Hussein in Iraq and the Assads in Syria; for all their brutality, they protected Christians. Syria's ten million Christians under Assad were free to evangelize, publish religious material, and build churches. However, after the American intervention in Iraq and the Syrian civil war, Christians began leaving the Middle East in record numbers, driven out by terrorism, violence, and discriminatory laws. According to Cardinal Kurt Koch, prefect of the Vatican Congregation for Christian Unity, "Christians represented 20 percent of the population in the region before World War I, today, they are only 4 percent."[9]

In 1987, there were more than 1.4 million Christians in Iraq (about 6 percent of the population), but after the post-Saddam chaos and Islamic State (ISIS) violence, numbers had fallen to about 150,000, though after the defeat of ISIS some Christians have begun to return. In a speech at Georgetown on February 15, 2018, Chaldean Archbishop Bashar Warda of Erbil said, "Without an end to this persecution and violence, there is no future for religious pluralism in Iraq or anywhere else in the Middle East for that matter." He argued that it is not enough to say, "ISIS does not represent Islam," adding that "there is a fundamental crisis within Islam itself and if this crisis is not acknowledged, addressed and fixed then there can be no future for Christians in the Middle East."[10]

In Syria, the number of Christians has declined by 70 percent. Although the Obama administration refused to name as genocide the ISIS persecution of Christians, Yazidis, Shia Muslims, and other religious minorities,

---

[8] See Kimberly Winston, "The Top 10 Worst Countries for Christian Persecution," *Religious News Service*, January 1, 2018.

[9] Quoted in Inés San Martín, "Francis Brings Walls down with the Orthodox for Middle East Peace," *Crux*, July 3, 2018.

[10] Quoted in Courtney Grogan, "Archbishop of Erbil: Christians in Iraq Are 'Scourged, Wounded, But Still There,'" Catholic News Agency, February 19, 2018.

Secretary of State John Kerry did so in March 2016. After the April 14, 2018, Western air strikes on suspected Syrian chemical sites, three patriarchs—two Orthodox and one Catholic—co-signed a statement strongly condemning the air strikes while reasserting their support for the Assad regime and its Russian and Iranian allies.[11]

Not all persecution of Christians is the work of ISIS and other extreme groups; some of it has government or popular support, even in countries the United States considers allies. There are at least 1.5–2 million Christians in Saudi Arabia, but they are not allowed to have churches or visits from their clergy. Non-Muslim worship is forbidden, though some worship in embassies or private homes; nor can non-Muslims become Saudi citizens. Catholics number more than one million, mostly Filipinos, 60 percent of them women, but they are not allowed to hold mass on Sundays.

Christians are frequently victims of violence in Egypt. In May 2017, at least twenty-eight Coptic Christians traveling to visit a monastery were killed when gunmen ordered the passengers to get out of the bus. Separating the men from the women and children, they told the men to recite the Shahada, the Islamic declaration of faith, an attempt to make them deny their Christian faith and become Muslims. When the men refused, the gunmen opened fire. Among the dead were several children. Over one hundred died in Egypt in 2017 because of anti-Christian violence.

In Pakistan, the application of the so-called blasphemy laws frequently victimize Christians and others who belong to minority religions. Personal grudges or disputes over land can trigger charges of desecrating the Qur'an or insulting the prophet, generating popular outrage that intimidates police and judges who then frequently fail to intervene. The penalty is life imprisonment or death. Asia Bibi, an illiterate Christian woman accused of blasphemy by her neighbors, spent almost ten years under a sentence of death by hanging. Two Christian ministers challenging the blasphemy laws were assassinated. Pakistan's Supreme Court finally overturned Bibi's conviction in 2018. In January 2019, the chief justice of Pakistan's Supreme Court definitively dismissed a petition to overturn the acquittal of Asia Bibi, leaving her free to leave the country. She was finally reunited with her family in Canada in May 2019.

In its 2018 report the United States Commission on International Religious Freedom (USCIRF) "again finds that Pakistan should be designated

---

[11] Samuel Lieven, "Why Syria's Patriarchs Back Assad," *La Croix International*, April 17, 2018.

as a 'country of particular concern.' . . . Despite USCIRF's longstanding recommendation, the State Department has never so designated Pakistan."[12] The *2018 World Watch List* published by Open Doors lists Pakistan as the fifth-most-dangerous country for Christians. In 2019, Pakistani authorities blocked a number of young Pakistani Catholics from attending World Youth Day in Panama City after they had paid for the plane tickets. Christians are frequently discriminated against in hiring, educational opportunities, and housing; some assume Muslim-sounding names to hide their identity. A 2014 Supreme Court ruling set aside 5 percent of government positions for religious minorities, but less than 2 percent apply.

Persecution of Christians comes not just from fundamentalist Islamic movements but often from ordinary Pakistanis. Much of it is caste based, because many low-caste Hindus became Christian during the period of British rule. Women are especially vulnerable. Each year between one hundred and seven hundred Christian girls are forced into marriage and conversion to Islam, often after sexual assault. Some are sold to men in China. There are no laws against forced conversions, and little protection from civil authorities.[13] One hopeful sign, in January 2019, Father James Channan, a Pakistani Dominican, was invited to preach in the Royal Mosque in Lahore, memorializing the late Grand Imam Abdul Qadir Azad.

The Islamic Republic of Afghanistan does not recognize any of its citizens as Christians. Their only legally recognized place of worship is a Catholic chapel in the Italian embassy, completed in the 1950s. A Protestant church in Kabul, built in 1970 for the diplomatic and expatriate community, was destroyed in 1973 and not rebuilt. The constitution adopted in January 2004 provides for non-Muslim groups to exercise their faith, but it does not explicitly extend freedom to minority religious communities or to individual Afghans. Those who convert to Christianity are often threatened with death.

The numbers of Catholics in the Middle East are not large. Pakistan has one million Catholics, less than 1 percent of the population, though the church is respected for its educational, community service, and health work. Syria has some 375,000 Catholics, mostly belonging to the Melkite Rites; the rest are Latins, Maronite, Armenian, or Syrian.

---

[12] United States Commission on International Religious Freedom, *2018 Annual Report*, 64.

[13] Usman Ahmad, "Is Pakistan Safe for Christians?" The South Asia Channel, May 16, 2016.

Iraq has roughly 150,000 Christians today, most Chaldean Catholics. Iran has approximately 21,000 from the Chaldean, Armenian, and Latin rites. Israel has roughly 108,000 Catholics from the Melkite, Maronite, and Latin rites, with some from other rites included. Counting both the state of Israel and the Palestinian territories, 85 percent of Catholics there are Arabic speaking.

China

Although Christians from the Assyrian Church of the East had visited China in the seventh century and some Franciscans came in the thirteenth century, neither mission survived. Modern Christianity in China dates from 1601, when Jesuit Fathers Matteo Ricci and Michele Ruggieri arrived in Beijing during the Ming Dynasty. They were chosen for the mission by Alessandro Valignano, who had learned the value of language fluency and cultural accommodation from his experience in Japan. Ricci and Ruggieri were both Italians. They devoted themselves for several years to their studies in the city of Zhaoqing, Guangdong province, focusing on the Mandarin of the Chinese literati. Initially, they dressed in the manner of Buddhist monks; later they adopted the silk robes of the literati. After a first visit to Beijing in 1598, Ricci returned three years later to stay, charming his hosts with gifts of clocks, scientific instruments, and his map of the world. In fact, his *A Treatise on Friendship,* which was composed in Chinese, is still considered a classic of Chinese literature. Ricci and his convert Xu Guangqi (1562–1633) translated Euclid's Elements into Chinese. Ricci's cause for beatification is under way in Rome, and many would like to see the addition of his friend Xu.

A succession of Jesuits followed Ricci. Nicolò Longobardo (1559–1654) succeeded Ricci as superior of the mission and worked until almost ninety years of age. Johann Adam Schall von Bell (1592–1666) worked with Xu Guangqi to revise the Chinese calendar, making it more accurate at predicting eclipses. He became a trusted counselor to the third emperor of the Qing dynasty, the first to rule over all of China. Ferdinand Verbiest (1623–88) continued von Bell's work on the calendar and was appointed director of the Beijing Observatory. He was an adviser and close friend of the emperor, Kangxi. Because the Jesuits were accepted by the literati, the Christian mission—embracing merchants, craftsmen, and peasants—

flourished in China. Franciscan and Dominican friars who arrived in 1633 also joined the mission.

However, imperial support was soon lost. In 1715, after the Vatican's negative judgment on the "rites controversy," which among other things allowed the veneration of ancestors, the emperor banned Christianity in China. The Jesuits, at least until the suppression of their order in 1773, received permission to remain in Beijing as scientific assistants, but the Christian mission was effectively over. Cultural accommodation, which had proved so successful in China and India, also ended, meaning that a "Eurocentric perspective and uniform Romanization prevailed within the Church."[14] As Andrew Ross writes, "The Catholic Church did not die in China, but it became a harassed sect appealing to people at the periphery of society. Christianity was no longer Chinese but a foreign religion associated essentially with foreigners and foreignness."[15]

The identification of the Catholic and Protestant missions with European military and colonial power in the nineteenth century made the situation for Christians worse. Today, however, there is a new appreciation of the work of the missionaries. During the Second World War, missionaries from five different European countries, among them the Dutch bishop Frans Schraven and eight companions, were killed protecting Chinese girls and women from Japanese soldiers. In October 2017, scientists and professors of the Chinese Academy of Social Sciences, the largest historical and social research center in the People's Republic of China, acknowledged the sacrifice of these missionaries for the Chinese people, as well as the contribution of missionaries in general to the development of Chinese society. The academy called particular attention to their work in the areas of education and culture and their work in favor of those most in need.

Catholics numbered about three million when the Communists came to power in 1949, Protestants about one million. Today the Catholic Church is still largely rural, while Protestant congregations are multiplying with well-educated professionals in China's mushrooming cities. While exact numbers are hard to obtain, estimates put Protestant Christians at between fifty and sixty million, with twelve million Catholics.

---

[14]Thomas Banchoff and José Casanova, eds., *The Jesuits and Globalization: Historical Legacies and Contemporary Challenges* (Washington, DC: Georgetown University Press, 2016), 12.

[15]Andrew C. Ross, *A Vision Betrayed: The Jesuits in China and Japan 1542–1742* (Maryknoll, NY: Orbis Books, 1994), 198.

Contemporary China

The Catholic Church in China, acting under orders from Rome, initially opposed the Communist movement.[16] Archbishop Antonio Riberi, who was appointed nuncio to China in 1946, forbade Catholics to cooperate with the new Communist regime, thinking it would not be long lasting. This put Catholics, and especially their clergy, in a difficult position. However, the Maoist regime was also opposed to the church in principle. Itself a hierarchical organization, it could not tolerate a rival, one that challenged it symbolically or in terms of authority. To place the church under its own control, it established Catholic reform committees, eventually called Patriotic Associations, to make the church independent of all foreign influence in the areas of the "three autonomies," that is, all the churches were to be self-governing, self-financed, and self-propagating.

Riberi urged resistance and was forced to leave China in 1952. While not all Catholics opposed the government, bishops, priests, and nuns were especially vulnerable, and some Catholics continued to resist. The government insisted that priests join the state-sponsored Patriotic Associations, while the Vatican threatened them with excommunication if they did. In 1955, the most influential Catholic bishop (later cardinal), Kung Pin-Mei, was arrested, along with fifteen hundred Shanghai Catholics.[17] Some priests and even bishops joined the Patriotic Associations, some to keep the church alive, others for more personal reasons.

In 1957, the government organized a single Chinese Catholic Patriotic Association (CCPA). As foreign bishops and clergy were expelled, and Chinese bishops who resisted the CCPA's insistence on independence from Rome were arrested or not allowed to function, an increasing number of dioceses lost their ordinaries. In several dioceses the clergy elected candidates to fill the office of bishop, telegraphing the names to Rome for papal approval. However, the Congregation for the Propagation of the Faith refused to approve the candidates, objecting that those chosen by the CCPA would represent the government rather than the church. Judging that the Holy See did not understand the situation of the church in China, Bishop Li Daonan of the Diocese of Puqi, a bishop aligned with the CCPA, ordained two bishops. Thus began the practice of ordaining

---

[16] See Richard Madsen, *China's Catholics; Tragedy and Hope in an Emerging Civil Society* (Berkeley and Los Angeles: University of California Press, 1998), 34–39.

[17] See Paul Philip Mariani, *Church Militant: Bishop Kung and the Catholic Resistance in Communist Shanghai* (Cambridge, MA: Harvard University Press, 2011).

bishops approved by the CCPA but not by Rome.[18] Others continued to resist, suffering persecution, imprisonment, even martyrdom. The result was a divided church, a government-recognized public church, and an unrecognized underground church.

During the chaotic days of the Cultural Revolution (1966–76), all religious activity in China was suspended. Religious practice was proscribed; churches, temples, and mosques were closed or destroyed; church members were persecuted; most of their leaders were imprisoned or killed. To this day people in China are reluctant to talk about the Cultural Revolution because it was so painful. But it also led to an unexpected growth of the church. Perhaps 80 percent of Catholics lived in rural, largely Catholic villages or communities. Without priests, the laity were forced to assume leadership roles previously foreign to them. The communities began to organize themselves, with the laity conducting traditional devotions, especially the Rosary, while mothers and grandmothers taught Catholic prayers and doctrines. By the time the Cultural Revolution ended, the Catholic population had grown from about three million to ten million.

Under Deng Xiaoping's policy of Reform and Opening, the country went through a religious revival. Mosques and temples were able to reopen and churches rebuilt, sometimes with government assistance. Protestant churches, especially evangelical and Pentecostal, increased as much as twentyfold between the early 1980s and the mid 1990s. The number of Catholics increased also, though not as dramatically, and the old divisions reemerged. Within five years, there were forty-two CCPA bishops, approved by the government but not recognized by the pope. In the underground church there were more than fifty bishops by 1989.[19]

Since the 1990s, the underground church has become more confrontational. In late 1979, Rome gave a series of exemptions from canonical regulations to help the church. However, without Roman supervision many priests were ordained without proper theological education, and some priests and bishops spent their energies denouncing those in the public church, exacerbating tensions between the two. They instructed Catholics not to receive sacraments from them, lest they commit serious sin. Some saw this as permission to build an opposing church, accusing public-church priests and bishops of being tools of the government. Too many priests and even bishops were secretly ordained, far beyond what

---

[18] Jean-Paul Wiest, "Catholics in China: The Bumpy Road toward Reconciliation," *International Bulletin of Missionary Research* 27, no. 1 (2003): 2.

[19] Wiest, 2–4.

Rome intended. Instead of a formal academic education, many candidates for the priesthood went through an apprenticeship with an older priest. While at home in rural life, they lacked familiarity with cultural changes and the increasing urbanization of Chinese life. Some became bishops without pastoral experience and lacked good relations with other priests. Occasionally a diocese had several bishops claiming to be the ordinary.[20]

Over the years things have improved. By the end of the 1980s the public church restored the prayer for the pope in the liturgy, which had been removed in 1958. Many of the bishops have expressed their communion with the pope privately, and in recent years some priests have been ordained to the episcopate with the approval of both the CCPA and Rome. At the beginning of the twenty-first century there were twenty-four major seminaries operating with government permission and another ten in the underground church. There are over forty novitiates for sisters in the open church and twenty in the underground church.[21]

In some parts of the country the underground and public churches cooperate as much as they are able, with candidates studying together in the same seminaries, sharing buildings and churches, and sometimes even with pastors living together. However, there are provinces where the underground church is persecuted, with bishops and priests confined for years in jails—all dependent on the local mandarins and changing policy from Beijing. The Vatican has been wise in seeking to reconcile both churches, insisting that there is only one church in China. However, some traditionalist Catholics in the United States maintain that the public church is schismatic.

The appointment of bishops has continued to block a reconciliation between the Vatican and thus the universal Catholic Church and the Chinese government. Always sensitive to foreign influence in its domestic affairs, the CCPA has claimed the right to appoint a bishop without Roman approval. Nor can the Chinese bishops attend assemblies of the international Synod of Bishops in Rome or take their part in the Federation of Asian Bishops' Conference (FABC). The case of Thaddeus Ma Daqin, approved by both Rome and the CCPA as auxiliary bishop of Shanghai, was immediately complicated when Ma publicly resigned from the CCPA at his 2012 episcopal ordination. He immediately disappeared into house

---

[20] See Edmund Tang, "The Church in the 1990s," in *The Catholic Church in Modern China*, ed. Edmund Tang and Jean-Paul Wiest (Maryknoll, NY: Orbis Books, 1993), 28–49.

[21] Wiest, "Catholics in China," 5.

arrest, and though he has since publicly acknowledged his mistake, he has not been allowed to assume his office.

On September 22, 2018, the Vatican and the People's Republic of China signed a Provisional Agreement. A "pastoral not political" agreement, according to the Vatican, the full text has not been made public. It gives the pope final authority to veto any candidate for the episcopal office proposed by the official church. Rome agreed to recognize eight bishops ordained in China without papal approval, requiring several underground bishops to step aside, and both sides have agreed not to exercise their rights separately. The Provisional Agreement remains controversial. There is opposition from some within China, notably Cardinal Zen in Hong Kong. The Agreement is supposed to end the division between the underground and public churches that has existed since 1957, though making this effective will take time.[22]

Some opposition comes from those in the Vatican opposed to Francis's reforms. Other Catholics see it as a risk to the church's freedom, limited as it is. Francis sees it as the first step in a long process, one that marks a step forward in relations between the Catholic Church and the Chinese government. How it will work out remains to be seen. On June 28, 2019, the Vatican published pastoral guidelines allowing bishops and priests to register with the government, as long as they made clear that they would remain faithful to Catholic doctrine.

As of 2016, there were 112 dioceses in China, another 32 administrative regions, and more than 109 bishops, 72 in the open church and perhaps 37 in the underground. The open church has 2,500 priests, the underground 1,300.[23] Though the public church enjoys some freedom, it operates under tight controls. The church cannot operate schools, except for those forming priests and sisters. However, it sponsors several publishing houses and newspapers, and the bishops now send some of their priests and nuns to study in Taiwan, Europe, or the United States. Over 100 priests, nuns, and laity have studied at Taiwan's Fu Jen Faculty of Theology. There is a growing group of Chinese priests and nuns with professional degrees, ready to move into leadership positions in ecclesial and educational ministries. Thus, the public church is now more progressive

---

[22] Federico Lombardi, SJ, "The Agreement between the Holy See and China: Whence and Whither?" *La Civiltá Cattolica*, October 17, 2019.

[23] Katharina Wenzel-Teuber, "Statistics on Religions and Churches in China 2016," China Zentrum, 44–45.

than the underground church which has long been largely rural, though candidates for the priesthood are diminishing in both.

Contemporary Challenges

Beyond bringing the underground and public churches together into one community, the Catholic Church in China faces a number of challenges. Internal migration and the gradual transition from a rural to an urban church represents one of the greatest. Richard Madsen, who has written on the church in China for years, describes rural Catholicism as more of an ethnicity than a chosen faith; Catholics live in largely Catholic villages and receive the faith from their families or by marrying into one.[24] Transplanting rural Catholicism into the cities is difficult.

In the 1980s, hundreds of thousands of Chinese Catholics migrated from their rural villages into the growing cities. The transition has not always been easy, and in a largely secular culture, there are new challenges to their faith. Deng Xiaoping's "policy of openness" changed forever China's economic system and introduced a new prosperity, but in many ways it resulted in China embracing the worst values of the West—materialism, consumerism, and individualism. Those recently arrived in the cities had to find new ways to remain Catholic. Some could not find churches in their local communities and stopped attending church. Others continued their traditional devotions, saying the Rosary at home in the evening and receiving the sacraments when visiting their home villages, often for the New Year's holidays. Still others, rural migrants, found it difficult integrating their rural Catholicism with the urban churches, often with differences rooted in language or social status. Frequently they would gather in someone's home or later small chapels for prayer meetings, forming networks where they could meet. They tended to send their children back to their villages to be raised by grandparents and were suspicious of the more rationalized approach of modern catechisms.

By the twenty-first century these new urban migrants had become well established urban dwellers. More prosperous, they chose increasingly to keep a son or daughter with them. Some would help support a priest for ministry in their networks, often independently of the bishop. Sunday mass became more important. In one diocese with four downtown churches, they have more than ten chapels in the outlying suburbs, though

---

[24] Madsen, *China's Catholics*, 53–58.

they recognize that the majority of their fellow believers no longer go to church. If an unofficial church were present and accessible, they would eventually join it, or attend the public church, while staying involved with their unofficial networks.[25]

Dialogue with Culture

A related challenge is the dialogue with culture so important today for urban Catholic life. Because priests from the underground church are generally comfortable with the conservative piety of rural Catholicism, they have little to say to better-educated urban Catholics. What does the church have to say to modern culture, to urban life, to the difficult relationship between the church and state? Television, the internet, karaoke, and other urban entertainments allow little time to gather at the local church to pray the Rosary, as in rural China. The late Aloysius Jin Luxian, a Jesuit priest who spent twenty-seven years in prison before becoming the public-church bishop of ultra-modern Shanghai, was quite aware of this challenge: "We feel very weak and powerless against the tide of modernization that brings a lot of products like corruption, idolatry of money, spiritual vacuum."[26] How can Catholics help their fellow Chinese to find meaning in the extroversion of modern life? The internet, so popular in China today for its social media, is an underutilized resource, though largely controlled by the Communist Party.

Programs for training candidates for the priesthood in both the underground and the open church are ill-equipped to form priests to meet the challenges of contemporary Chinese society. Seminaries lack up-to-date Chinese textbooks, professionally trained faculty, and competent spiritual directors. Candidates are not always carefully screened, and intellectual formation is minimal. Too often, candidates see priesthood as a job path to a better life. Some bishops use church funds to set up private businesses.

Spiritual formation fails to develop a strong sense of priestly identity; it is rigidly traditional, emphasizing oral prayers and devotions, while issues of psychological and psychosexual development are rarely addressed. Seminarians have little personal freedom, and faculty enjoy better food

---

[25] Michel Chambon and Antonio Spadaro, SJ, "Urban Catholicism in China," *La Civiltà Cattolica*, January 7, 2019.

[26] Cited in Madsen, *China's Catholics*, 123. See also Kin Sheung Chiaretto Yan, *Evangelization in China: Challenges and Prospects* (Maryknoll, NY: Orbis Books, 2014).

and special privileges. In the underground church, formation usually means an apprenticeship or tutorial program; candidates live with an older priest or bishop. Still, some underground candidates are able to study in open-church seminaries.

Another challenge is finding ways to work with the authorities in the Community Party to develop a "Christianity with Chinese characteristics," as Ambrose Ih-Ren Mong urges and government policy now demands. While the Christianity that came to China with Ricci and the Jesuits in the late sixteenth century saw no conflict between the gospel and Chinese culture, especially in its Confucian expression, this approach of the early missionaries was replaced two centuries later by the "gunboat Christianity" of European colonialism. A Christianity freed of its colonial past may find common ground with a Chinese Marxism that is unlikely to disappear in the near future and that shares with Christians a concern for social harmony, stability, and improving the life of its citizens. Certainly, there are gospel values in this approach. Here dialogue, both with Communist Party officials and with the academy, can be important. The challenge for the church is to witness to the social dimensions of the kingdom without losing its transcendental vision and eschatological hope.[27]

Some Chinese intellectuals, particularly in the universities, find Christianity attractive, precisely because they see Christianity with its transcendent vision as grounding a social ethic and its stress on the importance of a civil society and the rule of law as counterpoint to the vacuum of values underlying contemporary Chinese society. Often referred to as cultural Christians because most are not formally church members, they believe that with this vision, Christianity may be the secret behind the strength of the West. Still, Chinese Catholics are slow to develop an effective program of evangelization.

Another challenge is the diminishing number of vocations. While vocations surged in the 1990s, Anthony Lam of the Holy Spirit Study Center in Hong Kong notes a loss in both the public and underground churches. "Between 1996 and 2014 the number of male vocations has dropped from 2,300 to 1,260, while the number of female vocations has

---

[27] Ambrose Ih-Ren Mong, "The Task of Religion in Secular Society: The Challenges Ahead for Christianity in China," in *Catholicism in China, 1900–Present: The Development of the Chinese Church*, ed. Cindy Yik-Yi Chu, 237–51 (New York: Palgrave Macmillan, 2014).

plummeted from 2,500 to 156. He [Lam] also writes that the number of ordinations dropped from 134 in 2000 to 78 in 2014."[28] One contributing factor has been the One Child policy that makes parents less willing to encourage a son or daughter to consider priesthood or religious life. Because of this policy China has thirty million more young men than women. After 2016 the policy was changed; couples are free now to have two children. Another deterrent to vocations is the attraction of modern urban life, with its many distractions.

The apostolic formation of the laity is another critical need. Estimates put the number of Catholics at between ten and twelve million, probably closer to ten million today, and that number seems to be diminishing rather than growing because of low birth rates, failures to evangelize, and conflicts with the government. The Catholic Church, without a theologically formed, engaged laity, or a spirituality shaped by Pope Francis's emphasis on a missionary discipleship, will continue to diminish. "The issue of formation of laity in some dioceses in China is in its infancy, while some other dioceses have no idea about this need or are not even aware of its importance."[29] A rural, "ethnic" church did not need to evangelize, and clerically dominated, it failed to develop lay ministries able to spread the faith; nor will its devotional Catholicism centered on rosaries and the saints appeal to the better educated and upwardly mobile in the cities. An urban church cannot count on conversions through marriage; it has to find ways to touch the young urban professions that populate China's cities. No longer the church of martyrs, it needs urban Bible study programs, university ministries, and intentional Christian communities to reach a new generation.

Thus, Chinese Catholicism has not shared in the religious explosion that China has experienced recently. Buddhism and Taoism, which almost disappeared during the Cultural Revolution, now have members in the millions. Moreover, the growth of Chinese Protestantism has been even more spectacular. Estimated at fifty-eight million in 2010, numbers today, though difficult to determine, range between sixty and eighty million. Some scholars judge Protestant numbers to be inflated. The enormous "house church" movement drives much of the growth with new believers

---

[28] Cited in Ian Johnson, "How the Top-Heavy Catholic Church Is Losing the Ground Game in China," *America*, September 18, 2017.

[29] Joseph You Guo Jiang, SJ, "Catholicism in 21st Century China," *La Civiltà Cattolica*, May 2017, 4.

rapidly becoming pastors, evangelizing, and starting new churches that are decentralized and independent of government control. Still, the growth of Chinese Protestantism is both enormous and highly diverse, with most Protestants practicing a simple form of Christianity in autonomous communities that are nonsacramental, minimal in structure, theologically conservative, and lay centered.[30] Many are neo-Pentecostal.

The recent efforts of the government to impose tighter controls over religion represent a final challenge. In a three-hour speech at the 19th National Congress of the Communist Party of China in 2017, President Xi Jinping insisted on the "Sinicization of religions," stressing that the Communist Party will fully "uphold the principle that religions in China must be Chinese in orientation, and provide active guidance to religions so that they can adapt themselves to socialist society."[31] "Sinicization of religions" really means state oversight and control, and thus a loss of religious freedom. Since then, Chinese officials have placed more than one million ethnic Muslims in the Xinjiang region in internment camps, more than 10 percent of the Uyghur population. Chinese authorities euphemistically call these camps educational training centers. They have also destroyed over twenty churches, both Protestant and Catholic, claiming violations of property regulations. The unregistered churches are particularly at risk. At least one hundred crosses have been removed from churches in Henan Province, and many Christians have had their bibles confiscated. New restrictions prescribe sharing religious material online.

In Henan, Jiangxi, Zhejiang, Liaoning, and Hebei, churches have been ordered to fly the Chinese flag, destroy banners and images with religious messages, and sing the national anthem and Communist Party songs at their services. Government-installed television cameras with facial-recognition technology monitor congregations. Children under eighteen have been forbidden to attend churches, and local people have been threatened with expulsion from education and employment if they "believe in religions." In some parts of the country the faithful have been asked to replace paintings of Jesus with portraits of President Xi Jinping. Thus, Xi's New Regulations on Religious Affairs, described by Amnesty International as

---

[30] See Kim-Kwong Chan, *Understanding World Christianity: China* (Minneapolis: Fortress Press, 2019), 32–36 (on numbers), 186–200 (on diversity).

[31] Li Yuan, "At the Congress Xi Reaffirms: Sinicization of Religions under the Communist Party," AsiaNews.it, October 19, 2017; see also Benoit Vermander, "Sinicizing Religions, Sinicizing Religious Studies," *Religions* 10, no. 137 (2019): 1–23.

"draconian," are causing considerable concern.[32] Catholics in Hong Kong are particularly worried.

A document issued by authorities in Fujian seeks to prevent any outside influence: Catholics are "to consciously boycott foreigners' interventions; not to contact foreign powers, not to welcome foreigners, not to accept any delegation from foreign religious communities or institutions, not to accept interviews, formation or invitations to conferences abroad, not to violate state regulations by accepting national and international donations."[33] This is to isolate them from the universal church. The church needs to find ways to cooperate with the state and still work toward greater independence.

Taiwan

The Vatican's efforts to establish a diplomatic relationship with the government of China will certainly affect the church in Taiwan, probably forcing a move of the nunciature from Taipei to Beijing.[34] Catholics in Taiwan constitute only 1 percent of the population, but their number has been decreasing year by year. The 2014 *Catholic Directory* reports about 230,000 Catholics in seven dioceses in Taiwan, a 20 percent drop from 2008, when the number was 290,000.

Unfortunately, many of the original inhabitants of the island tend to identify the Catholic Church with those who fled China after the Communist takeover with Chiang Kai-shek in 1949. Many Catholic parishes that were established at that time gave priority to the exiled mainlanders. However, the church has made a significant impact on Taiwan's indigenous or Aboriginal community. People in Taiwan also appreciate the Catholic Church's institutions—schools, hospitals, and social-services centers—but few want to enter the church. Moreover, the culture is becoming more secular, though still socially conservative. On November 24, 2018, the voters overwhelmingly affirmed a traditional definition of marriage and voted to remove from elementary and junior high school curricula material reflecting gender ideology.

---

[32]Verna Yu, "Chinese Christian Churches Face New Threats as State Religious Code Is Revised," *America*, January 25, 2018.

[33] Bernard Cervellera, "Suffocating Chinese Church with 'Independence,' while Applauding the Chinese-Vatican Agreement," AsiaNews.it, June 25, 2019.

[34] See Francis K. H. So, Beatrice K. F. Leung, and Mary Ellen Mylod, eds., *The Catholic Church in Taiwan* (New York: Palgrave Macmillan, 2018).

Vietnam

Catholicism first came to Vietnam in the early sixteenth century with occasional visits from Spanish Franciscans and Dominicans from Malacca in Malaysia and from the Philippines. A stable Catholic presence came only when Jesuit missionaries, mostly Portuguese, arrived at Cochinchina (the southern part of present Vietnam) in 1615 and Tonkin in 1626. Foremost among them was Alexandre de Rhodes (1593–1660), the French Jesuit whose legacy included a Latin-script alphabet, a Vietnamese catechism, and a continuing French influence, with the majority of Rhodes's successors being missionaries from the Societé des Missions Étrangères de Paris.

After the French invaded Vietnam in 1858, they established a colonial administration, briefly interrupted by the Japanese during the Second World War and by Ho Chi Minh's short-lived declaration of independence afterward. The latter was initially supported by the Catholic Church before the Viet Minh began purging non-Communist parties from the government in 1946.[35] The French struggled without success to regain control, but after the Communist victory at Dien Bien Phu in 1954 the country was partitioned into a Communist regime in the North and a pro-Western government in the South.

The terms of the settlement called for a popular election to determine the type of government for the unification of the country, but the election was never held; it also allowed people to move from either half of the country to the other. The Vietnamese Communist Party shared the common Marxist attitude toward religion, especially Christianity, holding it responsible for capitalism, colonialism, and imperialism. The government of North Vietnam imposed severe restrictions on the Catholic Church, expelling missionaries, restricting the ordination of both priests and bishops, arresting prominent religious leaders, and frequently denying the civil rights of the faithful. Despite the government's official claims to respect religious freedom, some 700,000 Catholics moved from the North to the South, beginning a gradual shift of the Catholic population.

After the long, devastating civil war and the North Vietnamese victory in 1975, another exodus of Christians took place; approximately four hundred priests and fifty-six thousand Catholics fled the country. In the now united Socialist Republic of Vietnam, the triumphant Communist

---

[35] Lan T. Chu, "Catholicism vs. Communism, Continued: The Catholic Church in Vietnam," *Journal of Vietnamese Studies* 3, no. 1 (Winter 2008): 157–58.

government sought to bring the Christian churches under its control. Archbishop (later cardinal) Nguyen Van Thuan was not allowed to take up his position as bishop of Saigon; six days after the North Vietnamese victory, he was arrested and spent thirteen years in prison.[36] The apostolic nuncio Henri Lemaitre was expelled, as were any remaining foreign clergy. Some three hundred priests were sent to "reeducation" camps, several dioceses were left without bishops, properties belonging the religious orders were confiscated, and Catholic schools and social ministries were closed. A long struggle between the Communist Party and the church followed.

The Church and the Communist Party

The unification of the country brought the bishops of the North and South together into one episcopal body. In 1975, recognizing the new situation the country faced, church leaders urged the faithful through pastoral letters to cooperate with the government in building a just, peaceful, and prosperous country. The archbishop of Saigon stressed the importance of maintaining communion with Rome, thus rejecting any idea of a "patriotic" church on the Chinese model, but also urging Catholics to recognize the contributions of socialism toward social justice. In July 1976, the bishops of the South pointed out the differences between the Marxist-Leninist ideology and Christian faith, but at the same time they encouraged Christians to cooperate with the government for the common good of the country.

With the reestablishment of the Catholic Bishops' Conference of Vietnam in 1980, the bishops of both North and South issued a pastoral letter, calling on Catholics in Vietnam to serve as both citizens and members of the people of God. However, the government remained suspicious of the church's organizational strength and its anti-Communism. It feared the church's strength as an organization and tended to see it as "a state within a state," opposed to its social programs.[37] The result was a protracted struggle for religious liberty. As Peter Phan notes, in the period from 1975 to 1989 the government continued its triple strategy toward religion: elimination

---

[36] See Francis Xavier Nguyen Van Thuan, *The Road of Hope: A Gospel from Prison* (Hyde Park, NY: New City Press, 2013). Pope Francis has cautiously promoted Vān Thuan for canonization, but his cause remains controversial because he was a nephew of South Vietnam's President Ngo Dinh Diem.

[37] Nguyen Van Canh, *Vietnam under Communism, 1975–1982* (Stanford, CA: Hoover Institution Press, 1983), 169.

of the leadership, demolition of organizational structures, and restrictions of religious activities.[38]

With the collapse of the Soviet Union in 1989, relations between the Catholic Church and the Communist government began to improve remarkably. With the economy near collapse, the government as early as 1982 had begun to introduce a number of reforms, permitting some "capitalist" accommodations, especially in the South. A 1986 Five-Year Plan sought to introduce a "socialist-oriented market economy." Farmers were allowed to keep whatever surplus they produced and to sell it on the free market or to the government. Agriculture collectives were abandoned, as were price control on agriculture goods, and both private businesses and foreign investments were encouraged, meaning in practice a move toward a free-market system. The United States lifted its embargo in 1994 and reestablished diplomatic relations in 2000.

While the government was reluctant to give up its exclusive grip on power, relations toward religious freedom improved considerably, with some diplomatic relations established with the Vatican. Directives issued by the government in 1998, 1999, and 2004 relaxed slightly the list of unlawful religious activities, though the government continued to require registration of religions as well as a strict oversight of their activities; for the church, this meant requiring government approval for establishing seminaries, choosing candidates for the priesthood, and appointing bishops.

President Bill Clinton reestablished normal diplomatic relations with Vietnam in 1995 with the strong support of two veterans of the war, Senator John Kerry and Senator John McCain. The latter had suffered terribly as a prisoner of war in Vietnam. The first US ambassador to Vietnam was also a former POW, Douglas "Pete" Peterson. Continuing concern over violations of religious freedom led U.S. Secretary of State Colin Powell to include Vietnam among "countries of particular concern" in 2004; his successor, Condoleezza Rice, removed Vietnam from the list in 2006.

In 2011, the Vatican named Archbishop Leopoldo Girelli as a nonresidential papal representative for Vietnam, though the archbishop's status was really that of an apostolic delegate. Significantly, in 2012, the FABC held its Tenth Plenary Assembly at the Xuan Loc Pastoral Centre, just east of

---

[38] Peter C. Phan, "Christianity in Vietnam Today (1975–2013): Contemporary Challenges and Opportunities," *International Journal for the Study of the Christian Church* 14, no. 1 (2014): 5.

Ho Chi Minh City, the former Saigon. And a delegation from Vietnam's government met with Pope Benedict in January 2013.

As in China, the government considers Protestantism a different religion from Catholicism, and it continues to demand registration of the Protestant churches. The reluctance of many in the rapidly growing house church movement to seek official recognition and the fact that the government is frequently reluctant to recognize them remain sources of tension. The present generation of Communist leaders no longer sees the churches, Protestant or Catholic, as a threat to national security, though relations between the churches and local governments are more difficult in some provinces than in others. Many Communist Party members recognize that the churches can be an ally for the economic and social development of the country, though the government continues to struggle to exercise some control over them. In 2017, the United States Commission on International Religious Freedom again designated Vietnam a "country of particular concern," as it has every year since 2002. This status could improve depending on how the new Law on Beliefs and Religions, which became effective on January 1, 2018, is implemented.[39]

Present Challenges

While the churches continue to struggle for greater religious liberty, they face new challenges. As religious minorities they are only beginning to enter into interreligious dialogue, especially with Buddhists; many of the Protestant churches remain closed to such dialogue. The forces of globalization as well as the new consumerism and materialism, exacerbated by the now-dominant market economy, are bringing about considerable cultural changes. Few take communism as a philosophy seriously. As Peter Phan says:

> Communism as an ideology, though still spouted and propped up by the Communist party, is fast becoming an empty shell, and party leaders are quite cognizant of this state of affairs and are busy preserving their interests in an eventual post-socialist state. Today the greatest threat to Christianity in the Asian socialist countries is . . . complete indifference to Christianity as well as to any other religious

---

[39] United States Commission on International Religious Freedom, *2017 Annual Report* (Washington, DC: US Commission on International Religious Freedom, April 2017), 114.

way of life as the result of a relentless pursuit of wealth and all the pleasures it promises.[40]

Like Christians in many other countries, Catholics in Vietnam try to witness to their faith in a secular, often hostile culture. They have many strengths. Their churches are full, vocations plentiful, and the church has recently received permission to establish a university-level theological institute. Catholics hold positions in the government and Party members frequently send their children to Catholic preschool programs or to US Catholic universities. Nevertheless, as Tom Reese says, Oscar Romero would not be better treated in Vietnam than he was in El Salvador.[41] Playing a prophetic role—for example, criticizing Communist Party policy or advocating for democracy or human rights—is generally not possible. Restraints on efforts at evangelization and limitations on Catholic ministries remain in place. Catechists must instruct those interested in the faith privately. Access to public media is restricted, but the church can circulate its own publications. In some provinces it is difficult to get approval for new churches or religious activities. Thus, the church in Vietnam remains a church in some tension with the government.[42]

Today, the Catholic Church in Vietnam has twenty-six dioceses divided into three ecclesiastical provinces: Hanoi, Hue, and Ho Chi Minh City. As of 2016, the 6,332,700 Catholics in Vietnam make up roughly 7 percent of the population of the country, the fifth largest Catholic population in Asia. The cultural changes brought on by modernity affect not just traditional Vietnamese society but also the Catholic Church. In an October 2017 pastoral letter, the bishops encouraged Vietnamese Catholics to uphold the traditional values of Catholic marriages, resisting social trends toward abortion, cohabitation, same-sex marriage, and divorce.[43]

Korea

The origins of Catholicism and Christianity in Korea are difficult to discern, but a central theme is that the faith was brought by the laity. One

---

[40] Phan, "Christianity in Vietnam Today," 17.

[41] Thomas J. Reese and Mary Ann Glendon, "How Vietnam Respects and Protects Religious Freedom Has Implications beyond Its Own Borders," *America*, February 18, 2016.

[42] Reese and Glendon.

[43] "Vietnamese Bishops Journey with Young Families," UCAN India, October 18, 2017.

account says that the first Christians were Korean Catholic slaves; they had been captured by the Japanese during their invasion of Korea (1592–98) and later sold to the Portuguese.[44] The traditional story dates the beginning of the Catholic Church in Korea to the return of Yi Seung-hun to Korea in 1784 with Christian literature produced by the Jesuits in China. Baptized in Beijing as Peter Yi, he is said to have baptized some of his countrymen on his return.[45]

The faith spread principally through family relationships, and thus, thorough the laity. After the formation of the Apostolic Vicariate of Korea in 1831, missionaries from the Société des Missions Étrangères de Paris arrived in 1836, and the first Korean priest, Andrew Kim Taegon, was ordained in Shanghai in 1844; he was martyred after returning to Korea in 1846. Today he is the patron saint of Korea.

Persecution

The nineteenth century saw a fierce persecution of Christians. An initial tension was controversy over what is inaccurately referred to as ancestor worship, a Confucian practice that the early Jesuits in China had given a Christian interpretation; however, in 1704 and again in 1742, Rome ruled that these rites represented idolatry. Korean authorities saw the rejection of this practice as undermining the moral foundations of Korea's Confucian state. The gathering of a group of friends and relatives of Yi Pyok to read Catholic books brought from Beijing by Yi Seung-hun led to a small group fascinated with Catholicism as they learned about the creation of the universe and the difference between material and spiritual beings. This ultimately led to a conflict between the supernatural orientation of Catholicism and Confucian moral demands, especially the obligation to place God first. By 1791, Catholics were being executed for their faith.[46]

Other persecutions followed, with mass executions of Christians in 1801, 1839, and 1846; perhaps as many as ten thousand were martyred. In 1984, Pope John Paul II canonized 103 of the men and women killed during the persecutions. Pope Francis beatified an additional 124 martyrs

---

[44] Kaijian Tang, *Setting Off from Macau; Essays on Jesuit History during the Ming and Qing Dynasties* (Boston: Brill, 2016), 93.

[45] Don Baker, with Franklin Rausch, *Catholics and Anti-Catholicism in Choson Korea* (Honolulu: University of Hawaii Press, 2017), 48.

[46] See Baker, with Rausch, 67–82.

during a visit to Korea in August 2014. Thus, the tradition of martyrdom plays a strong role in Korean Catholicism.

The first Protestant missionaries arrived in 1884 after the signing of a treaty two years before establishing diplomatic relations with the United States. Henry Appenzeller and his wife were Methodists. Horace Underwood was Presbyterian; his interpreter, when baptized, became the first Korean Protestant. Evangelization took place through the circulation of Christian literature. The Korean churches and missionaries played an important role in developing Korean nationalism and ethnic identity, especially during the colonial era (1910–45).[47] The majority of Christians lived in the north. During the Korean War (1950–53), one-half of Protestant pastors disappeared or were killed by the Communists; many Christians fled to the south. Nevertheless, Christianity continued to spread. Both Protestants and Catholics were active in opposing the denial of human rights under the military governments of the 1960s and 1970s.

Christianity Today

Korea has no single religious majority, with 45 percent of the population lacking any religious affiliation, 30 percent Christian, and 22 percent Buddhist. Protestantism now numbers nine million adherents, about 18 percent of the total population. Among the 170 denominations, Presbyterianism is the largest. About 10 percent of Korean Christians belong to independent churches, many of them Pentecostal. According to a North Korean Protestant pastor, there are five hundred house churches and ten thousand Christians in North Korea. The evangelical zeal of Protestant Christians in Korea tops most other countries in terms of the missionaries they send abroad.

The Yoido Full Gospel Church in Seoul, South Korea, a Pentecostal megachurch, may be the largest congregation in the world. Founded in 1958 by David Yonggi Cho and five others, the church today numbers over half a million. Affiliated with the Assemblies of God, the congregation gathers each Sunday for seven services in a vast theater-style auditorium. When one service ends, the next begins, with twelve thousand congregants streaming in to take their places on the ground floor or in upper tiers facing the platform where the ministers gather. Overhead, a bare wooden

---

[47] Edward J. W. Park, "Global Religion and Local Faith: Korean Churches in Beijing and Tokyo," *Journal of Global and Area Studies* 2, no. 2 (2018): 66.

cross and television monitors with notices, video clips on the church's ministries, or words to songs supported by a robed choir and orchestra. When called to pray, all do so at once, with noise and enthusiasm. One of its features is the Prayer Mountain, established in 1973, where people can come to fast and pray in tiny cubicles; it receives a million visitors a year. The church's message promises a threefold blessing of spirit, soul, and body, including both physical health and financial prosperity, a message shared with many Korean Protestant churches.

Christian missionaries, both Catholic and Protestant, contributed much to the development of Korea. From the beginning they established a network of schools, from kindergarten to universities, many of them first rate. They introduced studies in science and modern medicine as well as a network of social services, including healthcare for the disadvantaged and hospitals, orphanages, daycare and job-training centers, often with governmental support. For many Koreans, Christianity represents a path to modernity. No other organization offers more social-services agencies. The churches have also contributed enormously to the country's political life, promoting values such as freedom, human rights, and democracy, especially during the period in the 1970s and 1980s when the country suffered under oppressive military governments guilty of human rights abuse, though some Protestant churches have been more tolerant of authoritarian regimes. Both Catholics and Protestants continue to play significant roles in the country's political life to an extent unknown in much of Asia.

The Catholic Church in South Korea has seen enormous growth. By the end of 2017, Korean Catholics numbered approximately 5.8 million, or 11 percent of the population. That year alone there were seventy-five thousand adult baptisms. The church enjoys great respect for its social and educational works, for its support of democracy, and for its respectful approach to interreligious dialogue. Vocations to the priesthood and religious life have increased.

Though religious practice remains exceptionally high for both Catholics and Protestants, Peter Kim writes that Christian expansion may have reached a plateau. While he sees a decline in Christianity's political and social influence as well as in its levels of religious practice, he remains optimistic that Christianity will remain strong and continue to spread its influence.[48]

---

[48] Peter Andrew Eungi Kim, "South Korea," in Phan, *Christianities in Asia*, 229.

The Indian Subcontinent

The Indian subcontinent is a vast area the size of Europe. It is isolated from the rest of Asia by the Himalayas, save for the Khyber Pass in the Northwest, through which Muslim armies moved in the eleventh century. While Christianity is still seen as a foreign import in this part of the world, Christian communities have been present there since at least the second century. Tradition attributes the introduction of Christianity to the northern part of the subcontinent to the apostle Thomas. Today the subcontinent embraces the nations of India, Pakistan, Bangladesh, Nepal, Bhutan, with the island of Sri Lanka usually included.

The first Christian communities on the subcontinent were those of the so-called Thomas Christians, communities established by Nestorian missionaries who arrived somewhere between 52 and 356, thus before the Council of Chalcedon (451). Thomas Christians were Orthodox, members of communities that in the fourth century came under the jurisdiction of the Church of the East, centered in Persia. Virtually self-governing and integrated into the Hindu state, they adopted a number of Hindu and Muslim customs involving purity, rituals for prayer, and eventually the caste system. Even today Thomas Christians are recognized as truly Indian or "local."

With the arrival of the Portuguese in the early sixteenth century, along with Dominican and Franciscan missionaries, most of the subcontinent fell under the jurisdiction of the Archdiocese of Lisbon. The Jesuits came with Francis Xavier in 1540; Xavier worked out of Goa, which became an independent archdiocese in 1557. Known as the primate of the Indies, Goa's archbishop exercised jurisdiction over India, Burma, China, and Japan.

Today, there are 1.2 million Catholics in Sri Lanka, about 6 percent of the population. Pakistan has a little over one million Catholics, less than 1 percent, while Myanmar (formerly Burma) has approximately 450,000 Catholics. Bangladesh has 350,000 Catholics or 0.2 percent of the population; Nepal 10,000, 1.4 percent; while Bhutan has only one thousand, or 9 percent.

India

Two Jesuits, Roberto de Nobili (1577–1656) and John de Britto (1647–93) played a significant role in shaping Indian Catholicism. De Nobili, an Italian, moved from Goa to Tamil Nadu in 1606. Not unlike Matteo Ricci in

China, he adopted the method of inculturation. Mastering Sanskrit and Tamil, he took on the role of a sannyasi or holy man, with Indian dress and manners, and sought out high-caste scholars for dialogue about the truths of Christianity. However, these methods were controversial with other Jesuits and church authorities such as the archbishop of Goa. John de Britto also adopted sannyasi customs and dress, but he focused on Indian society's warrior class and the lower-class Shanars.

Both de Nobili and de Britto sought an inculturation of Christianity, with the unfortunate consequence of accepting the caste system; more positively they sought to distance Indian Christianity from Portuguese colonialism. As later missionaries increasingly sought to Latinize the Thomas Christians, they split into two separate churches, the Syro-Malabar Church, in communion with Rome, and the Malankara Church, an Oriental Orthodox community. They further divided in modern times into a number of different communities.

Conflicts over Caste

From the beginning Christian missionaries and their churches have been ambivalent about the caste system. The Thomas Christians have always claimed high-caste status, and de Nobili addressed himself only to the high-caste Brahmins, hoping that conversion of the lower castes would follow. Other Catholic missionaries, accustomed to the social stratification of Portugal or Italy, easily adapted to it in India. In 1623, the papal bull of Gregory XV granted the requests of the missionaries to accept certain caste practices as a temporary measure, while insisting on showing charity and respect for Dalit Christians. Protestant missionaries opposed the caste system as incompatible with Christianity. Low-caste peoples, known by various terms, prefer the common term Dalit ("oppressed" in Sanskrit), commonly translated as "untouchable." The constitution of India, recognizing Dalits as socially disadvantaged, designates them as "Scheduled Caste" and "Scheduled Tribe" peoples, with various subdivisions among them.

Caste consciousness and discrimination, so deeply embedded in the culture, remains a problem not only in India, but also in Sri Lanka and parts of Pakistan.[49] Considered outside the caste system and bound by taboos, the Dalits suffer social, economic, and religious oppression. They are thought

---

[49] See Felix Wilfred, "South Asian Christianity in Context," in *The Oxford Handbook of Christianity in Asia*, ed. Felix Wilfred (New York: Oxford University Press, 2014), 41–44.

to pollute others by contact and hence are prohibited from normal contact in temple, using public wells, or even hotels. While the cities have seen some progress toward equality, Dalits in rural areas still face persecution. Dalit women, sometimes referred to as "the Dalits among the Dalits," face even greater discrimination. Efforts at inculturation—such as uncritically accepting local cultural mores, adopting indigenous music, or reading from Sanskrit texts—often has the unhappy effect of reinforcing the caste system.

Dalits have experienced prejudice even among Catholics. Because upper-class Indian converts tended to interpret their new faith in terms of Brahmanic culture, Dalit converts were excluded from mainstream church life and theology. In Tamil Nadu they had separate places in the churches or had to sit on the floor; in some places they had separate chapels and services, as well as different communion lines, cemeteries, even hearses. In Kerala there is no intermarriage between castes. Even Dalit priests sometimes face caste-based discrimination; one parish priest suffered a brutal beating when he spoke out in support of Dalits.[50] One Catholic commentator notes that in his travels he had seen discrimination "among congregations and even among priests. I have seen separate graveyards for lower-caste Catholics who, when alive, were relegated to the back corners of the church. A priest once told me that he wished he had tweezers to distribute communion to those from the back of the church, lest he be contaminated."[51]

Of the twenty-eight million Christians in India, Dalits make up about 60 percent, though the exact figure is difficult to establish. Of the more than 240 bishops in India, only 12 are Dalits (5 percent), while of the over nineteen million Indian Catholics, over twelve million are Dalits (63 percent). But prejudice against Dalits persists. One challenge is to develop an Indian theology that incorporates the experience of Christians of Dalit origin, a theology based not on Marxist analysis, as in Latin America, but on the complex reality of the caste system.[52]

On December 13, 2016, the Catholic Bishops' Conference of India for the first time published a report acknowledging prejudice against Dalit Christians as a social sin, asking each diocese to submit a plan on how

---

[50] See C. V. Vinod, "A Critical Reflection on the Theological Realm of Dalit Christian Exclusion in Catholicism in India," *Voice of Dalit* 5, no. 1 (2012): 45–51.

[51] Ivan Fernandes, "Not Even the Church Escapes India's Caste System," UCAnews, September 11, 2013.

[52] Vinod, "A Critical Reflection on the Theological Realm of Dalit Christian Exclusion in Catholicism in India," 53.

to end caste-based discrimination. Dalits also face discrimination from the government, which refuses to extend laws outlawing discrimination against those of a Scheduled Caste that are not Hindus, Sikhs, or Buddhist.[53] Christians and Muslims of Dalit origin are ineligible for social welfare benefits such as reservations (affirmative action quotas) in government jobs, educational institutions, and financial help with studies, because, according to a 1950 government policy, their religions do not follow the caste system.

Contemporary Tensions

Although India is officially a secular state, since the Hindu nationalist Bharatiya Janata Party (BJP) came to power in 2014 persecution of Christians as well as Muslims has increased. In 2017, there were some six hundred cases, according to Christian records. The New Delhi-based Alliance Defending Freedom reports a rising number of violent episodes: 147 in 2014, 177 in 2015, 208 in 2016, 240 in 2017, and 292 in 2018. The report noted that many attacks are not reported because of inaction by police and local officials or fear of reprisals.

Churches have been burned, priests, ministers, and nuns have been attacked, and Indian Christians, especially Dalits, have been forcibly "reconverted" to Hinduism. Some have returned to Hinduism to be eligible for the benefits denied them as Christians. Physical violence against Christians was up 40 percent in 2016, and the number of murders doubled. Women and girls are particularly at risk. In August 2017, the US Commission on International Religious Freedom ranked India's persecution at "Tier 2," along with Iraq and Afghanistan. Uttar Pradesh, India's most populous state and home to almost 17 percent of the country's total population, recorded the most attacks against Christians and their churches in 2018.

In early September 2019, a mob of over five hundred radicals armed with various weapons attacked St. John Berchmans Inter College and the Loyola Adivasi Hostel in Mundi, two Jesuit institutions in a state governed by the BJP. They vandalized both institutions, doing extensive damage, beating some of the boys from the Hostel, and threatened the college and women staff. After a week, no arrests had been made.

---

[53] "Policy of Dalit Empowerment in the Catholic Church in India: an Ethical Imperative to Build Inclusive Communities," http://www.cbci.in/DownloadMat/dalit-policy.pdf.

Altogether, there are some 28 million Christians in India, making Christianity the third largest religion (after Hinduism and Islam). There are over 19.9 million Roman Catholics, with 174 dioceses, 132 of them Latin, 31 Syro-Malabar, and 11 Syro-Malankara. While collectively they represent the largest Christian church in India, they make up only 2.5 percent of India's huge population. Besides those churches split off from the Thomas Christians, Protestant Christians have been present since the nineteenth century. The largest after the Catholic Church is the Church of South India, formed out of Anglican and a number of Protestant churches, numbering today approximately four million.

But ecumenical efforts are minimal in India. One Indian Jesuit told me that ecumenism is a forgotten issue; there are occasional meetings of people from different churches to address secular issues, but there is so much anger on both sides that there are no efforts to discuss or do scholarship on ecumenical issues. Another highly placed source said that hardly anyone was directly and actively involved in ecumenism, though some Indian institutes did have ecumenical collaboration. In 2020, the COVID-19 pandemic led to one helpful sign—when representatives of five Indian churches came together on Pentecost Sunday to pray for an end to the crisis. With its overcrowding in cramped slums, shortage of healthcare workers and testing kits, and lack of centralized management for fighting the pandemic, India has been particularly hard hit. Only the United States, Brazil, and Russia have more cases. The Catholic Church has been working to help provide the hungry with food.

Another issue that is only beginning to surface is sexual abuse both of minors and of women. The abuse of women, widespread in India, is a taboo subject, but women are nonetheless beginning to speak out against it. In a recent AP report "nuns described in detail the sexual pressure they endured from priests, and nearly two dozen other people—nuns, former nuns and priests, and others—said they had direct knowledge of such incidents." One said she had been repeatedly raped by her bishop.[54] One positive sign was the creation of a service wing of the National Council of Churches in India. "Understanding and Responding to the Sexual Abuse Crisis in the Indian Church—An Ecumenical Consultation" was the title of the program organized by the Church Auxiliary for Social Action (CASA); it included Catholic, Protestant and Orthodox churches.

---

[54]Tim Sullivan, "Nuns in India Tell AP of Enduring Abuse in Catholic Church," AP, January 2, 2019.

From the earliest days of the Catholic mission efforts the churches have established schools, hospitals, and social services, playing a major role in the development of the country. Protestant mission schools are responsible for introducing the English language to the country. The members of the Hindu nationalist party, the BJP, in spite of their hostility to Christianity, continue to send their children to Catholic schools.

Beyond its educational and social ministries, the Catholic Church in India is providing a model for the rest of the church for an engaged mission. Theologians such as Michael Amaladoss, Felix Wilfred, and Jacques Dupuis have worked to recast Christian proclamation within the context of India's religious pluralism. The Catholic Bishops' Conference of India calls for the church to be a church of dialogue, inviting Catholics into a "dialogue of life" with those of other religious traditions, and they continue to work for the rights of Dalits and women. The bishops reaffirm their commitment to the protection of nature and the sustainable development of peoples.

Conclusion

Though present across the vast continent of Asia, Christianity remains a minority religion. There are some exceptions. Christianity continues to grow dramatically in China, mostly among evangelical and especially neo-Pentecostal communities that emphasize "signs and wonders," the struggle against demons and spirits, and often the prosperity gospel. In China the Catholic Church is undergoing a difficult transition from being a largely rural church to an urban church in the country's rapidly developing cities, with their largely secular cultures. The academic as well as spiritual formation of priests remains a challenge. Concerns also remain about recent efforts to bring the churches under greater control of the Communist Party.

Christians constitute the largest religion in Korea, some 30 percent of the population, of which Catholics represent slightly more than 10 percent.

The 900,000 Catholics in East Timor, a former Portuguese colony, represent 96 percent of the population. In Sri Lanka, Catholics make up 6.1 percent of the population; in Vietnam they constitute 7 percent. Catholics in Macau, another former Portuguese colony, and also in Hong Kong make up 5 percent of the population. Singapore is 5.7 percent

Catholic. There is a strong Catholic presence in Indonesia, with 7.5 million Catholics, though they make up only 2.9 percent of the population.

In India, the Latin, Syro-Malabar, and Syro-Malankara Catholics together constitute the largest Christian church but make up only 2.5 percent of India's vast population. Indian Catholicism is strong, though like other minority religions, Catholics frequently experience discrimination and even violence from the Hindu Nationalist Party. Many fault Prime Minister Narendra Modi for lack of action in response to BJP-sponsored violence. The church continues to struggle against the cultural effects of the caste system, with prejudice and discrimination against those from the lower castes, the Dalits, sometimes even in the church itself.

The ancient Catholic churches of the Middle East are in danger of disappearing, while both Catholics and Protestants lack full religious freedom in China and Vietnam, as well as actual persecution in India from the Hindu Nationalist Party. In Pakistan, Christians are frequently victimized by the application of laws against blasphemy.

The churches of Asia have been glacially slow in addressing the sexual abuse crisis. In most Asian countries there is a deep cultural reluctance to address issues as sensitive as sexuality. At the meeting of the heads of episcopal conferences to focus on sexual abuse, called by Pope Francis in Rome, February 21–24, 2019, a press briefing on the first day reported that the bishops of Asia and Africa stated that sex abuse was not a problem in their countries. However, Virginia Saldanha, former executive secretary for the FABC Office of the Laity said that there was considerable evidence to the contrary, including the abuse of nuns and vulnerable women by priests in Asia.[55]

Though some of the non-Catholic Asian churches are reluctant to enter into interreligious dialogue, the FABC continues to emphasize it, along with dialogue with the poor and with culture. If successful, it may be able to teach all Christians how to live in harmony with those of other religions.

---

[55]Virginia Saldanha, "Bishops' Summit on Sex Abuse: An Asian Perspective," *La Croix International,* April 10, 2019.

6

The Pacific

While Christianity remains a minority religion in most of Asia, it is often the majority in the many nations stretching across the vast Pacific Ocean. The region referred to as Oceania covers an area of 8,525,989 square miles. It includes the continent of Australia; Polynesia; the huge triangle formed by Hawaii, New Zealand, and Easter Island; Melanesia, the island groups south of the equator and north and east of Australia from Papua New Guinea to the Fijis; and Micronesia, stretching northward from the equator to the Marianas and eastward from Palau to the Gilbert Islands.

The fathers of the Sacred Hearts of Jesus and Mary were among the first missionaries to Eastern Oceania, coming first to Hawaii in 1825. Among their members was Father Damien De Veuster (1840–89), the famous "Leper Priest," now honored as a saint. The Marist Fathers evangelized Western Oceania, embracing Melanesia and the Caroline, Marshall, and the Gilbert islands of Micronesia. It was a difficult mission, with not a few martyrs. They include Saint Pierre Chanel, martyred at Fatuna in 1841; Bishop Jean-Baptiste Epalle, killed on Santa Isabel in 1845; and Brother Blaise Marmoiton, killed in New Caledonia in 1847. That same year another two Marist priests and a brother were killed in the Solomon Islands. Having lost so many men, the Marists decided to withdraw from the archipelago.

On other islands priests, nuns, and brothers continued their missionary work, often at great sacrifice. Many lost their lives to disease or violence. The Missionaries of the Sacred Heart came to New Britain, New Guinea, and the Gilbert Islands in 1882, followed later by the Society of the Divine Word fathers. The Jesuits began a mission in the Caroline Islands in 1731, a work carried on by Spanish Capuchins after the suppression of the Jesuits. Missionary work in the Solomon Islands began again in 1897, assisted by Samoan and Fijian catechists. Not always culturally sensitive, the missionaries made many mistakes, tragically contributing to the disintegration of the native culture and to many deaths, though the impact of other Europeans—including whalers and slavers—would have been even worse without them.

By introducing education, written language, and reading, as well as various crafts, the missionaries not only established Christianity but helped to bring the peoples of the Pacific into the modern world. According to a report prepared by the United States Conference of Catholic Bishops, *Encountering Christ in Harmony,* the colonial and missionary history of these countries has shaped their religious and cultural identity.[1]

Catholics are in the minority on most of these Pacific island nations, but they form the majority faith in Australia, the Philippines, Timor-Leste, Wallis and Fortuna, and Guam. The Philippines and Timor-Leste each have a higher percentage of Catholics than any other country in the world, 93 percent and 96 percent respectively. Guam is 75 percent Catholic; the Federated States of Micronesia, 52.7 percent; Kiribati, 55 percent; New Caledonia, 50.8 percent; Northern Micronesia Island, 64.1 percent; and Palau, 55.1 percent. Malaysia has over a million Catholics, approximately 3.56 percent of the population. The island nation of Indonesia, the world's fourth most populated country, is mostly Muslim, but it is home also to ten million Christians. In parts of the country Christians are the dominant religion. Since we cannot treat all these countries, we focus on Australia and New Zealand, as well as the Philippines and Japan, which really belong to Asia but are also island nations in the Pacific.

Australia

The colonization of the great island continent of Australia began with the arrival in 1788 of the First Fleet, which comprised eleven ships carrying Irish convicts from England to its barren shores. By 1802, the number of convicts, most of them Catholics, had reached 2,086. Other convicts continued to arrive, and by 1868, there were approximately 161,700, of whom 25,000 were women. Sentenced to transportation "beyond the seas" under England's harsh penal code, they were exiled to the Australian

---

[1] United States Conference of Catholic Bishops, *Encountering Christ in Harmony: A Pastoral Response to Our Asian and Pacific Island Brothers and Sisters* (Washington, DC: USCCB, 2018), 14–15.

colonies of New South Wales, Van Diemen's Land (now Tasmania), and Western Australia.

While some were common criminals, perhaps the majority of them were guilty of theft and other crimes typical in an age of crushing poverty. The total includes thirty thousand men and nine thousand women transported directly from Ireland. Some were guilty of political crimes, though not the majority, as an Australian legend would have it. Robert Hughes suggests that no more than 20 percent were political rebels.[2] Most were nominal Catholics, if not irreligious, while others struggled to keep their faith alive without the ministry of priests.

The first priests, themselves convicts, arrived in 1800. Accused on shaky evidence of taking part in the Irish rebellion, James Dixon received permission to minister to the Catholics of Sydney, Liverpool, and Parramatta; after a few years he was able to return to Ireland. Finally, in 1820, two priests appointed by the London government arrived as chaplains, marking the official establishment of the church in Australia. The 1828 census reported a Catholic population of roughly ten thousand, the vast majority from England or Ireland. An English Benedictine monk, John Bede Polding, was the first bishop, with a vision of a church founded on a monastic model. However, the Irish priests and bishops who succeeded him were more practical; the church they helped form was very much an Irish church until shortly before the Second World War, when Australian-born priests began to replace them in the majority. Religious sisters, priests, and brothers arrived to staff the growing number of Catholic schools, especially after the various states between 1872 and 1893 withdrew state support for church schools. By 1900, the Christian Brothers staffed some thirty schools with 115 brothers; by 1910, more than five thousand religious sisters were teaching in church schools.

The real growth of the Catholic Church in Australia took place after the Second World War. As increasingly educated Catholics began moving into the middle class, they began to rival other groups in prosperity and social status, establishing parishes in the growing suburbs. Catholic piety flourished, with high attendance at mass, rich devotional life, and the flourishing of sodalities and Holy Name societies. However, the Irish dominance began to give way as a new wave of Catholic immigrants arrived from Italy, Malta, Germany, Croatia, and the Netherlands, bringing the Catholic culture of their home countries and often their own priests.

---

[2] Robert Hughes, *The Fatal Shore* (New York: Alfred A. Knopf, 1987), 195.

Post Vatican II

As in other countries, Catholic life in Australia changed considerably in the years following the Second Vatican Council. As the number of priests and sisters declined, mass attendance fell off precipitously, traditional devotions largely disappeared, and lay men and lay women took over roles previously filled by priests and religious. Schools and colleges were largely lay run, and not always by Catholics. As the country moved into the twenty-first century, Australia's population was becoming increasingly diverse. Asians made up the largest group of newcomers, with their percentage jumping from 32.9 percent in 2011 to 39.7 percent in 2016. Religious practice also dropped considerably. Fifty years ago more than 88 percent of the country was Christian, but according to the 2016 census, 30 percent reported "no religion," 23 percent "Catholic," and 13 percent "Anglican."

According to the 2011 census Catholics constitute the largest religious group in the country, with thirty-five dioceses spread out in five provinces: Sydney, Melbourne, Adelaide, Perth, and Brisbane. They make up just over one-quarter of Australia's population of 24.6 million people. In terms of ethnicity the Catholic population is highly diverse. Nearly one-quarter were born overseas, three-quarters of those in non-English-speaking countries. An additional 2.3 percent is of Aboriginal or Torres Strait Islander origin. Only about 12.5 percent of Australian Catholics will be in church on a typical weekend; of this number 85 percent attend every week, another 15 percent less regularly. The majority of those attending mass come from non-English-speaking countries, so mass on Sundays is celebrated in more than thirty languages. Of those priests in parish ministry, 51 percent are foreign born, with most coming from West Africa, India, the Philippines, and Vietnam.

Sexual Abuse

Though it surfaced late in Australia, the sexual abuse scandal has done great damage to the Catholic Church there, leaving in its wake thousands who have suffered. In 2013, the Australian government established a Royal Commission into Institutional Responses to Child Sexual Abuse. Its report, which appeared five years later, listed almost forty-four hundred cases of child sex abuse between 1950 and 2010; it identified eighteen hundred priests as perpetrators, 7 percent of all Catholic priests. A disproportionately high percentage of the abusers were religious brothers, with most incidents of abuse occurring between 1950 and 1989. The report generated disillusionment, rage, and negative reporting throughout the country.[3]

To make matters worse, the country's highest-ranking clergyman, Cardinal George Pell, a member of Pope Francis's special council of nine cardinals (C9), was himself accused. He had to return to Australia in 2017 to face charges, and in December 2018 he was convicted on five counts of abusing two thirteen-year-old boys. He denied the charges. After his appeal was rejected, he began serving his six-year sentence. In April 2020, the High Court of Australia dismissed his conviction on the basis of the evidence presented requiring a reasonable doubt. Another bishop, Archbishop Philip Wilson of Adelaide, received a sentence of up to twelve months' home detention on the charge of failing to report child abuse in the 1970s. After serving almost four months, his conviction was overturned on appeal.

Optional celibacy was one recommendation of the Royal Commission's report; another was that Catholic priests report to authorities any confession of child abuse made in the confessional, a recommendation strongly rejected by the bishops and other church leaders. The church estimates that it will be liable for AUS$1 billion in compensation, and it was the first to join the government-sponsored plan to compensate victims. Archbishop Coleridge has called for a plenary council of the Australian church to break away from its disastrous past and to begin again on a sound footing. In response to one of the recommendations of the Royal Commission, on May 2, 2019, the Australian Conference of Bishops and Catholic Religious Australia, an organization of the leaders of religious institutes and congregations, named a panel of experts to conduct a national review of the governance and management structures of Catholic dioceses and parishes, including issues of transparency, accountability, consultation, and lay participation.

The panel's response, dated May 1, 2020, was embargoed by the bishops for six months so they could study it. Entitled "The Light from the Southern Cross: Promoting Co-Responsible Governance in the Catholic Church in Australia," the document made eighty-six sweeping

---

[3] Royal Commission into Institutional Responses to Child Sexual Abuse, "Final Report," 17 vols. (December 15, 2017). The volumes and other helpful documentation, including "A Brief Guide to the Final Report" and a history of the commission's work, can be downloaded from www.childabuseroyalcommission.gov.au.

recommendations. Among them, inviting all the baptized into the church discernment and mission; stressing that all participate in the traditioning process of the church; recognizing that good governance will demand a change of culture stressing subsidiarity, stewardship, synodality, dialogue, and discernment; developing structures of accountability, including for bishops, with meaningful checks and balances; ensuring greater participation of clergy and laity in the appointing and assigning of bishops; reforming the seminary system; mandating pastoral councils on diocesan and parish levels, and expanding incorporation of lay women into governance structures.[4]

Today, Australia is becoming increasingly secular. The 2016 census showed "no religion" as the most popular response, nearly 30 percent. In November 2017, a solid majority of Australians voted to allow same-sex marriage. Immigration is another increasingly contentious issue, with a majority in favor of a slowdown. The country has accepted many immigrants from Lebanon, mostly Muslim, while the majority of immigrants today are coming from Asia.

Between 2011 and 2016 the Catholic population in Australia dropped by 2.7 percent, from 25.3 percent of the total population to 22.6 percent. The 2016 census showed nearly 5.5 million Australians identifying as Catholic, but fewer than 10 percent of them said they attend mass. A second, smaller group calls for reform, wanting the church to move "with the times." A third group is conservative, holding firmly to "the truths of the faith" and seeing the spirit of the world as antithetical to the Holy Spirit. They argue that the places most hostile to the faith are hospitals, schools, and universities with Catholic names.

A successful renewal for the Australian Catholic church will require—besides openness to the Spirit—"a focus on the horizontal rather than the vertical in Church life; recognition of lay leadership and the leading role of women in the Church, which actually exists already but is not acknowledged; but above all, an interior journey for those committed to the transformation of the Church."[5] The 208-page review commissioned by the bishops' conference, "The Light from the Southern Cross: Promoting Co-Responsible Governance in the Catholic Church in Australia," was leaked to the internet on June 1, 2020.

---

[4] Richard R. Gaillardetz, "May the Global Church Discover 'Light from the Southern Cross,'" *La Croix International,* June 3, 2020.

[5] Michael Kelly, "After the Tumult and the Shouting," *La Croix International,* August 23, 2019.

New Zealand

New Zealand and Australia share a common British colonial heritage and are members of the British Commonwealth. The first settlers in New Zealand were Polynesians; they arrived in the fourteenth century and developed a Māori culture. In the seventeenth century Dutch explorers charted the coastlines of the two major islands. Captain James Cook arrived there in 1769 on his first voyage, the first of many explorers, missionaries, and traders. The first Catholics arrived in the 1820s along with other British settlers. In 1840, the British signed the Treaty of Waitangi with various Māori chiefs, granting their people the same rights enjoyed by the British, but the imposition of a European economic and legal system eventually impoverished the native peoples.

According to a 2013 census, New Zealand is 48 percent Christian. For a long time Catholics constituted a subculture, looked down upon for their Irish working-class roots and their drinking. Lurid stories about the supposed sins of Catholics, including misbehavior between nuns and priests, were common. Today, the number of Catholics is growing, partly through immigration. In 2013, Catholics became the largest Christian community, 11.7 percent of the population, followed by the Anglicans, 10.33 percent, and the Presbyterians, 7.44 percent. However, the shortage of Catholic priests has reached a critical point. In March 2019, Cardinal John Dew of Wellington announced that he had no priests to replace those who were retiring and would seek lay people to lead parishes.

Wellington is the one archdiocese, followed by five other Catholic dioceses. Roughly 25 percent of New Zealand's Catholics regularly attend mass; attendance has declined in recent years, but at a slower rate because of the arrival of immigrants from India, Southeast Asia, and South America, who are more faithful in their practice. The country's Catholic schools are highly esteemed for their strong moral codes, small classes, low costs, and the high academic achievement of their students.

A More Inclusive Church

Today the Catholic Church in New Zealand is making an effort to become more inclusive. In 2017, the bishop of Auckland, Patrick Dunn wrote:

> Like many others, I have friends and family members who are gay. For some years I have been troubled by the sense of rejection they

often feel with regard to the Church. Could we find some new way to converse with the LGBT community? . . . Compassion calls us to "listen" to people. What is it really like growing up as a gay boy, or a lesbian girl, or a transgender person? Deeply embedded in Catholic Church teaching is the call to stand by all who feel marginalized or threatened.[6]

At a workshop for young people, Bishop Stephen Lowe of Hamilton said that the issue of homosexuality may be a "Galileo moment" for the church, reminding his listeners that, in 1633, Galileo Galilei was found "vehemently suspect of heresy" by the Inquisition for holding that the earth is not the center of the universe but actually revolves around the sun. "The psychology is still up for debate, but the church has got to engage with the science and engage with the experience of couples with same-sex attraction," Lowe said.[7]

The March 17, 2019, massacre at two mosques by a white supremacist, leaving fifty dead and thirty-four wounded, pulled the religious communities together. Orthodox Jews, Hindus, Christians, and Sikhs all came together to help survivors and victims' families. Shortly after, Prime Minister Jacinda Ardern outlawed the sale of assault rifles.

The Philippines

The Republic of the Philippines and East Timor are the only majority Catholic countries in the Far East. Catholicism came to the Philippine islands in 1521 with the arrival of Ferdinand Magellan in Cebu, and with it came Spanish colonialism. An agreement between the king of Spain and the papacy linked the Spanish state with the church to the extent that it was difficult to disentangle the two. With most of the native peoples living in small communities called *barangays* along the coasts or rivers, the Spanish authorities adopted the Latin American policy of "reductions," relocating the people into towns built around a plaza, with the church and civic building occupying a central place. The various religious orders received pastoral responsibility for the country's different regions.

---

[6] Bishop Patrick Dunn, "Building a Bridge: Our Gay Brothers and Sisters," *NZ Catholic*, September 26, 2017.

[7] "New Zealand Bishops Chat with Youth about Church, Controversial Issues," *National Catholic Reporter*, January 24, 2018.

The first Jesuits arrived in the Philippines from Spain in 1581 and shortly after founded one of the first colleges in the Philippines, the Colegio de Manila, which opened in 1595. The Dominicans founded the Colegio de Santo Tomás in 1611; it became a university in 1645. In 1859, the Jesuits founded the Ateneo de Manila in Quezon City, outside Manila. The Synod of Manila (1882) decided to use native languages rather than Spanish for preaching and evangelization, leading Franciscan, Dominican, and Jesuit missionaries to produce dictionaries and catechisms in native languages. They organized sodalities and confraternities like those in Europe and established social ministries, schools, clinics orphanages, and hospitals for the sick, and exercised both religious and civil authority. The story of Jesus, celebrated and often acted out in various ways, became part of the religious culture of the people. To this day some Filipinos try to replicate Christ's passion story in their own bodies, even fastening or nailing themselves to a cross during Holy Week.

Preserving the languages of the indigenous peoples was fortuitous; it helped embed the church in the social fabric of the people. It also kept alive a certain distance from colonial power, though the merger of Spanish colonialism with Catholic evangelization made it difficult to dissociate church and state. While the Spanish influence remained strong, currents of resistance remained beneath the surface, occasionally breaking into open conflict. As early as 1660, a revolt broke out in Manila protesting conscripted labor, and there were others, often caused by conflicts between the native clergy and their Spanish bishops.

While the clergy tended to support Spain, dubious charges of conspiracy led to the execution of three priests with nationalist sympathies in 1872. A revolution broke out in 1896, inspired in part by the writings of José Rizal; he faced a firing squad at the end of the year. As part of the 1898 Treaty of Paris that ended the Spanish American War, Spain ceded the Philippines to the United States. Resistance to the new American occupation on the part of some, including some native clergy, led to another bloody war that lasted for two years, resulting in the deaths of 200,000–250,000 Filipinos. American influence introduced the separation of church and state, and English became the official language.

American Influence

With the Americans came Protestant missionaries, officially beginning their work in 1901. Though they regarded the popular religion of Filipino Catholicism as superstitious, they soon adopted the approach of the earlier Catholic missionaries, dividing the country into different regions and using vernacular languages for their texts and biblical translations. They also opened schools and hospitals and recruited local leaders, many of them strongly committed to Filipino nationalism. One of them, Felix Manalo, founded an indigenous, independent denomination, the Iglesia ni Cristo (Church of Christ) in 1914.

While the Protestant churches generally taught in English and used American textbooks, the Catholic Church, shaped by its Hispanic past and lacking English speakers, continued to use Spanish in its schools and seminaries. The University of Santo Tomás finally changed to English instruction in 1923, while the official *Catholic Directory* appeared in English only in 1950. But the arrival of new missionaries from religious congregations with English-speaking members from 1905 on initiated a process that was to shape a popular culture that was more American than Hispanic. The Catholic Church was also more deeply rooted in Philippine culture, especially after the painful Japanese occupation during World War II.

Philippine Catholicism in the postwar period reflected the antisocialist and anticommunist posture of the global church under the leadership of Pope Pius XII, but social changes and a growing awareness of the poverty of so many contributed to an increased social consciousness in the 1960s. Catholic and Protestant schools began sending their students into poor communities to sensitize the students to the actual lives of the poor. The Catholic Church, influenced by the social encyclicals, began to take a more critical role toward the government and society, especially after the Second Vatican Council. Theology and even official church documents selectively adopted some of the themes of the theology of liberation, such as social analysis and structural sin. Pastorally, the church turned toward greater involvement with the poor through small communities; Bible-study groups, sometimes organized for different classes and workers; insertion programs for students and religious; and the defense of human rights. Conflict with the increasingly repressive Marcos regime (1965–86) was inevitable.

The Protestant National Council of Churches condemned the imposition of martial law in 1972, though the Iglesia ni Cristo continued to support Marcos. Manila's Cardinal Sin tried to avoid direct confrontation despite government raids on religious houses and the arrests of priests and lay leaders. However, after the assassination of opposition candidate Benigno Aquino in 1983, the Catholic hierarchy began openly to oppose the Marcos regime. The sham reelection of Marcos in 1986 was the last straw. The Philippine Conference of Bishops denounced the election as fraudulent and the government as illegitimate. When Defense Minister Enrile and General Ramos withdrew support for the government, beginning the EDSA Revolution, people poured into the streets; nuns and priests joined the protests. When soldiers refused to carry out government-ordered attacks on the demonstrators, the government collapsed.

Church of the Poor

Once the Marcos dictatorship was overthrown, the Philippine church—bishops, priests, religious, and laity—could seriously address the question of what the Second Vatican Council might mean for the Catholic Church in the Philippines. The result, after considerable controversy between progressive and conservative wings of a society deeply divided by social inequities, was the Second Plenary Council of the Philippines (PCPII), January 20–February 17, 1991. In the struggle to prepare for the council, one of the strongest voices for reform was that of Francisco Claver, a Jesuit called home from graduate studies in Colorado to become bishop of Malaybalay in 1969. Vatican II's vision, Claver insisted, called for a participatory church in which all had a voice—bishops, clergy, religious, the laity, and especially the poor. He was to help craft the documents that would give expression to the council's vision, stressing especially the role of the local church.

When the PCPII convened in 1991, its diversity was remarkable. Men and women lay people, religious sisters, members of the clergy, and bishops were represented. While more progressive voices were in the majority, the concluding "Message of the Council to the People of the Philippines" set before the church a number of "painful questions," among them "the poverty, dispossession, violence, and environmental degradation that afflict the Philippines and belie its claim to being a Christian nation." Its call to be a "church of the poor" was a radical challenge; it should be a church that lives in evangelical poverty, defends the rights of the poor, a church where "no one is so poor as to have nothing to give, and no one is so rich as to have nothing to receive."[8] It stressed that the poor were to become themselves evangelizers. The acts and decrees of the council

---

[8] Eleanor R. Dionisio, "Introduction," in *Becoming a Church of the Poor: Philippine Catholicism after the Second Plenary Council*, ed. Eleanor R. Dionisio (Quezon City, Philippines: John J. Carroll Institute on Church and Social Issues, 2011), 5.

acknowledged the many failings of the Philippine church and stated that it needed to remain open to the possibility of change.

In the years that followed the Philippine church has struggled to create a truly Asian church rather than "the church in Asia," as a representative of the Curia insisted. Efforts include an emphasis on developing basic ecclesial communities (BECs) to engage lay leadership at local levels, to help bishops and priests to see themselves as servant leaders rather than belonging to an entitled group, and to give civic and moral leadership without displacing the laity from their own role in the processes of government. Also, the church has worked to find some middle ground between conservative and liberal voices over the vexing problem of population growth, a controversy that too often is reduced to pitting some pro-life bishops against others who simply remain silent. Finally, lack of employment opportunities has driven some 10.2 million Filipinos to live or work abroad, about 10 percent of the country's total; this is one of the world's largest diaspora populations. Over 60 percent of them are women.

The Charismatic Movement

The charismatic movement is particularly strong in the Philippines. Of the 81 percent of the population that is Catholic, 15 percent are charismatics. Protestants number about 7 percent, with one-third of those Pentecostal or charismatic. A charismatic community established in 1981, the Manila-based Couples for Christ (CFC), is now present in all eighty-two Filipino provinces as well as in many other countries; its mission is to renew Christian family life. In 2000, the Holy See recognized it as an "international association of the faithful of pontifical right." Its leaders were present at the 2014 Extraordinary Synod on the Family.

One of the largest charismatic movements is El Shaddai, founded in 1982 by religious broadcaster Mike Velarde, whose inspiration came partly from the American evangelical preacher Pat Robertson. The movement now claims nine million members in the Philippines, with perhaps two million more among expatriates. Although its beginnings were nondenominational, Velarde now describes it as Catholic charismatic, and the Catholic Church, which provides a retired bishop as adviser or spiritual director, officially recognizes the movement. Its four-hour services at outdoor rallies combine evangelical and Catholic styles of worship and usually include the celebration of the mass. Brother Velarde, as he prefers to be known, preaches from the stage in a brightly colored jacket, using an evangelical call-and-response style.

While the movement has kept many Filipino Catholics from joining evangelical or Pentecostal churches, it remains controversial. It preaches the prosperity gospel, appealing to people from the impoverished lower classes; it emphasizes spiritual warfare and the "seed-faith principle," eliciting miracles with testimonies and cash offerings or "tithes" placed in wooden boxes; and it encourages the faithful to extend inverted umbrellas skyward to catch "blessings from heaven." In many ways it represents a Philippine version of neo-Pentecostalism. Some accuse the movement of seeking to influence Philippine politics.[9]

Brother Velarde claims that his El Shaddai movement seeks individual transformation, not social change. It promises personal blessings, miracles, healings, deliverance from vices, and material prosperity, gifts mediated by El Shaddai handkerchiefs, blessed eggs, holy oil, and the laying on of hands, all the work of a Holy Spirit no longer confined. From its origins as a radio program, El Shaddai has created a new sacred space, not in churches, but in outdoor rallies attended by hundreds of thousands and mediated electronically through radio waves and video signals.

Contemporary Challenges

Thus, one of the challenges facing Philippine Catholicism is the tension between two different ways of engaging with modernity: personal transformation or becoming a church of the poor. One falls back on shamanic traditions and spiritual power; the other seeks to build on the gospel call for ministry to the disadvantaged and witness to the values of the kingdom of God. Building on the Vatican II documents and the work of the Second Plenary Council of the Philippines, the Catholic Church in the Philippines seeks to develop a more just society. It stresses an engaged faithful who witness to God's reign, see the poor as blessed, reject attachment to material possessions, and embrace the cross as a symbol of God's transforming love that brings life out of death.

However, it is difficult to estimate how many Filipinos regularly attend mass or are involved in their parishes or BECs. Most parishes in the provinces have a network of barrio or village chapels or BECs, far from the

---

[9] See Katherine L. Wiegele, *Investing in Miracles: El Shaddai and the Transformation of Popular Catholicism in the Philippines* (Honolulu: University of Hawaii Press, 2005), 89–90.

parish center, with a priest present for mass only once a month or every two months. According to Father Amado Picardal, executive secretary of the Bishops' Conference Committee on Basic Ecclesial Communities, the majority of Catholics are either seasonal or nominal.[10]

The fact that Filipino Catholicism has frequently been too identified with political authority constitutes another challenge. The Philippines is the only member of the United Nations that does not allow divorce (except for its Muslim citizens whose religion permits it). In addition, it is one of the most over-populated places on earth. Its challenge today is to continue its efforts to become a church of the poor and address the economic divisions in a society where so many live in poverty, while families of even moderate means live in gated communities.

The Catholic Bishops' Conference has been largely silent in the face of President Rodrigo Duterte's attack on the confernce and on Catholic doctrine, unlike 1986 when the bishops played a significant role in delegitimizing the election, which led to the fall of Ferdinand Marcos. Duterte's rhetoric has dismissed God as a "stupid God" and "son of a whore." He has mocked the mystery of the Trinity and called the crucifixion "unworthy of belief." Describing the Catholic bishops as "useless fools," he has called for people to kill them. The church has openly criticized his war on drugs, with its extrajudicial killings, since he took office in 2016. In March 2019, the United Nations High Commissioner for Human Rights estimated that twenty-seven thousand people had been killed, with no one brought to justice except in one high-profile case. The police dispute this number but admit to killing more than sixty-six hundred people.[11]

Yet Duterte remains highly popular. He has exploited the weakened authority of the church, the result in large part of the sexual abuse crisis. Some see focusing on his abusive language as "missing the point" when the church remains "still mainly middle class," as one prominent priest described it. Reformers call on priests and bishops to live more simply and humbly, without air-conditioned churches, fancy cars, and episcopal palaces.[12]

The scandal of sexual abuse of minors is another challenge, just beginning to surface. With the Asian reluctance to discuss issues of sexuality,

[10]"Seasonal and Nominal Catholics in the Philippines," *La Croix International*, May 7, 2018.

[11]Laila Matar, "UN Needs to Act Now to End Philippines Killings," Human Rights Watch, June 24, 2019.

[12]John Neary, "In the Face of Duterte's Attacks, a Pattern of Silence," *La Croix International*, January 17, 2019.

sexual abuse by clergy long went unreported. Only in 2002 did the bishops' conference admit that it faced "cases of grave sexual misconduct" among the clergy. But despite promises of new rules, little was done. The church's guidelines did not require reporting priests charged with abuse until 2013. According to one bishop, no priest in the Philippines has ever been convicted of sexual abuse of a minor. In 2016, the bishops again promised change, committing themselves to "transparency, accountability, and cooperation with civil authorities," but it is still not clear if and when abusing priests should be reported to civil authorities.[13]

Japan

The Catholic Church in Japan traces its origins to the arrival of Francis Xavier and two Jesuit companions at Kagoshima, on the coast of Kyushu, in 1549. Impeded by his lack of fluency in the Japanese language, Francis was dependent on one of his companions, Brother Fernandez, who had learned some rudimentary Japanese, as well as some Japanese converts. Francis himself would read from translations of the catechism, using pictures of Jesus and the Madonna. Recognizing that evangelical poverty did not impress the Japanese, he quickly adopted a more elegant style with his companions as attendants, bringing with them European artifacts as gifts for the daimyo or feudal lords. Also helping the mission was the country's lack of unity; it was divided by years of war, famine, and social chaos.

The second-generation Jesuits, joined later by Franciscans, went far beyond Francis Xavier's work. In 1579, Father Alessandro Valignano arrived as visitor.[14] He insisted that Jesuits in the mission learn the Japanese language and follow the policy of inculturation that other Jesuits in China would use with great success. The Jesuits succeeded in laying the foundations for a genuinely Japanese church, with strong lay leadership that sought to bring Japanese culture and values into the faith of the people. It embraced all classes of people, including many members of the warrior class, the

---

[13]Tim Sullivan, "US Priest Accused of Abusing Boys for Decades in the Philippines," *Crux*, September 9, 2019.

[14]The Jesuit's superior general may, from time to time, appoint a "visitor" to a church or religious community to maintain discipline and correct abuses. In the mid-sixteenth century a visitor was endowed with the authority to act in the superior general's stead while the superior general himself remained at the Curia in Rome.

samurai. Scholars speak of seventeenth-century Japan as the Christian century; estimates put Japanese Christians between 300,000 and 500,000. The missionaries established numerous churches, schools, and homes to care for the elderly, sick, and orphans, as well as residences and a novitiate for the Japanese brothers. Without the help of their Japanese catechists and lay assistants, who translated for the missionaries and instructed the people, as well as lay women in associations engaged in social and medical ministries, the mission would not have succeeded.[15]

The Age of Martyrs

The toleration of Christianity began to change under the Tokugawa Shogunate. Toyotomi Hideyoshi (1537–98) unified the country, but in 1587, suspicious of Christians who professed a higher loyalty to Jesus and fearful of European expansion, issued a directive repeating earlier efforts to outlaw Catholicism. Initially it was not enforced, but in 1596, after hearing the story of a ship-wrecked Spanish captain who said that the Christian missions were a prelude to conquest, his attitude hardened. In 1597, six Franciscan missionaries, three Japanese Jesuits, and seventeen Japanese lay men were executed by crucifixion in Nagasaki. Hideyoshi died in 1598, but subsequent shoguns banned Catholicism. An edict in 1614 forbade its practice and ordered the expulsion of some prominent lay Christian leaders.

Expulsion of the missionaries and more executions soon followed. "Thousands of converts, including children, were crucified, beheaded, flung from cliffs, burnt at the stake with babies strapped to them, boiled alive in hot springs or hung upside down over pits of sewage, bleeding to death from cuts behind their ears. The number of martyrs is thought to have been between 4,000 and 6,000."[16] Thousands more were killed as part of a rebellion against Iemitsu Tokugawa in 1638.

After 1627, when the authorities recognized that lay martyrs only strengthened the faith of the Japanese Christians, they instituted a new system that focused on the Catholic community's leaders. Their priests were hunted down and brought before an inquisitor, the most famous being Inouye Masashige, who sought to make the priests apostatize—give

---

[15] See Andrew C. Ross, *A Vision Betrayed: The Jesuits in China and Japan 1542–1742* (Maryknoll, NY: Orbis Books, 1994), 65; see also Mark R. Mullins, "Japan," in *Christianities in Asia*, ed. Peter Phan (Malden, MA: Wiley-Blackwell, 2011), 199.

[16] Lucy Alexander, "Voices from a Quiet Church," *Tablet*, December 9, 2018; other sources give lower numbers for those killed.

up their faith—in an effort to undermine the faith of the people. Several did, including one Portuguese vice provincial.[17] In the effort to wipe out Christianity, Japan was ultimately closed to trade with the outside world, but close to sixty thousand Japanese Christians survived until modern times, the "hidden Christians" (*Kakure Kirishitan*) living around Nagasaki. They carried on their faith without priests, through oral tradition and lay leadership. Many returned to Catholicism once Japan opened again to the West.

Christianity Today

Japan today may be one of the most difficult countries to evangelize. Cardinal Maeda of Osaka says that the reticent Japanese are averse to proselytizing:

> In fact, the barriers to the spread of Christianity in Japan are legion. It does not fit with the country's core national characteristic, which is rigid social conformity. In school, children are taught to respect authority and submit to the group. The idea of prioritising a personal relationship with a foreign God—moreover, a social outcast who was executed as a common criminal—is seen by most Japanese as arrogant and utterly bizarre. Most Japanese Christians therefore keep their religion to themselves.[18]

Only about 30 percent of Japan's 127 million people claim to profess a religious faith today. Comfortable with religious pluralism and unable to accept the concept of absolute truth, many Japanese observe rituals from several different traditions, for example, Shinto rituals associated with birth and Buddhist rituals when someone dies. Westerners might see this as reducing religion to culture, but for the Japanese, it means a respect for religious values.

Both Catholics and Protestants in Japan are open to interfaith encounters, and both have adapted rituals and memorial services for the dead that resemble Buddhist practice. Interestingly, some 70 percent of Japanese choose Christian rituals for their marriages, though they continue to show little interest in becoming members of Christian churches. Statistically, about 27 percent of Japanese claim to be Buddhist, 3 percent Shinto, and 2 percent Christian. There are slighty more than half a million Catholics

---

[17] This is the story of Shūsaku Endō's 1967 novel, *The Silence*, which was made into a film by Martin Scorsese in 2016.

[18] Alexander, "Voices from a Quiet Church."

in Japan today, more if expatriates are included; the church comprises sixteen dioceses, just 0.42 percent of the population. In terms of mission, the church puts an emphasis on dialogue, emphasizing the common need for religious values.[19]

Nagasaki, the target of the second US atomic bomb on August 9, 1945, has Catholic roots going back to Francis Xavier, who visited the city in 1549. It was also the center for the "hidden Christians" of Japan, thousands of whom died from the bomb. The present Immaculate Conception Cathedral, widely known as the Urakami Cathedral, was at the epicenter of the blast. Rebuilt on the site where the original stood before the war, some of the statues in the new cathedral are scarred and burned. Takashi Nagai, a Catholic convert and physician, attended to victims after the blast; later he founded a hermitage and wrote about his experience. His book, *The Bells of Nagasaki*, became a best seller. He has been declared a servant of God, the first step on the way to canonization. When Pope Francis visited Japan in November 2019, he made an impassioned plea for peace and the banishing of nuclear weapons.

The global sexual abuse scandal has only begun to surface in Japan. In April 2019, the Catholic Bishops' Conference of Japan announced that it would initiate an internal investigation in all the country's sixteen dioceses of allegations of the sexual abuse of minors. According to the media, surveys in 2002 and 2012 reported five cases; another newspaper referred to an investigation that uncovered cases going back as far as 1965 at an international school run by a French order, the Brothers of Christian Instruction.

The country's rape laws are also out of date; they do not consider an alleged assault to be rape unless the woman resists.

The Japanese bishops have long struggled with the Roman Curia for greater freedom in developing their own pastoral approaches and liturgical texts. In September 2019, the emeritus archbishop of Tokyo, Takeo Okada, made public a letter he had sent to Pope Francis, complaining about the Curia's over-centralization of authority. He said that the Bishops' Conference of Japan, in an effort to better inculturate the liturgy, had "sent our new alternative plan to the Congregation for Divine Worship and the Discipline of the Sacraments some years ago," but, "until now we have had no response from the congregation."[20]

---

[19] See Shun'ichi Takayanagi, "Mission in a Secularized Japan," *La Civiltà Cattolica*, June 15, 2017.

[20] "Retired Tokyo Archbishop 'Takes the Plunge' to Publicize Criticism of Roman Curia," *La Croix International*, September 24, 2019.

The Christian churches in Japan seem to be losing members. Numbers of annual baptisms, church attendance, and enrollment in church schools are diminishing. In part, this reflects low birth rates and an aging population. These changes also affect the Catholic Church. Most of its priests are elderly. Attending Sunday mass is difficult, because many work or have school events on Sundays. The idea of a personal relationship with God is difficult. The presence of Catholics coming to work in Japan from other countries has helped maintain the number of Catholics at a little more than half a million. At the same time, these new arrivals and their ideas have also led to tensions with older Catholics over finances and the use of church facilities.

Preparation for the Extraordinary General Assembly of the Synod of Bishops (October 2014) showed additional tensions in the Catholic Church of Japan. The bishops and religious superiors reported that, in Japan, Catholics are either indifferent to or unaware of the church's teaching on artificial contraception. Cohabitation and civil marriage outside the church have become the norm; pastoral practice should start from here. While the questionnaire sent as part of the preparation for the assembly seems to presume countries where the entire family is Christian, approximately 76 percent of Catholics in Japan marry non-Catholics. The bishops also saw simplifying the process for annulments as essential.[21]

Young people in Japan live in a competitive society driven by consumerism. Many experience alienation and addiction, and they have a high suicide rate. Without a transcendent hope, there is little to give depth to their lives. The church has an opportunity here, but it has made little effort to reach out to young people.

Conclusion

The Catholic Church plays an important role in Pacific nations such as Australia, New Zealand, the Philippines, and in the lives of inhabitants of smaller island nations like Timor-Leste, Wallis and Fortuna, and Guam. Catholics on Fortuna celebrate their evangelist and martyr, Saint Pierre Chanel. In Indonesia and Malaysia, Catholics make up 3 percent of the populations. The once largely Irish Catholic Church of Australia

---

[21] Joshua J. McElwee, "Japanese Bishops: Vatican Mindset Doesn't Fit Asian Church," *National Catholic Reporter*, February 19, 2014.

is now highly diverse, with a high percentage of Asians. The church itself has suffered significantly from the sexual abuse crisis, and the number of Catholics is decreasing. In Guam, a long history of abuse going back decades has only recently come to light, with the archbishop of Agana, Anthony Apuron, being removed from his office by the Vatican in 2018. In 2019 the archdiocese filed for bankruptcy.

In New Zealand, the Catholic Church has overcome traditional prejudices to become the country's largest church. Today, it is making efforts to become more inclusive, with some bishops reaching out to the LGBTQ community. The church's membership is growing slightly, mostly through immigration. The Philippines, one of Asia's two most Catholic countries, faces internal tensions between strong charismatic movements focused on personal transformation and a church led by its bishop, theologians, and lay leaders that wants to become a church of the poor. The church continues to face a society sharply divided between the affluent and the very poor, with some 10.2 million working abroad, many of them young women.

In Japan, the Catholic Church has a proud history; it is rich in martyrs and had thousands cling to the faith for two centuries while cut off from the universal church and without priests. Today, Japanese Catholics constitute only 0.42 percent of the total population of Japan, and the number is decreasing.

7

Europe

Christianity spread to parts of Europe in New Testament times with the missionary journeys of the early apostles and evangelists. Preeminent among them were Peter and Paul, both of whom died in Rome. The Roman province of Gaul, today part of modern France, was an early center of Christianity. Irenaeus of Lyon, one of the apostolic fathers, came from Smyrna in Anatolia (Turkey); he succeeded Lyon's first bishop, the martyr Pothinus, in 177. A council at Arles in 314 is considered a forerunner of the Council of Nicaea (325). Attended by three bishops from Roman Britain, this is evidence that Christianity had already reached Britain by the early fourth century. Religious freedom for Christians came with the Roman Emperor Constantine's Edict of Milan in 313, ending the period of Roman persecution. The faith spread rapidly from that point on, becoming the state religion in 380.

As the power of the Roman Empire and its local officers declined in the Early Middle Ages, the Catholic Church played an increasingly important role in European life. So closely did Catholicism inform and become embedded in the developing culture of Europe that Hilaire Belloc once said epigrammatically, "The Church is Europe and Europe is the Church."[1] European culture was largely shaped by the church in the areas of law, government, economics, the fine arts, science, education, and healthcare. Some argued that it enhanced the status of women, established hospitals and universities, and stressed the dignity of labor.[2]

---

[1] Hilaire Belloc, *Europe and the Faith* (New York: Paulist Press, 1920), 1.
[2] See Alvin Schmidt, *How Christianity Changed the World* (Grand Rapids, MI: Zondervan, 2004).

A Growing Secularism

Nevertheless, Christianity in Europe is in trouble today as the majority of the Christian population shifts from Europe and North America to the Global South. In 1910, Europe was home to roughly two-thirds of the world's Christians (66.6 percent), but by 2010, that number had dropped to 25.5 percent and is projected to drop to 15.6 percent by 2050. The reasons are complex.

A major factor is diminishing fertility. Europe has the lowest fertility rate of any global region, while Muslims have the highest birth rate of any religious group. As Europe's population ages and people have fewer children, compared to, for example, Sub-Saharan Africa, the number of those professing to be Christian continues to drop. Other factors include religious switching or people simply ceasing to practice, joining the religiously unaffiliated, as well as immigration from other religious groups.[3] According to a 2018 report, "in 12 out of 21 European countries studied, plus Israel, most young people say they have no religion. This figure rises to 91 percent in the Czech Republic."[4]

A Pew Forum study in 2018 maintains that most Western Europeans still consider themselves Christians, even if they rarely go to church. In most countries surveyed many tended to respond that religion is "not too" or "not at all" important in their lives (a median of 40 percent). Many say they never pray. For those who do not attend church, if they believe in God, it is usually not the God of the Bible, though they might speak of a higher power or spiritual force. The majority of the unaffiliated favor abortion and same-sex marriage and are raising their children without any religion. Many do not believe in an afterlife. Many non-practicing European Christians describe themselves as neither spiritual nor religious, in contrast to the United States. For those who do claim to be spiritual, Eastern or New Age beliefs and practices are more common. Ireland, Italy, and Portugal are exceptions, with lower percentages of the unaffiliated (15 percent).

Both church-attending and non-practicing Christians in Europe are more likely than religiously unaffiliated adults to have anti-immigrant and

---

[3] David Masci, "Christianity Poised to Continue to Shift from Europe to Asia," Pew Research Center, April 7, 2015.

[4] Arnaud Beviliacqua and Gauthier Vaillant, "Young Europeans Increasingly Distant from Religion," *La Croix International*, August 9, 2018.

anti-minority views. They are also more likely to agree with highly negative statements about Jews. They tend to have higher levels of nationalist attitudes. Relatively few Europeans give money to religious organizations, with Norway and the Netherlands being exceptions, or share their faith with others. Interestingly, highly committed Christians are more likely than the "nones" (those without any religious affiliation) to volunteer with community groups, but "nones" are more engaged in sports clubs.[5]

As sociologist José Casanova reports, the religious situation in Europe is extremely diverse.[6] In general, the population in most European countries is secular and nonreligious. Religious practice in former communist countries, like the Czech Republic and the former East Germany, where only one-fourth of the population believes in God, is extremely low. These, along with France, are Europe's most secular societies. Casanova points to Ireland and Poland as the most religious, though this was before the sexual abuse crisis devastated Irish Catholicism. On the other hand, former communist countries like Russia and Ukraine have seen remarkable religious revivals since 1989.

Paradoxically, Casanova reports that the majority of people in most European countries continue to believe in life after death, a hope for transcendence even in a secularized Europe, excluding the former communist countries, and Denmark, where belief in the resurrection seems to be diminishing. Some report a new interest in Catholicism and for a faith less dominated by the Enlightenment in Sweden, where the church is growing. Britain and the Netherlands show the most sudden and dramatic decline in both church attendance and affiliation, while the former West Germany preserves a relatively high level of church affiliation, though with very low church attendance. This may be changing with the present rebellion against the government-mandated church tax.

Responsibility for the secularization of Europe falls most often on the triumph of the Enlightenment critique of religion:

---

[5] Pew Research Center, "Being Christian in Western Europe," May 29, 2018. The survey interviewed 24,599 randomly selected adults across fifteen countries in Western Europe in twelve languages. See also, "Highly Committed Christians More Likely Than 'Nones' to Volunteer with Community Groups, But More 'Nones' Engaged in SportsClubs," May 23, 2018.

[6] See José Casanova, "The Religious Situation in Europe," in *Secularization and the World Religions*, ed. Hans Joas and Klaus Wiegandt (Liverpool: Liverpool University Press, 2009), 206–28. See also Oliver Roy, *Is Europe Christian?* (New York: Oxford University Press, 2020).

The cognitive critique of religion as a primitive, pre-rational worldview to be superseded by the advancement of science and rational thought; the political critique of ecclesiastical religion as a conspiracy of rulers and priests to keep the people ignorant and oppressed, a condition to be superseded by the advancement of popular sovereignty and democratic freedoms; and the humanist critique of the very idea of God as human self-alienation and as a self-denying other-worldly projection of human aspirations and desires, a critique which postulated the death of God as the premise of human emancipation.[7]

From a global perspective Casanova argues that the thesis that modernization leads to secularization is no longer tenable. The European pattern is exceptional. He suggests that in post-World War II Europe the majority of the population seems to have accepted the premise that a modern, progressive society leads to a decline in religious practice. Along with this he suggests that the institutionalization of welfare states across Western Europe led to a transference of collective identity from the national or confessional church to the imagined community of the nation state, leading to the drastic decline in religious practice. This was particularly true for Britain and the Netherlands, though it happened also in West Germany, if less dramatically. Switzerland, with its cantonal structure and "somewhat provincial" isolation from the rest of Europe, seems to have protected the Swiss churches from the consequences of a similar secularization.

He contrasts the increasing secularization of Europe with a transformation of American religion. Some of this is due to new religious movements, whether self-realization, New Age, therapeutic, fundamentalist Protestant, Hindu, Buddhist, or Islamic. Furthermore, he sees a shift as the new millennium began from denominationalism to what he calls an "individual mysticism," best expressed in the claim to be "spiritual but not religious."[8] In Europe, the secularists have won out, having given to the secular states the communal role once carried by their churches, even if the people continue to remain nominal members. Nevertheless, in the United States, the "seeker" impulse is still strong. Europeans leave religion behind while Americans, still seeking salvation, look for new, often individualistic expressions.

---

[7] Casanova, "The Religious Situation in Europe," 219–20.
[8] Casanova, 221.

In his conclusion Casanova argues that as Europe seeks greater unity and integration, religion is again becoming a contentious issue. Even the possibility of Turkey joining the European Union seems now more remote; immigration today in Europe is largely Islamic, and therefore on multiple grounds "other." For the European Union's secular societies, accepting a new kind of multiculturalism is difficult. In the new European constitution the secularist refusal to acknowledge Christianity's historic role in the development of its cultural and political identity becomes increasingly problematic. Casanova writes, "One should certainly recognize that any genealogical reconstruction of the idea or social imaginary of Europe that makes reference to Graeco-Roman antiquity and the Enlightenment while erasing any memory of the role of medieval Christendom in the very constitution of Europe as a civilization evinces either historical ignorance or repressive amnesia."[9]

Both Pope Benedict XVI and Pope Francis trace Europe's malaise to its loss of faith. In *Spe salvi* (2007) Benedict points to the triumph of secular, Enlightenment reason, which is replacing Christian hope with hope in progress, driven by science and technology (no. 17). Francis's critique is similar. He speaks of a Europe that is "tired," with its declining birthrate, hidden forms of euthanasia, and high rates of unemployment; "it has disowned its roots" and needs to be rejuvenated.[10] Ultranationalist movements are also leading to an increase in racist, anti-Islamic, and anti-Semitic incidents, especially in France, Germany, and Italy.

In 2010, Catholics constituted the largest Christian group in Europe, 46 percent of the total, followed by the Orthodox at 35 percent (keeping in mind that largely Orthodox Russia is the largest country by population). Protestants in Europe constituted 18 percent of Christians.[11] But Europe's Catholic population continues to decline. According to a recent Pew Study, in 1910 it represented 65 percent of the world's Catholics. By 2015 it had fallen to 24 percent, some 267 million.[12] Many have left the church, and birth rates are low, except for non-Christian immigrants, most of them Muslim, and still Europe's secular ethos continues to grow.

---

[9] Casanova, 227.

[10] "Pope Francis: Europe Is Tired, Must Be Rejuvenated," Catholic News Agency, June 15, 2014.

[11] Pew Research Center, "Regional Distribution of Christians," December 19, 2011.

[12] "Europe's Catholic Population Sees Biggest Decline: Pew," *La Croix International*, January 17, 2019.

Diminishing Practice

The number of Catholics in Europe who attend mass continues to decline. One indication of this is the closing and consolidation of parishes. In Vienna, 660 parishes are being merged into 150 larger pastoral centers. In Italy, foreign-born clergy run up to 40 percent of the parishes. In Spain, only one in five Catholics attends mass, only one in ten in France. Many parishes are without a resident pastor. In Germany, the Archdiocese of Berlin merged 105 local parishes into 35 "pastoral spaces," while the Archdiocese of Hamburg reduced 900 parishes to 60, with lay people authorized to conduct funerals and preach at worship services. After a 2016 diocesan synod, the bishop of Trier announced plans to reduce 887 parishes to 35 larger ones, though the Vatican has requested a stay. In Belgium, a 2019 report showed that baptisms had decreased by 12 percent, confirmations by 4 percent, and Catholic marriages by 14 percent.

In the Netherlands, where only 5 percent of Catholics attend mass, 20 out of 170 monasteries have closed, while it is estimated that two churches per week are closing. In the Diocese of Utrecht, the bishop has proposed "melting down" 326 parishes into 48 larger units, each with a single church as a "eucharistic center." Luxembourg's 274 parishes have been reduced to 33. Regular mass attendance has plummeted in Ireland, and seven out of eight seminaries have closed. The revelation in the 1990s of widespread sexual abuse by clerics, priests, and brothers shattered the reputation of the church in Ireland. Mass attendance, which was then around 90 percent in the Catholic population, has dropped to about 30 percent. Even Poland has felt significant losses, with bishops talking of having "to withdraw priests from working abroad and begin merging some of the country's 11,000 parishes."[13]

According to the Pew Research Center, the level of religious observance has risen substantially in some historically Orthodox countries since the fall of the Iron Curtain, particularly in Russia, Ukraine, and Bulgaria. Far more people identify with Orthodox Christianity than in 1991. However, Catholicism in Central and Eastern Europe has not experienced similar growth. Some countries such as Poland, Hungry, Lithuania, and the Czech Republic retained their Catholic identity during the Communist period,

---

[13] Jonathan Luxmore, "Europe's Church Evolves: Dioceses Think Creatively as Numbers Plummet," *National Catholic Reporter* 54, no. 31 (November 17–30, 2017), 1, 14–15.

but since then there has been significant change in the direction of greater secularization, most dramatically in the Czech Republic, where those identifying as Catholic dropped from 41 percent in 1991 to 21 percent in 2015. The Czech Republic is now one of the most secular countries in Europe, where 72 percent of adults describe themselves as "atheist," "agnostic," or "nothing in particular." In Orthodox countries there is a closer relation between religious and national identity,[14] while Catholics in Central and Eastern Europe are more religiously observant in terms of weekly mass attendance, Lenten and Easter observances, sharing their religious views with others, and reading scripture.[15]

Snapshots

Germany

In Germany, Pope Francis has called attention to an "erosion" of Catholic faith. In Germany, Pope Francis has called attention to an "erosion" of Catholic faith. The number of German Catholics decreased from 23 million in 2018 to 22.6 million in 2019. Catholics now account for 27.2 percent of Germany's population of almost 84 million, down from 27.7 percent in 2018.[16] In 2016, 2,574 entered the church, mostly from Lutheranism, but over 160,000 departed. The church has lost hundreds of thousands in recent years, 118,000 in 2012, 178,000 in 2013, and 218,000 in 2014. Mass attendance is lowest in traditionally Catholic regions along the Rhine, where the dioceses of Aachen and Speyer report only 7.8 percent attendance. Average church attendance is down from 18.6 percent in 1995 to 10.4 percent in 2015. In 2015, only fifty-eight men were ordained for the country; the number of priests in 2016 dropped to 13,856, a fall of more than two hundred from the previous year. Marriages, confirmations, and other sacraments are all in decline. Protestant losses are similar. A study conducted by the University of Freiburg predicted that the combined membership of the Catholic and

---

[14] See Cyril Hovorum, *Political Orthodoxies: The Unorthodoxies of the Church Coerced* (Minneapolis: Fortress Press, 2018).

[15] Pew Research Center, "Religious Belief and National Belonging in Central and Eastern Europe," May 10, 2017.

[16] "Catholic Church in Germany Lost a Record Number of Members Last Year," *Catholic Telegraph,* June 27, 2020.

Protestant churches in Germany would drop from the present 45 million to 22.7 million by 2060 due to fewer births and people leaving the church.[17]

While the causes are many, including the fact that an increasing number no longer practice their faith, one significant cause in Germany is the church tax (*Kirchensteuer*) required of all those baptized as children. A recent decision to add an 8–9 percent charge to capital-gains income or any profit made from the sale of an asset has led to a spike in departures from the church, a process that requires formally renouncing church membership. Those who have done so cannot receive the sacraments, including the sacrament of the sick unless they are on the point of death, nor can they attend state-sponsored church schools. These recent departures have not just been young adults who have joined the ranks of the nonaffiliated, but older pensioners as well, fearful of additional taxes on the income from their savings.

The revenue from the church tax makes the church in Germany financially powerful, but many criticize it as a structure heavy in bureaucracy, without real life. Nevertheless, it is able to fund numerous charitable works both in Germany and abroad. The Catholic Church, together with the Evangelical Lutheran Church (EKD), is the second largest employer in the country, second only to the public sector. From kindergartens to schools, hospitals to retirement homes, meals on wheels to many more services funded by Caritas, the charitable association of the German bishops' conference, the church is involved with German life in every area.

The German church is generally quite liberal. In April 2015, the German bishops began receiving the responses to the questionnaire sent to all the dioceses of the world in preparation for the synods on the family. The response showed that most Catholics in Germany hope for an openness to divorce and remarriage as well as to homosexual partners. In their summary the bishops write:

> A large number of faithful would like to see clearer steps being taken towards overcoming the "divide between the reality practiced in families in our parishes and associations and the Church's teachings" and that there is "criticism . . . of the lack of a really appreciative language for forms of relationship which neither conform to the Church's ideal nor take marriage and the family as an exclusive orientation."[18]

---

[17] Anita Rüffer, "Catholicism in Transition," Public Relations, University of Freiburg, February 1, 2018.

[18] Carl Bunderson, "A Crisis in the German Church? Synod Questionnaire Would Suggest So," Catholic News Agency, May 2, 2015.

While German Catholics agreed with the values of monogamy, faithfulness, fertility, and marriage itself and rejected abortion, they want non-moralizing pastoral care for those who do not or do not yet live up to the demands of the gospel; among those are the many who are civilly married because one partner was divorced. Stressing the need for a further development of the church's sexual morals and an enhanced appreciation of the responsibility of individuals to form personal conscience-based judgments, the bishops raised the frequently mentioned exclusion from communion of a partner belonging to another denomination as a problem, especially for the Christian upbringing of children.

On the question of homosexuality, only a small number of respondents saw homosexual relationships as a grave sin. And several bishops have called for a reconsideration of church teaching on homosexuality. Cardinal Reinhard Marx, of Munich/Freising, president of the conference, said there were "certain expectations" of Germany helping the church to open new doors, learning from life. He added: "We are not a branch of Rome. Each conference of bishops is responsible for pastoral care in its cultural context and must preach the Gospel in its own, original way."[19]

After Pope Francis responded to the synods on the family in his apostolic exhortation *Amoris laetitia*, the bishops' conference published guidelines that allowed for divorced and remarried Catholics in certain cases to receive communion. Nevertheless, the decision has divided the hierarchy. Some bishops, having already advocated admitting the divorced and remarried in certain cases to communion, supported the decision, among them Cardinal Walter Kasper, Cardinal Reinhard Marx, Bishop Franz-Josef Body, and Archbishop Heiner Koch. However, others spoke out against it. Cardinal Gerhard Müller, then prefect of the Congregation for the Doctrine of the Faith, argued that *Amoris laetitia* should be interpreted in light of the whole doctrine of the church, not just in terms of "little passages" in the document.[20]

In August 2018, *Spiegel Online* and *Die Zeit* leaked a study reporting some 3,677 cases of child abuse by clergy between 1946 and 2014. Commissioned by the German bishops and conducted by the universities of Giessen, Heidelberg, and Mannheim, the report took four years to assemble.

---

[19] Bunderson.

[20] Elise Harris, "The German Bishops Say the Divorced-and-Remarried May Receive Communion," Catholic News Agency, February 1, 2017.

The study's authors said the figure was "the tip of the iceberg," as many Church documents had been "destroyed or manipulated."[21]

A planned national reform consultation or "synodal path" in Germany hopes to address issues such as power in the church, priestly celibacy, the roles of women in the church, and sexuality. It opened on January 30, 2020, in Frankfurt, with 230 bishops and lay delegates. Klaus Nientiedt, former editor in chief of *Konradsblatt,* the weekly paper of the Diocese of Freiburg im Breisgau, writes: "The first image that struck me was the sight of the bishops wearing civilian clothes among the laity."[22]

Austria

The church in traditionally Catholic Austria faced considerable turmoil when Cardinal Hans Herman Gröer, archbishop of Vienna, resigned in 1995 after accusations surfaced that he had sexually abused students and some monks. The reaction was the formation of the People's Movement of the Church (*Kirchen VolksBewegung*) demanding reforms that include the ordination of married men, women deacons, local selection of bishops, expanded roles for laity, and more compassionate treatment of divorcees and homosexuals. The appointment of Christoph Schönborn as archbishop, named a cardinal in 1998, gave the archdiocese strong leadership.

In 2012 Schönborn unveiled a plan to reorganize the archdiocesan ministerial structure. The plan initially faced opposition from within the church, with a Priests Initiative arguing for women clergy and communion for the divorced and remarried. The plan was rejected as a ploy to maintain clerical power, but by late 2016 much of the opposition had dissipated. The archdiocese had reorganized thirty parishes into larger pastoral areas, with several communities run by lay volunteers authorized to conduct Services of the Word. Michael Pruller, a spokesman for the archdiocese, says missionary impulses have been reinvigorated and priests associated with the larger groupings are freer for pastoral work. He notes that as long as a priest is the proper pastor, the Code of Canon Law provides clear rules (Cann. 515–52) for lay administration of a community.[23]

---

[21] "Sexual Abuse of Minors by Catholic Priests, Deacons, and Male Members of Orders in the Domain of the German Bishops' Conference," MHG Study, September 12, 2018.

[22] In Claire Lesegretain, "In Germany, the Synodal Path Takes a First Step Forward," *La Croix International,* February 5, 2020.

[23] "Vienna Plans Massive Reduction in Parishes, "*Western Catholic Reporter,* October 22, 2012.

The Netherlands

When Pope John XXIII announced in 1959 that he was calling the church into what would be known as the Second Vatican Council, the Dutch bishops prepared themselves for it seriously, meeting together frequently, consulting with their theologians and sociologists, asking their input, and issuing joint communiqués to the faithful. During Lent in 1959, they published a letter stressing that while the hierarchy had a teaching role in the church, "the hierarchy only teaches what is already to be found living within the community of the faithful." The extensive network of Catholic media, with journalists and broadcasters trained in secular positions, began to bring a broader perspective to Dutch Catholics, previously locked into their own enclave or "pillars."[24]

In the years following the council, the Dutch church was the most avant garde. It was ahead of the rest of the church in introducing vernacular language and lay ministers into the liturgy; the reception of communion in the hand; pastoral councils at parish, diocesan, and national levels; and ecumenical initiatives. The *New Dutch Catechism for Adults,* published in 1966, was a model of a new, nontechnical, and irenic style of catechesis, though it was controversial from the beginning, with some finding its mood more subjunctive than indicative when discussing Catholic beliefs.

Nonetheless, the number of Catholics today continues to drop. In the 1960s, Catholics constituted 40 percent of the Dutch population. Though numbers vary, most report the Catholic percentage at 22–24 percent, though one government estimate puts it at 16 percent. In some parts of the country mass attendance for those under sixty-five is only 1–2 percent, though in the 1950s it was 90 percent. Between 2003 and 2015 the church lost 650,000 members. Churches have been closing at the rate of one or two a week, and the bishops told Pope Francis in 2013 that they expected that two-thirds of all Catholic churches in the Netherlands would have to be either sold or closed.

In 2010, the revelation of the sexual abuse crisis in Holland was a major cause of the departures; that year twenty-three thousand left the church. A report appearing in the *NRC Handelsblad,* the country's most prestigious newspaper, charged that, between 1945 and 2010, over half

---

[24] See John A. Coleman, *The Evolution of Dutch Catholicism, 1958–1974* (Berkeley and Los Angeles: University of California Press, 1978).

of the country's bishops either covered up abuse or, in the case of four, were suspected of abusing children themselves. When the report was published, all but one of the bishops had died. According to the bishops, a strict code of conduct has been in place since 2011.

The culture of Holland is pervasively secular; it was the first country to legalize brothels, marijuana, and same-sex marriage. Secularization has affected Catholic institutions; hospitals owned by the Brothers of Charity, under lay boards in both Holland and Belgium, have recently approved, under certain conditions, the performance of euthanasia. In Holland, that applies to psychiatric patients, as well as to those suffering from dementia, 141 of whom were killed in 2016. Still, Catholicism is the largest religious group in the country.

France

The Catholic Church in France, often called the eldest daughter of the church, is also in trouble. In 2007, Frederick Lenoir, editor in chief of *Le Monde des Religions,* said, "In its institutions, but also in its mentalities, France is no longer a Catholic country." While in the early 1990s, 80 percent of the French called themselves Catholic, by 2007, that number had fallen to 51 percent. Even if a majority of the French are cultural Catholics, only 5 percent or less go to church regularly, and only half claim they still believe in God; many said they were Catholic because of a family tradition. The reasons for the decline include an exodus from the countryside, changing values, individualism, and a lack of interest on the part of the younger generation.[25]

The number of ordinations continues to decline. In 2018, only 114 new priests were ordained, compared to 133 in 2017. Of ninety-six dioceses, fifty-eight had no ordinations at all.[26] A major seminary in Lille closed for a year in 2019 because of the lack of candidates. In May of the same year Cardinal Jean Pierre Ricard, archbishop of Bordeaux, announced its seminary would close, sending its few seminarians elsewhere. The country planned to ordain 126 priests in 2020, but close to 60 percent of its ninety-three dioceses expected no ordinations at all.

However, there are some signs of new life. One of them is the growth of "movements," many rooted in the Catholic charismatic renewal,

---

[25] Henry Samuel, "France 'No Longer a Catholic Country,'" *Telegraph,* January 10, 2007.

[26] Gauthier Vaillant and Julien Tranié, "France: Fewer Priests Ordained in 2018," *Le Croix International,* July 4, 2018.

communities like Emmanuel (1972), Chemin Neuf (1973), Foyer de Charité (1936), Béatitudes (1973), Fondacio (1974), and Verbe de Vie (1986). Some are lay movements; others are mixed communities of families, priests, sisters, and brothers. Their ministries include evangelization, forming lay leaders, and social ministries; from them have come a considerable number of vocations to the priesthood and religious life. Many have been canonically recognized as public associations of the faithful. Others are monastic communities, like the Monastic Fraternities of Jerusalem (1975) and the Communauté Saint-Jean (1975), or clerical, like the Communauté Saint-Martin (1976), an association of priests and seminarians.

The traditionalist movement, the Society of Saint Pius X founded by Archbishop Marcel Lefebvre in 1970, continues to exert an influence. As of April 2018, the society had 637 priests in thirty-seven countries, more than 772 mass centers, six seminaries with 204 seminarians, and more than one hundred schools. Both Pope Benedict XVI and Pope Francis have tried to reconcile the society to the church, giving local ordinaries permission to grant their priests faculties to hear confessions and celebrate marriages when no priest in full communion with the church is available. However, with the society's unwillingness to accept Vatican II's teaching on ecumenism, religious liberty, and collegiality, reconciliation has not been possible. Still, since Pope Benedict XVI's motu proprio *Summorum pontificum*, extending permission to celebrate the Latin mass, the society has become quite popular in France.

A number of commentators have suggested that a revival of an apparently dormant Catholicism is taking place. Sandro Magister, an Italian journalist, pointed to a sudden "turnaround" following a prayer in mid-August 2012 by Cardinal André Vingt-Trois, archbishop of Paris. The cardinal asked that children be able to enjoy the love of both a father and mother, entering into the controversy over same-sex marriage and gay couples adopting. As controversy exploded, the newspaper *Le Monde* defended the cardinal in a commentary signed by Patrick Kechichian, a well-known literary critic and convert to Catholicism. When the council of ministers approved a gay marriage initiative in November 2012, thousands marched in the streets, many Catholics among them.[27] Other commentators point to concern about the growth of Islam in French society, especially in light of the recent terrorist attacks. Some

---

[27] Sandro Magister, "The Reawakening of the Church of France," www.chiesa, December 7, 2012.

argue that France's distinct character cannot be understood apart from Catholicism.[28]

One journalist acknowledged that churches in the countryside were "desperately empty," but he attributed this to the movement of the young to the cities, where the people are. When he showed up ten minutes early for mass in Paris, he found the church full, with folding chairs in an adjacent room where parishioners watched the mass on a large TV screen. The priest was not particularly charismatic but "unapologetically orthodox," tactful but not afraid to raise controversial topics. For example, he was asked if the presence of people who were divorced and remarried or who were homosexual was a problem. He answered: "No, the real problem is people who go to church every Sunday and are not willing to see everyone as a child of God, are not willing to welcome them," a doctrinally sound yet welcoming approach he attributed to Pope John Paul II and Pope Francis.[29]

The term *Zombie Catholics,* coined in 2013 by sociologists Emmanuel Todd and Hervé Le Bras, describes those in France who are still influenced by traditional Catholic values, even if not actually "practicing." They see this as part of the traditional battle of the secularist left against the traditionalist right that is reflected in the parents who in the mid-1980s took to the streets to protest government efforts to merge Catholic and public schools as well as those who thirty years later did so again to protest government efforts to legalize gay marriage. Generally, they are highly educated, privilege a traditional approach to professional and domestic relationships, with strong attachments to their communities and families, and are wary about the role of the state in private and community affairs. Catholic values seem to persist, even if the church as an institution has vanished. In the words of Todd and Le Bras: "Catholicism seems to have attained a kind of life after death. But since it is a question of a this-worldly life, we will define it as 'zombie Catholicism.'"[30] This group includes François Fillon, an unsuccessful candidate in France's 2017 presidential election, open about his Catholic beliefs, and Emmanuel Macron, who was elected. Though not a regular churchgoer, Marcon asked to be baptized at the age of twelve.

Pascal-Emmanuel Gobry, who has been studying this phenomenon, has found churches in Paris and Lyon filled with young "upwardly mobile"

---

[28] Samuel Gregg, "France's Catholic Moment," *First Things* (February 2017): 21.

[29] Pascal-Emmanuel Gobry, "Is There a Christian Revival Starting in France?" *The Week*, January 15, 2015.

[30] Cited in Robert Zaretsky, "France's Zombie Catholics Have Risen—and They're Voting," *Foreign Policy*, December 1, 2016.

Catholics as well as immigrant families, and the decline in vocations to the priesthood has leveled off, with the Archdiocese of Paris showing an "uptick." These "new Catholics" (*néocatholiques*), a term apparently coined by *Le Figaro*, are not conservative in either the American or traditional French sense. Samuel Gregg sees them as critical of both progressivism and Lefebvrism. Newly observant, they are self-confident about their faith, often lay led, and frequently appear as commentators in the secular media.[31] According to Gobry, they see liberalism in the French sense of a drive for ever-greater individual liberty as the enemy, responsible for sexual depravity and the culture of death.

If there is a revival in France, Gobry suggests that it will come from the highly educated Catholics living in the cities. As an example, he cites the case of Jean-Marc Potdevin, an engineer who had left his faith behind, but after walking the *Camino* to Santiago de Compostela, had an encounter with Christ that changed his life. After some spiritual guidance he established an iPhone app called Entourage designed to provide a social network that reaches out to the homeless. Gobry is cautious; he sees this movement as still young, small, and sociologically elite; but he remains hopeful, thinking it may be a movement of the Spirit.[32] Samuel Gregg writes that something has changed in French Catholicism: "It is alive in ways one does not see in neighboring Germany, Belgium or Switzerland."[33] A number of observers claim that the April 2019 fire in Notre Dame Cathedral may have awakened French Catholics to a more open practice of their faith.

The church in France had been slow in responding to cases of sexual abuse, some quite controversial. In November 2018, at their plenary assembly at Lourdes, the French bishops acknowledged "the long-lasting and profound damage" caused by the acts of abuse themselves and by "the inadequate taking into account of these acts by ecclesial authorities, and the feeling of not being heard at all." After meeting with victims at their assembly, the bishops voted to establish an "independent commission to shed light on the sexual abuse of minors within the Catholic Church since 1950," as well as initiatives to gather accounts from those who had suffered, including "a financial gesture to the victims."[34] In March 2019,

---

[31] Samuel Gregg, "France's Catholic Revolution," *The Catholic World Report*, November 23, 2015.

[32] Pascal-Emmanuel Gobry, "Zombie Catholics vs. French Secularism," *America*, April 7, 2017.

[33] Gregg, "France's Catholic Revolution."

[34] Anne-Bénédicte Hoffner. "Bishops in France Set Up Commission on Sexual Abuse," *La Croix International*, November 9, 2018.

Cardinal Philippe Barbarin was convicted of failing to report accusations to juridical authorities and given a six-month suspended sentence. Though he was acquitted by the court of appeal, he offered his resignation, which Pope Francis later accepted.

Further damaging were revelations that several founders of new religious movements were guilty of the sexual abuse of women members. They included Gérard Croissant, known as Brother Éphraïm, founder of the Community of the Beatitudes; Father Marie-Dominic Philippe, founder of Communauté Saint-Jean; his brother, Father Thomas Philippe, spiritual adviser to Jean Vanier, the revered founder of L'Arche. Thomas Philippe was accused of sexually abusing a number of women. In 2020 L'Arche leaders acknowledged that Vanier had taken advantage of six women in manipulative sexual relationships.

England

In Britain, the Church of England and the Church of Scotland have each lost 75 percent of their membership over the last sixty years. Other historic Protestant churches—Methodists, Presbyterians, and Congregationalists—have suffered even more drastic losses. However, newer churches—evangelical, Pentecostal, and independent—are growing dramatically. Ian Bradley estimates that in England there are more Catholics attending church on Sunday than Anglicans, and in Scotland more Catholics than Presbyterians.[35]

A survey conducted by the National Center for Social Research

> found that 15 percent of people in Britain consider themselves to be Anglican, compared to about 30 percent in 2000. The proportion of people who say they are Catholic has remained consistent, however, at about 10 percent for the past three decades. . . . Fifty-three percent of nearly 3,000 adults interviewed for the British Social Attitudes survey said that they had 'no religion,' NatCen reported. That figure, covering 2016, is up from 48 percent in 2015. . . . Seventy-one percent of people ages 18–24 said they had no religion, up from 62 percent in 2015.[36]

---

[35] Ian Bradley, "The Strange Death of Protestant Britain," *Tablet*, December 13, 2017.

[36] Simon Caldwell, "New Data from Britain: 53 Percent of Adults Say They Have 'No Religion,'" Catholic News Service, September 6, 2017.

According to a survey produced by St. Mary's University, Twickenham, Catholics have the greatest retention rate of any of the denominations, though they are making few converts today. Two of every five Catholics in England and Wales say that they rarely or never attend church, and almost one-quarter of those who attend mass weekly or more are women over the age of sixty-five.[37]

As a religious community Britain's Catholics are highly diverse, though those of Asian origin are underrepresented. Considerable prejudice against Catholics still exists among the most secular in Britain; at the same time, the country's secularism has generally made Catholics and Anglicans allies, though full diplomatic relations with Rome were reestablished only in 1982.

Poland

The Catholic Church in Poland, with a long history of resistance to persecution, was once a source of national unity. During the Second World War the Nazis murdered some 2,000 diocesan priests, 370 monks, and 280 nuns. Thousands were imprisoned in German extermination camps. In the postwar period the church stood as a bulwark against communist atheism. Today, however, the Polish church is in a period of decline.

While 92.9 percent of Poles claim to be Catholic, the number of those active in the church's life is diminishing. The decreasing number of vocations to the priesthood has led the bishops to begin consolidating some parishes. Few Poles pay attention to rules about sexual abstinence before marriage. As many as four-fifths of Polish Catholics object to the church's regular involvement in politics.[38] Church attendance is falling as well. The Statistic Office of the Catholic Church, run by the Pallotine order in Warsaw, reports that only 36.7 percent of Poles regularly come to mass, compared to more than 50 percent two decades ago. Admissions to Poland's 83 Catholic seminaries are also falling, along with vocations to its 104 female religious congregations, raising fears of a future clergy shortage.[39] In 2019, the number of those to be ordained was 20 percent lower than in 2018.

---

[37] Rose Gamble and Megan Cornwell, "Catholic Church in England and Wales Is Failing to Attract New Believers, Finds Report," *Tablet*, May 24, 2016.

[38] Jan Puhl, "The Catholic Church's Fading Influence in Poland," *Spiegel ONLINE*, July 11, 2012.

[39] Jonathan Luxmore, "Poland's Catholic Church Takes on Its Critics," *National Catholic Reporter*, February 16, 2018.

The situation has worsened since the right-wing Law and Justice Party (PiS) under the firm control of Jaroslaw Kaczynski won both the presidential and parliamentary elections in 2015. From the beginning, Kaczynski has awarded the Catholic Church even more privileges than in the past; he has given money to dioceses, parishes, and other Catholic institutions; granted more power to priests in the running of schools and determining their curricula; and appointed a conservative Catholic as health minister, who has imposed further limits on abortions beyond Poland's already restrictive laws.

On January 26, 2018, Kaczynski's nationalist conservatives adopted a new law that prohibits the use of the expression "Polish death camps," or implications of any Polish "responsibility or co-responsibility" for crimes of the Third Reich. As a result, Polish secondary-school teachers speak of a "tense atmosphere" that prevents them from teaching honestly about examples of anti-Semitism, victimizing Jews in Poland during the war.[40]

Of particular concern is the support the state has given to Father Tadeusz Rydzyk's Radio Maryja and the media empire that has developed around it. Today, Radio Maryja includes a television station, various business enterprises, and a university, all of which receive millions of euros from the government. Its university, despite its poor academic standards, wins prestigious government grants at the expense of Poland's best secular institutions. Radio Maryja is widely recognized as a right-wing, anti-Semitic voice that is hostile to the post–Vatican II church's efforts to address more effectively the modern world.

> The language that Fr. Rydzyk and his various media use is full of unequivocal hatred towards other people and nationalities (most of all Jews, but also Germans) and although it excoriates all kinds of political "enemies," including the members of the "progressive open Church," its message resonates with many Polish Catholics.[41]

---

[40] Jean-Baptiste François, "Polish Schools Promote Nationalist History," *La Croix International*, February 1, 2018.

[41] Cezary Michalski, "The Right Stuff," *Tablet*, December 16, 2017, 6. See also Ireneusz Krzemiński, "Radio Maryja and Fr. Rydzyk as a Creator of the National-Catholic Ideology," in *Religion, Politics, and Values in Poland: Continuity and Change Since 1989*, ed. Sabrina P. Ramet and Irena Borowik, 85–112 (New York: Palgrave Macmillan, 2017).

While the total listening audience is small, Radio Maryja plays a dispro-portionate role in mobilizing people and shaping opinion, and too often it finds support from the Polish hierarchy.

The church in Poland had long avoided addressing the issue of sexual abuse, something the Polish bishops themselves acknowledged in 2014. In 2009 they published a framework for combatting abuse, helping victims, and training future priests, but the measures were somewhat general. Vatican-mandated guidelines were not introduced until 2015; by 2018, only one diocese had implemented them. Protests by defenders of victims and internet posts have evoked dozens of appeals by victims.[42] A two-hour documentary, "Don't Tell Anyone," by Polish journalist Tomasz Sekielski, shocked the Polish public and was widely viewed after its release in May 2019.[43]

In March 2019, the Secretariat of the Episcopal Conference of Poland published a study on sexual abuse of minors for all the country's dioceses and religious orders, listing 382 cases. In most of the cases reported the canonical process had been completed (74.6 percent), though another 25.4 percent were still in process. All forty-four Polish dioceses now have child-protection officers in place, and more than three thousand clergy have undergone training at a Center for Child Protection run by the Jesuits in Krakow, specializing in protecting young people and providing psychological, spiritual, and legal help for victims. A letter sent by the bishops to all the parishes acknowledged that they had "not done enough to prevent these harms" and asked those who had suffered to report of-fenses to church superiors and state authorities. In October 2019, the bishops established a foundation with "listening posts" in several cities to support those abused by clergy.[44]

And there are other signs that the culture is beginning to change. In May 2020, Sekielski released a second film, which was focused on Ed-ward Janiak, bishop of the Diocese of Kalisz. It accused him of failing to suspend an accused priest or inform the Vatican as he was obliged to do. Archbishop Wojciech Polak of Gniezno, the primate of Poland and

[42] Marie Malzak, "In Poland, Admission of Sex Abuse Is Causing 'a Revolution' in the Church," *La Croix International*, February 21, 2019.

[43] See Hadrien Genieys, "New Documentary Exposes Sexual Abuse in Polish Church," *La Croix International*, May 15, 2019.

[44] Augustine Passilly, "Polish Church Establishes Foundation to Support Abuse Victims," *La Croix International*, October 17, 2019.

delegate for child protection of the bishops' conference, asked the Vatican to investigate him.

The Polish Catholic Church is still divided today between its more progressive intellectuals and "Vatican II bishops" and its majority of more conservative priests and bishops, who see the government as defending Poland from contemporary secularism. Kaczynski skillfully exploits this division, appealing to those groups uncomfortable both with the reforms of the Second Vatican Council, and even more, with the direction set by Pope Francis. As a result, many see the church to be in close alliance with Kaczynski's right-wing, anti-Western government. Meanwhile, the number of Catholics regularly attending mass continues to decline.

Italy

Italy has 225 dioceses and archdioceses, more than any other country in the world with the exception of Brazil. It also has the largest number of parishes, roughly 25,694. Yet, according to a 2016 poll, only 50 percent of Italians consider themselves Catholic, with another 13 percent claiming to be Christian. Of the fifteen hundred respondents, 64 percent said they did not feel part of any religious community, while some said they believed in horoscopes, reincarnation, Tarot readings and miracle cures. Many Catholics are withdrawing from their parishes, using forms provided by the Italian Union of Atheists; in 2012, they downloaded 45,797 forms, while in 2015, the number was a record 47,726.[45] Foreign-born clergy now run up to 40 percent of Catholic parishes.

Nevertheless, if many are inactive, the church in Italy, following Pope Francis, has been very involved in working with the enormous influx of refugees. In 2015, some 153,600 arrived in Italy, fleeing war and political unrest. Italian religious communities have been working directly with migrants. At the Gregorian University, Jesuit Father René Micallef has developed classes around refugees, looked at immigration policies from a biblical and ethical perspective, hoping to sensitize his students, many of them seminarians, to the issues facing migrants. Jesuit Refugee Services (JRS), an international organization founded by Father General Pedro Arrupe in 1989, now has fifteen national offices in Europe, including one in Rome. Working with migrants and asylum

---

[45]"The Pope's Still Catholic—But Half of Italians Aren't," *Local*, March 30, 2016.

seekers is its primary mission. Micallef, from Malta, worked with JRS before becoming a Jesuit.

Caritas Italiana, a pastoral organization of the Italian Bishops' Conference, is another Catholic agency working directly with refugees in 220 Italian dioceses, providing them with food and clothing. In Sicily, Archbishop Domenico Mogavero, known as the Migrant Bishop, established a diocesan program to help integrate migrants into Italian culture. The program offers cooking classes that incorporate native ingredients of the migrants into typical Italian dishes. Local sisters working together with Caritas help migrant children with their homework.

Citing a United Nations Refugee Agency report, Mogavero states that 39 percent of the world's displaced people find hosts in the Middle East and North Africa, while only 6 percent are hosted in Europe, and that political movements that caution about the "Islamification of Europe" are based on outdated "racist and xenophobic" assumptions. He says it is not a Christian Europe anymore; "the world is for everyone." Elsewhere in Sicily, in the town of Agrigento, an international group of sisters from several congregations is working to provide emotional support to migrants, beginning with one-on-one relationships, in a program called Migrant Project/Sicily, begun by the International Union of Superiors General.[46] While Catholic authorities and publications criticize Matteo Salvini, the Minister of the Interior (2018–19), for his hostile attitude toward immigrants, an increasing number of lay Catholics support his nationalist policies.

The Community of Saint'Egidio represents another positive sign. A worldwide movement of lay people founded in Rome in 1968 shortly after the close of Vatican II, it is now a network of communities in some seventy countries. Based on a careful listening to the word of God, it focuses on prayer, serving the poor—including the elderly, homeless, migrants, disabled people, prisoners, street children—and working for peace.

The sexual abuse scandal has also surfaced in Italy, though the number of victims is difficult to obtain. In February 2014, the United Nations Committee on the Rights of the Child issued a blistering report accusing the Vatican of fostering a "code of silence" that "systematically" put the reputation of the church over the protection of child victims. In 2019, the same committee again questioned the Italian government about

---

[46]Tracy Badalucco, "Catholic Church's Presence Strong among Migrant Work in Italy," *National Catholic Reporter*, September 7, 2016.

clerical sex abuse, concerned that civil laws protected predator priests from criminal charges.

The Italian Bishops' Conference recently created a Clerical Sexual Abuse Network, to provide information and support victims, but the secretary general of the conference was not able to give any numbers. Some estimates put the number of victims in the thousands. In September 2019 the Vatican's Promotor of Justice requested the indictment of two Italian priests: one for sexual abuse in a minor seminary in which he was living; the other for "aiding and abetting" it.

Ireland

The Catholic Church in Ireland is in serious need of healing. For years the alliance of church and state dominated Irish social life. A senator from the Labor Party, Aodhán Ó Ríordáin said, "In the '40s and '50s, people replaced the colonialism of the Brits with a kind of colonialism of the church."[47] The higher clergy dominated Irish life in the Republic. Divorce was forbidden, the sale of contraceptives was restricted, and abortion and homosexuality were forbidden by law.

In recent years much of that has changed. Revelations about abuse in Irish schools, orphanages, Magdalene asylums (state-supported institutions run by nuns where unwed pregnant girls often were sent to live and work), and residential reform schools for poor, unwanted boys have caused outrage. A ten-year twenty-six-hundred-page report of Ireland's Commission to Inquire into Child Abuse, the Ryan Report, released in May 2009, stated that thousands of boys and girls suffered from beatings, humiliation, sexual abuse, and rape in institutions run by religious. Most of the institutions in question were closed in the 1990s.[48]

Though criticized by many leaders of the religious congregations involved, the Irish Catholic Bishops' Conference stated:

> The Ryan report represents the most recent disturbing indictment of a culture that was prevalent in the Catholic Church in Ireland for far

---

[47] Aodhán Ó Ríordáin, quoted in Liam Stack, "How Ireland Moved to the Left: 'The Demise of the Church,'" *New York Times*, December 2, 2017.

[48] For an overview of the five-volume commission report, see Commission to Inquire into Child Abuse, "Executive Summary," May 20, 2009.

too long. Heinous crimes were perpetrated against the most innocent and vulnerable, and vile acts with life-lasting effects were carried out under the guise of the mission of Jesus Christ. This abuse represents a serious betrayal of the trust which was placed in the church.[49]

In 2017, the conference published guidelines on the responsibilities of priests who had fathered children.

The stories of the sexual abuse of young people in Catholic institutions and other stories of abuse by priests, brothers, and even sisters caused many to lose confidence in the church. At least four bishops have resigned over criticism of how they dealt with allegations of sexual abuse. Some point to lifestyle changes brought on by economic prosperity during the boom days of the "Celtic Tiger," from the mid 1990s until 2008. These changes brought about the end of a dominating Catholic culture in Ireland, with its concern to regulate people's private lives. In 1992, the country decriminalized homosexuality; in 1993, it removed restrictions on the sale of contraceptives; and in 1996, it legalized divorce. In 2015, 62 percent of the population voted to legalize same-sex marriage, and the country passed a law on gender identity supported by transgender rights groups. The 2011 census identified 78 percent of the Irish population as Catholic, but Archbishop Diarmuid Martin says that he believes "the figure for true believers is closer to 20 percent."[50]

There are few young men studying today for the priesthood and, as already noted, seven out of the country's eight seminaries have closed since 1993. The one remaining, St. Patrick's College at Maynooth, the largest seminary in the world when it was begun in 1795, is an enormous Gothic facility that was built to accommodate five hundred seminarians, but in 2017, there were only thirty-six students in residence, with another twenty-five living elsewhere. Another twelve study at the Irish College in Rome.

"Since 1995, the number of Catholic priests in active ministry in Ireland had dropped by 43 percent, from 3,550 to 2,019." The average age of Irish priests "is approaching 65."[51]

---

[49] Shay Cullen, "The Catholic Church's March of Misery in Ireland," Spero News, June 24, 2009.

[50] Stack, "How Ireland Moved to the Left."

[51] Patsy McGarry, "Irish Priests' Group to Discuss Vocation Crisis with Bishops," *Irish Times*, May 19, 2016.

In Dublin, estimates put the weekly mass attendance at about 20–22 percent of the population, with attendance in some working-class neighborhoods as low as 2–3 percent. Indeed, the decline in church attendance is true for all churches in Ireland, with the Presbyterian Church in the North experiencing the most dramatic losses.

Ireland has also experienced cultural changes; EU membership has resulted in immigration that has brought a new diversity in culture, creed, and ethnicity to the country's previously homogenous population. Where in the past a cultural Catholicism was considered sufficient for handing on the faith, in today's changing society the need for a new evangelization is becoming apparent. As Ireland changes from a largely rural society to a modern, upwardly mobile urban one, new methods are becoming necessary.

As Archbishop Martin has said, "We learned all the rules and the norms, and it was presumed that the basic elements of faith were there. . . . People felt that there was really very little need to evangelize, that being born into Irish society made you a Catholic."[52] Lay people need to take a more active part in the life of the church; the role of women has changed enormously; and the country does not have a number of deacons such as the number that has appeared in the United States. With fewer priests, Ireland, like other countries in Europe, will be consolidating parishes and calling on professionally trained lay ministers.

Spain

The Catholic Church still dominates religion in Spain, at least in terms of its religious culture. Neither the charismatic renewal nor evangelical or Pentecostal churches play significant roles. Opus Dei, founded in Spain in 1928 by Josémaria Escrivá de Balaguer y Albás, still has considerable influence. Some argue that the long years in which the Catholic Church supported Francisco Franco's regime explains the secular liberalism of contemporary Spain.

While Catholics in Spain make up roughly 68.3 percent of the population, mass attendance has been low. Yet, a recent study by the Centro de Investagaciones Sociológicas (CIS) shows that the number of Spaniards attending mass increased from 12.1 to 15 percent between 2011 and 2012, and a further 23 percent from 2012 to 2013. According to the Pew

---

[52] Cited in James T. Keane, "The Uncertain Future of Catholic Ireland," *America*, February 23, 2018.

Research Center, Spain has a relatively large share of highly observant people: 21 percent. The number of diocesan seminarians, 1,227 in 2010–11, increased to 1,321 in 2013–14, a steady growth, while congregations of sisters, both active and contemplative, are also experiencing a slow but steady growth. Filip Mazurczak attributes this at least in part to a growing dissatisfaction with the policies of José Luis Rodríguez Zapatero's socialist government (2004–11) over same-sex marriage, relaxed divorce and abortion laws, and a secularized education.[53] In 2018, 135 men were ordained priests, compared to 109 in 2017.

Eastern Europe

While religious life in Eastern Europe suffered under communism, there has been a significant revival since the fall of the Iron Curtain and the collapse of the Soviet Union. In many Eastern European countries religion is an important part of individual and national identity, with Orthodoxy and Roman Catholicism being the major faiths, even if few in either tradition regularly attend church services. Poland, here, is an exception, but Poland is also changing, as we have noted. Orthodoxy is generally the largest tradition; Moldova and Greece have the highest percentage of Orthodox believers, while the most numerous Orthodox populations are in Russia and Ukraine.

A number of Eastern European countries have large Catholic populations—Poland (92.9 percent), Croatia (84 percent), Lithuania (75 percent), and Hungary (56 percent)—with a small percentage in these countries identifying as Orthodox. In the Czech Republic 29 percent were raised Catholic, though only 21 percent identified as Catholics in 2015. According to a Pew Forum study, noted earlier, 72 percent of respondents identified as "atheist," "agnostic," or "nothing in particular." Bosnia, Estonia, and Latvia are religiously diverse, without a clear majority, but also with sizable Orthodox minorities.[54]

Catholics in Central and Eastern Europe tend to be more religiously observant than Orthodox Christians or their co-religionists in the West.

---

[53] Filip Mazurczak, "Is Spain Regaining Its Faith? And Why Isn't Anyone Else?" *First Things*, June 11, 2014.

[54] Pew Research Center, "Religious Belief and National Belonging in Central and Eastern Europe," May 10, 2017. See also Erasmus, "Religion after Communism: Eastern Europe's Patriotic Faith," *Economist*, May 14, 2017.

They are also more socially conservative. Most oppose gay marriage, and though some might favor abortion, it is at substantially lower rates than Catholics in Western Europe (47 percent vs. 71 percent). They are much less open to accepting a Muslim family member. Politically, they tend to look to the West and the United States, while the Orthodox, whose faith is more closely related to their national identity, identify more with Russia, though Greece is an exception to this and now also Ukraine.

Scandinavia

The Scandinavian countries—Norway, Denmark, Sweden, and some add Finland—are Lutheran countries but today largely secular. All are members of the Porvoo Communion, a significant ecumenical agreement joining the Anglican churches of the British Isles, the Baltic Lutheran churches, the Lutheran churches of Scandinavia, the Church of Iceland, and the Anglican churches of Spain and Portugal in full communion.

Lutheranism is no longer the established church in Sweden or Norway. In Sweden, Lutherans constitute 59.3 percent of the population, but that number is deceptive, with any newborn with at least one parent a member of the Lutheran Church automatically registered as a member. Membership continues to decline, with fewer baptisms and new members. Estimates put Catholics at 4 percent, largely immigrants—Poles, Croatians, and Latin Americans—working in the country. In 1998, Stockholm got its first Swedish bishop since the Reformation, Anders Aborelius, born a Lutheran. He was named a cardinal by Pope Francis in June 2017. Today, the Catholic Church is the fastest growing church in Sweden, with converts from Lutheranism. Each year some four thousand new Catholics register.

In Norway, 71.5 percent of the population belong to the Evangelical Lutheran Church, but practice is minimal, with 3 percent attending services every Sunday, and another 10 percent roughly once a month. Though no longer the official church, it still receives support from the state. The Catholic Church is the next largest church, at 2.9 percent, though lately it has been accused of inflating its numbers, with fines levied. The Evangelical Lutheran Church of Denmark is the state church; 75.3 percent of the population are registered members, but only 3 percent regularly attend on Sundays and only 19 percent of Danes consider religion an important part of their lives. Catholics make up about 1.3 percent of the population.

The Evangelical Lutheran Church of Finland, governed by bishops, is one of the largest Lutheran churches in the world, with 70.9 percent of the population, though its membership is declining. Most Finns attend services only on special occasions—Christmas, Easter, weddings, and funerals. As of 2018, Finland had a total of more than fifteen thousand registered Catholics and perhaps another ten thousand unregistered. The Finnish Orthodox Church has about sixty thousand members, 1.1 percent of the population.

Conclusion

Will European Christianity simply fade away as the church continues to expand in the Global South? Is it possible to see God's hand in the diminishments in the church's onetime European home? There are some signs of renewal. In France, a popular reaction to what is perceived as government interference in community life at the expense of traditional values, concern over the growth of Islam, and increasing secularization has led some young, upwardly mobile professionals to be more public about their faith and to an increased attendance at mass in the cities. And the popular movements in the French church, with their concern for evangelization and ministry to the disadvantaged, have also brought a new energy as well as vocations.

A recent book by French historian Guillaume Cuchet, drawing on a series of surveys carried out by Fernand Boulard, suggests that the rupture in French practice was inevitable, given cultural changes to authority in family and education. Still, he argues that the effect of Vatican II triggered and intensified changes in French religious life. He sees the council as establishing a new hierarchy of values, not the popular Catholicism, based on attendance at mass, popular prayers, and the sacrament of reconciliation, but one geared more to educated, ultra-conscious elites. The threat of mortal sin was gone. Involvement in social and community life and freedom of conscience appealed to these elites, but the popular sacramental piety that sustained the less committed churchgoers became less important.[55]

---

[55] Guillaume Cuchet, *Comment notre monde a cessé d'être chrétien* (Paris: Éditions du Seuil, 2018).

Catholicism is also growing in Sweden, and Spain also seems to be experiencing a similar revival, with reaction to the secular policies of the former socialist government, an increased attendance at mass, and an increase in candidates for the priesthood and religious life. While Italy has fewer priests and is increasingly reliant on priests from abroad, its social ministry to migrants provides a model for the rest of Europe.

One positive outcome to European diminishments, particularly the shortage of vocations, may be the emergence of a more lay-centered church. In Britain, lay men and lay women are increasingly helping with administrative tasks, while priests are working together across traditional parish boundaries. In Germany, in the Archdiocese of Hamburg, designated lay people conduct funerals, proclaim, and preach in different worship forms. Priests still have overall responsibility, but work with a team that assigns various tasks and duties to lay ministers.

Cardinal Christoph Schönborn has done much to channel reform movements in Vienna in spite of some initial opposition. His reforms consolidated parishes into pastoral areas and give considerable responsibility to lay ministers. These responsibilities include being parish administrators, giving priests greater freedom for pastoral work. Cardinal Willem Ejik, president of the Dutch bishops' conference, has proposed a similar consolidation of 326 parishes into 48 larger territorial unities, with each one having a single church as a "eucharistic center."

The scandal of the sexual abuse of minors was late emerging in Europe and has been acknowledged in most countries. Many have established procedures for dealing with it. Since Pope Francis published mandatory procedural norms for reporting sexual abuse to competent civil authorities in *Vos estis lux mundi* in 2019, the situation in Europe has changed considerably. Laws or protocols dealing with family issues, domestic violence or child protection, and codes of ethics for specific professions, have established the obligation or duty to report for those professionals working in contact with children in Austria, Bosnia, Croatia, Denmark, Finland, France, Greece, Herzegovina, Iceland, Italy, Lithuania, Luxembourg, the Republic of Moldova, the Netherlands, the Republic of Macedonia, as well as for *any* person with such knowledge in Iceland, Lithuania, and Malta.[56] Hungary and Poland now have child-protection protocols in place.

---

[56] See Lanzarote Committee, "Committee of the Parties to the Council of Europe Convention on the Protection of Children against Sexual Exploitation and Sexual Abuse," May 30, 2016, 4.

It is also clear that a cultural Catholicism will no longer suffice for handing on the faith to the next generation. The church must find new and effective ways to evangelize. The church in Germany is placing greater emphasis on all sharing in the universal priesthood. As Stefan Foerner, the spokesman for the Archdiocese of Berlin, stated: "The era of a popular folk church is over—we've had to reshape our structures and find new ways of working with each other."[57] With a strongly secular culture, the life of faith places new demands on European Christians, one that requires a more personal, appropriated faith rather than a merely cultural one. Reform movements have called for greater lay involvement and increasingly, public witness. Yet, how to share that faith with others to evangelize effectively in an often hostile culture remains a challenge.

---

[57] Cited in Jonathan Luxmoore, "Berlin Archdiocese to Restructure for Administrative, Spiritual Reasons," Catholic News Service, December 7, 2012.

8

A Tentative Look Ahead

From the beginning of his pontificate Pope Francis has sought to move the church forward, away from focusing on itself and its own problems, as he told the cardinals in his brief remarks at the congregation prior to the conclave. Instead, it should focus on the risen Christ. Having played a key role in drafting the final document of the Fifth General CELAM Conference at Aparecida in 2007, the new pope was calling the church to a pastoral conversion, one that would lead to a new understanding of the church's mission, to a new evangelization.

Such an evangelization was not to be a moralistic focus on sexuality and a concern for correct doctrine. It has to find ways to move beyond what he calls in *Laudato si'* the "myths of modernity grounded in a utilitarian mindset (individualism, unlimited progress, competition, consumerism, and unregulated markets)" (LS, no. 210). Christians are called to be missionary disciples, to bring the good news to the peripheries, to all the excluded—the poor, the suffering, migrants. The church should be described by what it is for, not what it is against, building bridges instead of walls. It needed to rediscover the grace and the mercy of God.

To better meet the challenges of today, Pope Francis has sought to reimagine the church as a synodal church, acknowledging that Catholics can learn much about synodality from our Orthodox brothers and sisters.[1] A synodal church grants more authority to national and regional conferences to make decisions concerning their lives, liturgy, and mission. It gives them both voice and agency. To facilitate this, Francis wants to

---

[1] See Pope Francis, "Ceremony Commemorating the Fiftieth Anniversary of the Institution of the Synod of Bishops," October 17, 2015.

give greater expression to the authority of episcopal conferences, even doctrinal authority.

For example, in his motu proprio *Magnum principium*, he restored to regional episcopal conferences their proper role in preparing and approving liturgical translations according to the vision of Vatican II's *Sacrosanctum concilium* (*Constitution on the Sacred Liturgy*) (SC, no. 36). Thus, he essentially moved beyond the conservative 2001 instruction of the Vatican's Congregation on Divine Worship, *Liturgiam authenticam*, which gave all authority to the Curia in Rome.

Beyond conversion in the lives of all Catholic Christians as well as in the structures of the church itself, he stresses the importance of inculturation and the social dimensions of evangelization. Always evident is his special concern for the poor and the disadvantaged. The October 2019 Synod of Bishops for the Pan-Amazon region, even though it met in Rome, was an example of the pope's efforts to empower regional churches to better address the pastoral issues they face, listening to one another and journeying together.[2]

Future Church

In surveying global Catholicism we have seen its rich diversity, the challenges it faces in so many different parts of the world, and those challenges that are common to so many of its local churches. We have considered the demographic changes that are changing the church's face. And we have seen areas where change is not only appropriate but increasingly necessary, though, as Massimo Faggioli observes, global Catholicism means not just an enlargement of boundaries, but also a deepening of divisions.[3]

In Europe and North America all the churches continue to lose members, though Christianity is expanding in remarkable ways in the Global South. Much of its growth is in its Pentecostal or neo-Pentecostal expressions. The disaffiliation of young people is a concern in many countries. The scandal of the sexual abuse of minors, now recognized as a global problem, still brings new changes. There are new calls for declericalization

---

[2] Pope Francis.

[3] Massimo Faggioli, "In the Shadow of Vatican I: The Pope, Homosexuality, and Change in the Church," *La Croix International*, August 22, 2019.

and greater lay participation in decision making. So what does all this suggest for the church's future?

In 2009, John Allen published a book on the future church. Reflecting on the shift of the majority Christian population from Europe and North America to the Global South, he envisions that, while the churches of the West or Global North would continue to be important centers of Catholic thought and life, church leadership would increasingly come from the Global South, perhaps even a pope from Asia, Africa, or Latin America. With the election of Pope Francis that forecast has already proved true. He sees tomorrow's Catholicism as largely non-Western, non-white, and non-affluent. It will be more conservative on sexual issues, more liberal on questions of social justice; it will be antiwar, pro–United Nations, and suspicious of free-market capitalism; more biblical and evangelical in engaging with cultural issues; more concerned with a strong Catholic identity in the face of religious pluralism; younger and more optimistic; and more open to indigenous religious practice.[4]

Taking all this into account, including Francis's efforts to transform the church, we might submit that the Catholic Church of tomorrow will be a polycentric church. It will be more inclusive and participatory in its governance, while the face of its ministerial leadership will continue to change as more and more lay men and lay women take on ministerial responsibilities, some of them formerly reserved to priests. Without significant changes the number of priests will continue to diminish. The ecumenical movement continues to struggle, though in much of the Global South, it is still in its very early stages. These churches, many not interested in traditional ecumenism, are often looking forward to a new form of ecumenism, less restricted to specialists. Regardless, in many parts of the world, the ecumenical movement has led to greater mutual respect and even friendship across ecclesial boundaries.

Rome remains strongly committed to interreligious dialogue, particularly important in the Global South, where Catholics are often in a minority status or face tensions from those belonging to other religions, often with the threat of violence. Finally, in many places a more fluid ecclesial identity seems to be emerging, especially among the young. Let's now examine these and other trends and developments more closely.

---

[4] See John Allen, *The Future Church: How Ten Trends Are Revolutionizing the Catholic Church* (New York: Doubleday, 2009), 432–35.

A Polycentric Church

The shift of the Christian population from Europe and North America to the Global South, with 75 percent of all Christians projected to live south of the equator by 2050, means that the global church will be a polycentric church. This is especially true for the Catholic Church. As Karl Rahner predicted as early as 1954, the Catholic Church is no longer a church of Europe and North America, no longer a church exclusively of Rome. Rahner spoke of a "diaspora Christianity," fragmented, no longer representing a majority of a nation's inhabitants or supported by a Christian culture.[5] Vatican II represented the first assembly of this world church.[6]

Rahner's reflections were in many ways prophetic. If the Catholic Church today is truly global—a world church—it no longer reflects a homogeneous Christian culture. Thus, it must learn to be considerably more comfortable with diversity. Paul Murray speaks of an "intra-Catholic pluralism" of practice, debate, and disagreement. He argues that the word *catholic* cannot be understood simply as a spatio-temporal universality. The Greek *kath' holou* means "according to the whole." The earliest usage of the adjective *katholikos* in relation to the church suggests wholeness or fullness. Murray uses Cyril of Alexander as well as Möhler and Congar to argue that both meanings should be held together, embracing both universality and particularity. That means theological, liturgical, spiritual, and cultural diversity as well as gathering diverse particularities into one church, with lay and ordained, celibate and married, heterosexual and homosexual members, if the church is to grow into the fullness of catholicity.[7]

The variety of cultures in which the church is embedded, many of them secular, with different problems and challenges, contributes to the decentralization called for by Pope Francis. Such a church will increasingly be less Eurocentric, more dependent on the Spirit, enabling it to read the signs of the times in living out its faith and carrying out its mission.

The Second Vatican Council represented a rediscovery of the Spirit's animating presence, opening the Church to what Pope Francis called the

---

[5] In Massimo Faggioli, "Diaspora and the Globalization of the Catholic Church," *La Croix International*, July 30, 2019.

[6] Karl Rahner, "Towards a Fundamental Theological Interpretation of Vatican II," *Theological Studies* 40, no. 4 (1979): 716–27.

[7] Paul D. Murray, "Living Catholicity Differently: On Growing into the Plenitudinous Plurality of Catholic Communion in God," in *Envisioning Futures for the Catholic Church*, ed. Staf Hellemans and Peter Jonkers (Washington, DC: Council for Research in Values and Philosophy, 2018), 109–58.

Spirit's "inexhaustible novelties."[8] The Spirit's work is not limited to the ordained, to the magisterium, or to the papacy, but gifts all the baptized, giving them a share in the church's mission. Ultimately, this must find expression in the church's structures of governance.

The pope calls for greater recognition of the magisterial authority of national and regional episcopal conferences, and stresses the importance of the *sensus fidei* and thinking with the church, not just the hierarchy. He emphasizes synodality, resisting the temptation to govern in a "top down" fashion.[9] As a global communion embedded in a plurality of diverse cultures, the churches of Africa, Asia, and Latin America will play an increasingly important role in its life. Inculturation will mean more diversity in theology, liturgy, and pastoral practical. To some extent, this is already happening.

The emphasis on liberation theology and a preferential option for the poor have left a mark on new theologies of liberation and on what Pope John Paul II called in *Sollicitudo rei socialis* (*On Social Concern*) "the option of love or preference for the poor" (no. 42). The effectiveness of CELAM in revitalizing the churches of Latin America in the period after Vatican II illustrates the potential of regional episcopal conferences. Pentecostalism has left its mark on their liturgies and catechetics. Today, African theologians are striving to develop an authentically African theology, with women playing an increasingly important role. Asians churches, particularly in India, struggle with how to present Jesus as Word of God and savior in the face of religious pluralism and their minority status. They stress a threefold dialogue with the poor, with culture, and with other religions. And in China, Christianity is growing rapidly, despite government efforts to restrict it. The Chinese model of bishops nominated by local authority, with a possible veto by Rome, could provide a model for the universal church, giving local churches more say in their leadership.

Some have proposed a retrieval of the patriarchal ordering of the early church, for a more effective, decentralized government, a structure that was still developing at the time of the Council of Nicaea (325 CE). Prior to Nicaea, local bishops came together in synods, meeting usually in metropolitan centers to address common problems; they would gather under

---

[8] Pope Francis, "Theology after *Veritatis gaudium* in the Context of the Mediterranean," June 21, 2019.

[9] See Pope Francis, "Ceremony Commemorating the Fiftieth Anniversary of the Institution of the Synod of Bishops." See also International Theological Commission, "Synodality in the Life and Mission of the Church," March 2, 2018.

the authority of a *protos*, a first or presiding bishop. Nicaea referred to four preeminent sees: Rome, Alexandria, Antioch, and Jerusalem. From this was to develop the patriarchal office, though it survives today only in the Eastern Orthodox churches and in six of the Eastern Catholic churches: the Coptic, Melkite, Syrian, Maronite, Armenian, and Chaldean. The only patriarchate in the Latin church is the bishop of Rome, though Pope Benedict XVI suppressed the papal title Patriarch of the West in 2006.[10]

Before he became pope, Joseph Ratzinger had suggested establishing new patriarchal structures as a way to break down what he called an extreme centralization of church structure.[11] Such patriarchs—or better, presiding bishops—might summon and preside over local synods in Africa, the Americas, and Asia. The result would be the emergence of new centers of authority based on national or regional episcopal conferences such as the United States Conference of Catholic Bishops (USCCB) in Washington, DC, or the Federation of Asian Bishops' Conferences (FABC) in Asia. According to Massimo Faggioli, the church needs "a strengthening of the mid-level of authority between the local (diocesan) and the universal (Rome), that is, the continental level."[12] This may well develop if Francis's vision of a more synodal church can be realized.

A More Inclusive Governance

A decentralized, polycentric church will be characterized by more inclusive governance. It will speak with a plurality of voices, though to this point no structures exist to bring those different voices—of theologians and scholars; the laity, especially women; the poor and the excluded—into conversation. Some voices are being heard for the first time. They often bring new concerns, assisted by the simultaneity of modern communications and social media. Many local and regional Catholic churches are striving to be more inclusive of those who are different. Other churches in developing or religiously pluralistic countries are beginning to find their voices, addressing issues vital to their ecclesial life and mission.

---

[10] John R. Quinn, *Ever Ancient, Ever New: Structures of Communion in the Church* (New York: Paulist Press, 2013), 13–19.

[11] Quinn, 19.

[12] Massimo Faggioli, "The Running of a Multicultural World Church in Global Times," in Hellemans and Jonkers, *Envisioning Futures for the Catholic Church*, 290.

With over five thousand Catholic bishops today, the logistical difficulties of holding another general council could well be unsurmountable. Furthermore, as Staf Hellemans and Peter Jonkers warn, given the confusion and disagreement about how the church should move forward, "summoning a new council today would be no guarantee at all for reaching a lasting consensus, but would rather risk tearing the Church apart or to causing fateful paralysis."[13] This suggests that the Synod of Bishops, representing bishops from around the world, will play an increasingly important role in the future. Massimo Faggioli suggests that if Francis's turn or, more accurately, "re-turn towards synodality succeeds, it could be the beginning of a new chapter in the history of Church governance." Even more, it may require a change in the synod structure itself, to make it more than simply a synod of bishops in which voting rights belong only to clergy.[14] Lay men and lay women have sometimes taken part in the discussions of the language groups at synods, and more ways can be found for them to participate effectively.

The two synods on marriage and the family (2014–15) and the October 2019 Synod on the Amazon were very different from the synods that preceded them, carefully managed by the Curia. They reflected the free discussion on controverted issues not seen since Vatican II. Pope Francis encouraged the bishops to listen to one another and to speak about what was in their hearts, not simply say what they thought the pope wanted to hear them say. For genuine discernment, such honesty is essential. He emphasized the importance of experience, of focusing on real life and on God as a God of mercy.[15] These most recent synods were unique in seeking broad consultation with the faithful before the synods met and in the issues raised. In many ways these synods can provide a model for the future. We will consider the Synod on the Amazon more fully below.

And there are other examples. For example, in August 2019, the Chaldean Catholic Church held a synod in northern Iraq, bringing together church leaders and parishioners from Iraq, the United States, Syria, Iran, Lebanon, Egypt, Canada, Australia, and Europe to discuss the church's future in Iraq and elsewhere. In what they called a synodality exercise, the bishops of France opened their November 2019 plenary assembly for

---

[13] Hellemans and Jonkers, *Envisioning Futures for the Catholic Church*, 21.

[14] Massimo Faggioli, "What the Synod of Bishops Means for Vatican II . . . and 'Vatican III,'" *La Croix International*, October 30, 2019.

[15] See Austen Ivereigh, *Wounded Shepherd: Pope Francis and His Struggle to Convert the Catholic Church* (New York: Henry Holt, 2019), 252–57.

the first time to lay participation. Each bishop was allowed to bring two members of the faithful, men or women, ordained or lay, to reflect with them on the future mission of their diocese. The result is a far less clerical assembly. Germany also is developing a synodal process.

Lay men and lay women could also be better represented on Vatican dicasteries, and they should have some say in the choosing of their bishops. The present system is monarchical, with no provision for the consent of the governed. The result too often is a hierarchy that simply reflects the theology or particular approach of the ruling pontiff. A system of nominations from local dioceses, with the pope's right to make the final decision, respects both local participation and papal oversight.

And there are other voices that need to be heard. The churches of the Global South are increasingly finding their voices and bringing forward their own concerns. Their voices will find a place at international synods with more provision for lay participation. With them will come the voices of the laity, women, and especially the poor.

After the Pandemic

What can we expect for the church after the pandemic? Many commentators suggest that the church will never be the same. Churches around the world have had to suspend Sunday mass. Some scholars are worried that those who lost the habit of regular attendance are now accustomed to Sundays without it. With many parishes suffering from loss of revenues, making finances more transparent will be important in encouraging parishioners to offer renewed support. Parish ministers and staff will have to reach out to bring people together and learn to share responsibilities with lay people.[16]

Some suggest that more radical changes may lie ahead. They envision the collapse of the distinction between the baptized and the ordained, in effect denying the existence of the church's pastoral office. Instead of being dependent on remote clerical presiders, they ask why the laity gathered in their homes couldn't celebrate mass themselves? Wouldn't this be better than a clerical "virtual liturgy" or a "spiritual communion"?[17]

---

[16] Dennis Sandowski, "Prepare Now for Post-Pandemic Ministry, Church Professionals Urge," *Crux*, April 20, 2020.

[17] J. P. Grayland, "Ministry in the Post-Pandemic Church," *La Croix International*, May 14, 2020.

They see the "royal" or baptismal priesthood of 1 Peter 2:4–9 as rooting the priestly charism in baptism alone: "No extra laying on of hands is required. In baptism we receive the ordained task of leading and enriching the community as a regal, prophetic and priestly people."[18] They point out that Christians played a more active role in the sacraments until the Middle Ages, anointing the sick with blessed oil or even with some declaring to others the forgiveness of their sins. We know that Ignatius of Loyola before a battle declared his sins to a lay man.

Pope Francis has expressed the hope that the post-pandemic church can learn to be both institutional, with certain rules and regulations, and more free form, responding to pastoral needs in creative ways. Will it be a synodal church, able to address local problems with local initiatives? Will it be a less clerical church, serve by an ordained ministry modeled on that of Jesus? Will the faithful who have found new ways to pray, celebrate, and worship during the pandemic come to a new appreciation of their share in Christ's priesthood? Many argue that women, who at times presided over domestic liturgies, will be reluctant to return to a more passive role when traditional church life is restored.

The pandemic has shattered our usual complacency; it is something completely beyond our control. We sense the fragility of our human community, the social nature that binds us together but also puts us at risk. Positively, it has led to a new sense of our interrelatedness, sometimes on a global scale. Though we so often forget it, we are connected to one another, perhaps now more than ever. There has been an outpouring of prayers for healthcare workers, grocery store employees, and others on the front lines who are at risk.

Joachim von Braun, president of the Pontifical Academy of Sciences, warns that we cannot simply go back to our old ways after the pandemic is under control. "If we want to survive, we will need a society that is more responsible, more prepared to share, more caring, just and equal." Survival will demand more responsible societies, greater willingness to share, less selfishness and national egotism.[19] The church itself will have to change, becoming more welcoming, reaching out to the vulnerable, the poor, and the socially excluded. It cannot think simply of maintaining the status quo.

---

[18] Peter Maher, "Setting a New Course for Catholic Priestly Ministry," *La Croix International*, May 12, 2020.

[19] Christa Pongratz-Lippitt, "Leading Vatican Academic Says Pandemic Demands We Rethink Our Current Lifestyles," *La Croix International*, April 21, 2020.

The Peripheries

In his apostolic letter *Evangelii gaudium* Pope Francis challenges Catholics, indeed each Christian, to obey the Lord's call "to go forth from our own comfort zone in order to reach all the 'peripheries' in need of the light of the Gospel" (EG, no. 20). At the center of his concern are the poor, the disadvantaged, and migrants. And if the church is to evangelize the diverse cultures in which it lives successfully, it must become inculturated (EG, nos. 68, 116–28). No longer a European church, such a church should be greatly decentralized. His choice of cardinals from nontraditional sees and his inclusion of the concerns of regional episcopal conferences in his apostolic letters are other indications of this.

Most of all, as Faggioli notes, Francis sees the need to understand synodality as moving beyond the clerical sphere of ecclesial life, with the lines between lay and clerical identity becoming much less distinct. All are called to be missionary disciples.[20] It also concerns more than institutional governance. It means "a synodality that ensures that 'small but powerful groups'"—whether well-funded conservative groups on the right or liberal advocacy groups on the left—"are prohibited from running the church."[21]

Francis's emphasis on synodality is, in part, an effort to go to the peripheries, to better meet the needs of the poor and the disadvantaged. The recent Synod of Bishops for the Pan-Amazon region is an example of this. The Amazon region embraces all or parts of Bolivia, Brazil, Colombia, Ecuador, French Guiana, Guyana, Peru, Venezuela, and Suriname, and is home to thirty-four million people, including three million indigenous. Most in these countries are Roman Catholic. Jesuit Father Antonio Spadaro describes the synod as an example of a church seeking a form of synodal government, "a more participatory, collegial Church, characterized by a greater and stronger communion, a Church that establishes new criteria and structures to advance with greater adherence to the rhythm of reality."[22]

The Vatican's preparatory document (*lineamenta*) stresses "new paths for the church and for an integral ecology." The Amazon region is under threat, with thousands of acres of rainforest, often referred to as "the planet's lungs," destroyed by fires caused largely by slash-and-burn methods

---

[20] Massimo Faggioli, *The Liminal Papacy of Pope Francis: Moving toward Global Catholicism* (Maryknoll, NY: Orbis Books, 2020), 124–28.

[21] Faggioli, *The Liminal Papacy of Pope Francis*, 138.

[22] In Mauricio López Oropeza and Antonio Spadaro, "Sinodo Amazonico," *La Civiltá Cattolica*, October 15, 2019.

of clearing the land for agriculture and raising cattle. Brazil's National Institute for Space Research (INPE) reported 72,843 fires in the country's Amazon region in 2019. Other threats come from the use of agro-toxins; the polluting of rivers, lakes, and waterways; and illegal mining. Social problems include the displacing of indigenous peoples; criminalization of refugees and migrants; the sex trafficking of persons, especially women; and increased use of alcohol and drugs.

Thus, proclaiming the gospel in Amazonia has ecological as well as biblical-theological, social, sacramental, and ecclesial-missionary dimensions, hopefully leading to a new church with an Amazonian face. One proposal is for the ordination of married men recognized as religious leaders in the communities without priests. The working document for the synod, *Instrumentum laboris*, was described by Cardinal Lorenzo Baldisseri, secretary general of the Synod of Bishops, not as a papal document but rather as a compilation of the questions and petitions of the Amazonian peoples. Cardinal Cláudio Hummes, archbishop emeritus of São Paulo, Brazil, added that it represents "the voice of the local church, the voice of the church of Amazonia, the church of the people and of the Earth."[23]

The synod represented an important determination on the part of the regional church to differentiate itself from new colonizing efforts by listening to the Amazonian peoples themselves, to assist migrants and combat human trafficking, to protect the rights of indigenous communities, and to defend the threatened ecology of the Amazon region. About three hundred listening sessions were held in preparation for the synod, along with some twenty-two thousand sessions in territorial assemblies and another sixty-five thousand in parish groups.

There has been considerable opposition. German Cardinal Brandmüller called the working document heretical, accusing its drafters of trying to change the church into a secular NGO. Cardinal Burke described it as an attack on the Lordship of Christ. Other attacks came from a number of right-wing groups.

One of the primary hubs of resistance to the October gathering is the Pan-Amazonian Synod Watch, which was created by the Plinio Corrêa de Oliveira Institute (IPCO) and its "sister organizations," the right-wing Societies for the Defense of Tradition, Family and

---

[23] Rosa Die Alcolea, "Synod on the Amazon: The *Instrumentum Laboris* Is Not a Papal Document," Zenit, October 3, 2019.

Property (TFP). Oliveira founded the TFP in 1960 as a bulwark against "communist" influences in society and the Church. . . . The Pan-Amazon Synod Watch website cautions that "the Indigenist Theology now being promoted is nothing more than a radicalization, behind the mask of ecology."[24]

The 120 paragraphs of the synod's final document were approved by a two-thirds majority, including 128 yes votes to 41 no votes for married priests—the so-called *viri probati* or older men of proven virtue—as well as 137 yes votes to 30 no votes for women deacons. Also recommended was a special rite for the Amazon, though with some dissenting votes.[25] Either with a call for further study or recommendations to the pope with significant reservations on the part of some, the recommendations are now in the pope's hands. Some were disappointed when Francis's post-synodal apostolic exhortation failed to address these two recommendations and with his setting up a second commission to study the women's diaconate that seems to include only more conservative scholars.

Also of concern for Francis are the millions of migrants and refugees abandoned at the peripheries. Today the whole world is on the move, with families fleeing violence and war, religious persecution, crushing poverty, or climate change; Francis mentions them in his encyclical *Laudato si'* (no. 25). The UN Refugee Agency reported that the number of people forcibly displaced in 2018 as a result of persecution, conflict, violence, or human rights violations had reached almost 70.8 million. This is the highest level on record.[26]

On the southern border of the United States, immigration officials under the Trump administration are separating children from their families as well as denying migrants and asylum seekers access to pastoral care and the sacraments. For Christians, all human life is sacred; it needs to be nurtured and protected, not just prior to birth but after as well.[27]

---

[24] Christopher White, "Catholic Reactionary Group Raising Its Profile Ahead of Amazon Synod," *Crux*, September 25, 2019. See also Heidi Schlumpf, "Head of Liturgy Commission Criticizes Amazon Synod of Social Media," *National Catholic Reporter*, December 5, 2019.

[25] Luke Hansen, "Top 5 Takeaways from the Amazon Synod," *America*, November 11, 2019.

[26] UNHCR, the UN Refugee Agency, "Global Trends: Forced Displacement in 2018," June 20, 2019.

[27] See David Hollenbach, *Humanity in Crisis: Ethical and Religious Response to Refugees* (Washington, DC: Georgetown University Press, 2020). See also Linda Dakin-Grimm,

Ministerial Leadership

As the number of priests continues to decrease and more lay men and lay women seek ministerial positions, the face of ministerial leadership will continue to change. Vatican II sought to develop a theology of the laity, expressing the share of all the baptized in the priesthood of Christ and the mission of the church, but few expected the explosion of lay ministries that followed the council. Today, positions of leadership in local communities and dioceses are increasingly filled by lay men and especially lay women. In Africa and Latin America, lay catechists and pastoral agents have long been leading local communities. In churches in Europe, Latin America, and Africa, lay ministers conduct funerals, lead services of the Word, and preach at prayer services when a priest is not available. Some churches in the United States have lay parish administrators who function as lay pastors in all but sacramental ministry.

According to statistics on the Center for Applied Research in the Apostolate (CARA) website, in 2019 the United States had 35,929 priests, 18,193 permanent deacons, and, in 2015, 36,651 lay ecclesial ministers.[28] These lay ministers are full-time or part-time and salaried, and they often have a graduate degree in theology or pastoral studies and some spiritual formation. In addition, there are other lay ministers, paid or unpaid, who bring a specific professional competence to church life, such as administrators. This means that lay men and lay women outnumber priests. The increasing age of the priests makes this significant. Further, some dioceses have more permanent deacons than priests.

In 2018, of the 17,007 parishes in the United States (less than in 2015 because of consolidation), 3,363 lacked a priest pastor, and 341 had been entrusted to non-clergy for pastoral care, that is, to a religious sister, brother, or deacon, or to a trained lay person. Though some bishops are not comfortable with the laity in these positions, these parish life directors coordinate the various ministries of the parish and oversee its maintenance. In Africa, the number is considerably less, with only 161 parishes administered by non-clergy. In Europe, Asia, and Latin America, it is also far less common, though CARA indicates some change in Asia since 2012, when sisters received responsibility for ninety-five parishes. In New Zealand lay men and lay women are also beginning to lead parishes.

Dignity and Justice: Welcoming the Stranger at Our Border (Maryknoll, NY: Orbis Books, 2020).

[28] CARA website, "FAQ->Frequently Requested Church Statistics." See also CARA, "Global Catholicism: Trends and Forecasts," June 4, 2015.

In Africa, Asia, and Latin America, pastoral leadership is often in the hands of lay catechists; in these areas, lay catechists and lay missionaries number in the hundreds of thousands.[29] However, it is important to note that in Africa and Latin America, catechists do more than catechesis; in many countries they are congregational leaders and perform many of the ministries reserved to priests and deacons in the United States and Europe. In Latin America, women frequently serve as leaders of communities, catechists, ministers of the Word, and extraordinary ministers of baptism and the Eucharist.

In Africa, catechists are usually supported by the communities they serve; they are not necessarily salaried but are provided with housing, food, motorcycles, and so on. They work closely with their pastors, solidarity groups, or basic ecclesial communities, and frequently have distinctive religious garb. Africa also has a new generation of theologians and church professionals, men and women, priests and sisters, even bishops, many of them trained in Europe or the United States. Their concerns are not simply inner ecclesial issues, but social problems that affect the lives of all Africans. The same is true of the church in China.

The Shortage of Priests

Even with an expanded ministry, the priest shortage remains a critical problem in many parts of the church. In 2017, the global number of priests decreased for the first time since 2010. In countries where flourishing Pentecostal churches continue to draw away Catholics, the long education and formation required for priests puts the Catholic Church at a disadvantage. The emphasis for Pentecostal churches is on charisms for preaching and ministry, though their pastors often lack a theological formation.

Much of the Amazon today is becoming evangelical, with few priests to minister to the area's Catholics. In one diocese in northern Brazil, 70 percent of the communities see a priest only once or twice a year, so baptism becomes the basic sacrament. Pope Francis has suggested he does

---

[29]According to CARA, in 2012 Africa had 393,580 catechists and 7,195 lay missionaries; Asia had 365,720 catechists and 31,341 lay missionaries; Europe had 549,878 catechists and 16,456 lay missionaries; the Americas had 1,846,107 catechists and 317,403 lay missionaries (CARA does not distinguish between North and South America); and Oceania had 15,358 catechists and 90 lay missionaries.

not necessarily oppose ordaining married men where there is serious need, and the bishops at the Synod on the Amazon recommended it, though with some reservations. More changes may lie ahead.

Certainly the church has considerably more freedom over its sacramental discipline than it has been willing to acknowledge. There is no substantive reason why it couldn't authorize deacons, many of whom do excellent hospital ministry, to celebrate the sacrament of the sick. There is at least a historical precedent for admitting women to the order of deacons, though as Pope Francis revealed in May 2019, the commission set up to examine the question could not reach an agreement, saying there is a need for further study.

And the church needs at least to investigate more carefully the possibility of ordaining women to the presbyteral office. Few Catholics are convinced by the arguments brought against the ordination of women, nor are statements from church authorities sufficient. The issue has never been discussed by the whole church, using all its theological and pastoral resources, nor has any effort been made to assess the *sensus fidelium* on the question. After the pandemic, some social distancing will probably be required for some time, and thus more masses, which might lead to changed attitudes toward a more inclusive ministry.

Renewing Priestly Formation

The seminary system for forming diocesan priests, established by the Council of Trent in its Decree on Seminaries (1563), was an important reform in what is often called the Counter-Reformation, but today's candidates face different challenges.[30] As the sexual abuse crisis has so clearly demonstrated, affective and psychosexual maturity are crucial issues to address. So is the culture of clericalism, as Pope Francis has repeatedly emphasized.

The present system, usually in all-male, semi-cloistered seminaries, often means a "formation by isolation." Those formed in this system often have little sense of the challenges of family life, or of equitable working relationships with lay ministers, especially women. The shortage of priests also can lead to a less careful selection of candidates. The theology of an

---

[30] See Thomas P. Rausch, "Vatican II on the Priesthood: Fifty Years Later," *The Seminary Journal* 18, no. 3 (2012): 4–18.

"ontological change" based on ordination makes little sense today; it developed from the notion of a sacramental "seal" or "character" originally associated with the unrepeatability of baptism, confirmation, and ordination. But as currently used, it fosters a false elitism based on a supposed unique status. The wearing of cassocks and Roman collars by seminarians also serves to reinforce clerical attitudes.

Those preparing for priesthood should demonstrate a charism for shared ministry and the ability to listen to others and enable their gifts, including those of women. Their formation should include classes with men and women preparing for ecclesial ministry; work in parishes and with other ministers; and professors that include both men and women, ordained and lay, as is the case for most candidates for orders in religious congregations.[31] Issues of sexuality, sexual identity, cultural difference, and clericalism need to be addressed openly in order to prepare future priests for healthy celibate living. They should learn how to include these sensitive topics in their preaching. Their teachers and *formatores* should also have some say in approving them for ordination.

Addressing Sexual Abuse

In February 2019, Pope Francis called a conference of the heads of the world's episcopal conferences to address the problem, bringing 190 bishops, representatives of religious communities, and experts to Rome. Following the conference he put in place a policy for the Vatican. Then, in May 2019, he announced a new law, making it mandatory for all clerics and members of religious orders to report cases of clerical sexual abuse to church authorities.

The pope's motu proprio *Vos estis lux mundi* establishes new procedural rules to combat sexual abuse and to ensure that bishops and religious superiors are held accountable for their actions. The norms "apply without prejudice to the rights and obligations established in each place by state laws, particularly those concerning any reporting obligations to the competent civil authorities" (art. 19). In other words, church authorities must follow civil laws about reporting abuse. Every diocese must have a system that allows the public to submit reports easily. *Vos estis lux mundi*

---

[31] Boston College Seminar on Priesthood and Ministry, "To Serve the People of God: Renewing the Conversation on Priesthood and Ministry," *Origins* 48, no. 31 (2018): 484–93.

also addresses the question of episcopal accountability. The response has generally been positive.

The sexual abuse crisis has demonstrated the liabilities of the church's clerical culture and has led to calls for substantive reform. Genuine reform means not just eliminating corruption, but also reforming structures, as Yves Congar pointed out long before Vatican II.[32] An immediate step toward greater transparency would be to ensure lay participation on diocesan review boards and as episcopal consultants. The February 2019 meeting in Rome on sexual abuse bought victims from around the world into the conversation. Some were heard in Rome; others spoke from a distance. The highly respected Father Hans Zollner, a German Jesuit who is one of the church's leading experts on abuse prevention and a member of Pope Francis's commission on the protection of minors, said that, even a year ago, it would have been unthinkable in Africa to talk about prevention. But in most places that is changing. It is a journey, "not as fast as we would like it to be, but I see signs of hope."[33]

Women's voices are also being heard more frequently, with religious women from African, India, and Europe beginning to address the sexual abuse of sisters by clergy. In the fall of 2018, the International Union of Superiors General urged sisters to denounce the "culture of silence and secrecy" and speak out. Many have. Doris Wagner, a former German nun, wrote about being raped by a priest when she was twenty-four. Another case involved a nun in India who claimed a bishop had raped her more than twelve times. Her charge split her community, with some of her sisters rising to her defense and others taking the side of the bishop, on whom they were dependent. Two of the sisters claimed that they had sent letters to the Vatican, but without a response. The bishop was imprisoned for three weeks; after his release the local clergy threw him a party. He has since been charged.

Other sisters have spoken out, including a French Dominican teaching at the Pontifical University of St. Thomas in Rome, the secretary general of the Higher Superiors of Female Religious Orders in Poland, and several sisters from Nigeria, including the superior of the Society of the Holy Child Jesus. Lucetta Scaraffia, editor of the Vatican's *Women Church World*, published an article denouncing the sexual abuse of nuns

---

[32] Yves Congar, *True and False Reform in the Church* (Collegeville, MN: Liturgical Press, 2010; French edition, 1950), 52.

[33] Quoted in Shannon Levitt Ines San Martín, "Sex Abuse Expert Expresses Cautious Optimism," *Crux*, November 14, 2019.

by priests, sometimes leading to abortions or to the birth of children not acknowledged by their priest-fathers. The article claimed that the Vatican has long known about this but not acted, and that sisters fearing retaliation against themselves or their communities have kept silent.

Pope Francis has acknowledged this problem. Today, communities of religious women are urging that reports of abuse be brought to the police. In September 2019, a Togolese nun, Sister Makamatine Lembo, successfully defended a dissertation at the Gregorian University on the subject, studying nine nuns who had been abused by priests in five different African countries. She graduated *summa cum laude*.

Loss of Privilege

As Massimo Faggioli notes, the sexual abuse crisis, the impact of which we've seen throughout this book, is only one of a number of challenges that modernity poses for the church. "They include the following: the effects of transparency and accountability on organized religion; the ability of the church to handle the psychology of indignation in the age of social media; and the huge re-negotiation of the relations between church and State." Faggioli describes it as the taking down the divine right of the Catholic hierarchy.[34] I call it here the loss of privilege, a leveling that denies to the church its special status among institutions.

Regardless of the reforms that have been instituted, the tendency of Catholic churches around the world, and even the Vatican, to deal with cases of the abuse of minors as an internal matter is over. That policy has led to considerable anger among the faithful as well as to accusations of cover-ups and a lack of transparency on the part of numerous bishops in dealing with the scandal. Significantly, in an increasing number of countries the church is no longer trusted to deal with these cases on its own. It is increasingly held accountable to civil laws.

In Australia, the states of Victoria, Tasmania, Queensland, and Western Australia have passed legislation criminalizing priests who fail to report the abuse of children disclosed during confession, with other states proposing similar laws. Several bishops and senior priests have said they would not obey these new laws, since it involves the sacred character of the seal of

---

[34] Massimo Faggioli, "Roma Locuta? Ecclesiology of the Vatican Summit on Sexual Abuse," *La Croix International,* August 8, 2019.

confession. Some have argued that breaking the seal won't prevent abuse, or that those guilty usually consider themselves innocent and so do not confess it.

In Argentina, Australia, Belgium, Canada, Chile, India, Ireland, and the United States, civil authorities have initiated investigations of local churches, demanding access to chancery records. Church officials, bishops, even cardinals, have been subjected to criminal prosecution. Cardinals in France and Australia have faced jail sentences or served time. For the church, it means a significant loss of privilege.

Faggioli has written that the church's response is still in its early stages. The church needs changes that are not just structural but also theological. Structurally, its response cannot be simply "top down," as was typical in the past. Some churches, especially in Africa, Asia, and even Italy, are only beginning to confront the crisis. The church needs to look more closely at how it forms its priests. It should also reflect theologically on the role of women and its theology of the sacraments, especially holy orders, addressing the false mystique that frequently surrounds it.[35]

The secular culture of many Western countries has also challenged longstanding policies of Catholic institutions because of church teaching on questions of life, sexuality, and family. While many Catholics see these efforts as an attack on their religious liberty, it means in practical terms that relations between church and state will have to be renegotiated. Thus, Catholic Charities offices or adoption services have lost state funding because of their unwillingness to place children with same-sex couples. Catholic colleges and universities have been required to provide coverage for birth control or abortion as part of their employee healthcare packages. The unwillingness of Catholic hospitals to provide sterilization and abortion services has been challenged. Some, arguing on the basis of the separation of church and state, have attempted to deny Catholic institutions their tax-exempt status or force compliance with what is seen as the rights of women, homosexuals, or transgender people. Some countries have passed laws against anti-gay comments, putting the expression of Christian teaching on homosexuality in the category of hate speech. The pandemic crisis has also led to new conflicts with civil authorities over closing or opening churches.

In other countries the church faces discrimination or persecution, some of it political or based on its minority status. In India, Catholics

---

[35] Faggioli.

face violence from Hindu fundamentalists. Christians frequently experience intolerance and violence in countries with an Islamic majority. In Pakistan, where Christians are only 2 percent of the population, they are frequently victimized by anti-blasphemy laws, which often entail capital punishment for allegedly insulting the Prophet or the Qur'an.

In China, the church struggles for religious liberty in the face of a government that remains suspicious of religion and seeks to control it. Jesuit Father General Arturo Sosa acknowledges that the church comes without privilege:

> For the Church to be inculturated in the reality of China implies her abandoning every claim to wisdom or social recognition in order to move to the new reality in which she desires to live fully. Inculturation involves leaving one's own home to go and live in the house of another, and so learn to live in a house other than the one you are used to.[36]

Dialogue with Culture

The church's loss of privilege also means a loss of authority, and thus, it must learn a new way to teach. It does no good to lament an increasing secularity; a loss of traditional morality; or new attitudes toward sexuality, gender, medical ethics, and end-of-life issues. The days when the church could simply impose its morality on a society through civil law—the ancient alliance of throne and altar—are gone, at least in the post-Enlightenment West and in much of the world.

For example, until recent times the Republic of Ireland prohibited abortion, divorce, selling contraceptives, and same-sex marriage. In the United States, what is perceived by conservative Catholics as Pope Francis's lack of support for their issues in the culture wars has led to his unpopularity and to considerable pushback against his efforts to reform the church. Some seem close to schism. However, the church needs to inspire and convince; it cannot compel. This applies even more in the Global South, where Christianity is a minority religion. The age of Christendom is gone forever.

---

[36] Arturo Sosa, SJ, "The Church in China: Notes for 'Writing the Future,'" *La Civiltà Cattolica,* August 20, 2019.

The church itself is divided in many countries. Some conservative Catholics appropriate the terms *orthodox* or *authentic* for themselves, claiming faithfulness to the magisterium and traditional doctrines. Others represent more *progressive* positions; they see themselves as reformers. These divisions can be found in other traditions as well. Mainstream Protestant traditions tend to be more liberal, while evangelical and Pentecostal communities are generally more conservative, especially on social issues, holding to an often literal interpretation of the Bible.

The Orthodox have tensions between many of their monastics and laity and their more reformist theologians. Churches in the West often reflect cultural concerns; many are open to homosexuality, abortion, as well as feminist and gender issues, while those in the Global South take more conservative positions on these questions but are concerned with the influence of the United States, free-market capitalism, peace, the environment, and international cooperation.

So how does an effective dialogue with culture take place? Contemporary culture appeals not to the authority of doctrine but to experience. It prizes individual rights, self-determination, and the freedom and authenticity of the person. In a pluralist, largely secular society, it is counterproductive simply to denounce the ambient culture as godless or anti-life. For example, when the University of Notre Dame invited President Barak Obama to speak on campus and receive an honorary doctorate in 2009, conservative Catholics, including some eighty bishops, denounced the university for not upholding Catholic values because of Obama's position on abortion.

A better approach is to focus on shared values—those that are also values of Christianity. In a pluralist society the church needs to enter into conversation, bringing in the church's scholars and theologians, those involved in its many social ministries and in its vast network of educational and healthcare institutions. As we noted in Chapter 1, Pope Francis wants theology to enter into "a sincere dialogue with social and civil institutions, with university and research centers, with religious leaders and with all women and men of good will, for the construction in peace of an inclusive and fraternal society, and also for the care of creation."[37] There must be an effort to explore common concerns, attempting to find common ground, as well as a willingness to let others make their own decisions without attempting to legislate morality on disputed issues.

---

[37] See Pope Francis, "Theology after *Veritatis Gaudium* in the Context of the Mediterranean," June 21, 2019.

At the same time, the church cannot simply embrace the ethos of the culture. Much of it is indeed contrary to the gospel. An extreme individualism works against the deep Catholic commitment to the common good, the dignity of the person, and its emphasis on the importance of community. The gap between the poor and the affluent continues to grow, and the powerless are ignored, as Pope Francis continues to point out. In the United States the problem of systemic racism surfaced in 2020 in the case of the tragic death of George Floyd, who died under the knee of an arresting policeman.

The church's voice needs to be in the public square to address these issues. But today there are many competing voices that are contrary to the gospel and the wisdom of the church's long experience. In many countries exclusionary nationalist movements are growing, based not just on national identity but sometimes also on race or religion. Fundamentalist religious voices, terrified by the impact of globalization, are transforming their religions into a kind of civil religion or ideology, often resorting to violence in God's name. Such efforts only serve to give religion a bad name. In the United States, many young people—not just Catholics—think that being Christian means joining the religious right, and so disaffiliate.

The church does not have the answer to all questions, something Rome too often seems reluctant to acknowledge. The church needs to consult the sense of the faith (*sensus fidei*) and of the faithful (*sensus fidelium*), as a recent paper of the International Theological Commission insisted. The bipartite image of a teaching church (*ecclesia docens*) and a learning church (*ecclesia discens*) is no longer appropriate, if it ever was.[38] The church needs to listen to its theologians, its scholars, and to other churches.

The church needs to think more seriously about its sexual morality, taking into account new knowledge. Changing attitudes toward the LGBTQ community have led to increasing conflicts between local church leadership and Catholic institutions, for example, in regard to gay and lesbian employees, some of whom are in same-sex relationships. We can expect more of these conflicts in the future. The voice of the laity also needs to be heard on these questions.

The Catholic Church in the West has tended to reduce the message of the gospel to its doctrinal tradition, rich as that is. But doctrine without

---

[38] International Theological Commission, "The *Sensus Fidei* in the Life of the Church," nos. 4, 43, 67, 72, 74. See also Thomas P. Rausch and Roberto Dell'Oro, eds., *Pope Francis on the Joy of Love: Theological and Pastoral Reflections on* Amoris laetitia (New York: Paulist Press, 2018).

a clear sense of the church's living tradition remains static, lifeless, and somewhat abstract. Context is always important. The new evangelical and Pentecostal churches of the Global South are not for the most part focused on doctrine; they stress experience, story, and personal testimony. What is most important is the encounter with the person of Jesus, the Christ.

This has long been the message of our most recent popes. In his apostolic exhortation *Ecclesia in America*, following the Special Assembly of the Synod of Bishops for America (1997), Pope John Paul II speaks of the assembly's theme as an encounter with the living Jesus Christ (no. 3), "the human face of God" (no. 67). At the beginning of his encyclical *Deus caritas est* (2005), Pope Benedict XVI wrote that being a Christian "is not the result of an ethical choice or a lofty idea, but the encounter with an event, a person, which gives life a new horizon and a decisive direction" (no. 1). Unfortunately, with the enormous theological output of both popes, this theme has often been overlooked. The Catholic Church needs very much to recover this personal christological focus.

Certainly, it is foundational to the teaching of Pope Francis. As he says in his *Evangelii gaudium*, important as the central truths of Christianity are, "Christian morality is not a form of stoicism, or self-denial, or merely a practical philosophy or a catalogue of sins and faults. Before all else, the Gospel invites us to respond to the God of love who saves us, to see God in others and to go forth from ourselves to seek the good of others" (no. 39).

A New Ecumenism

Much of the explosive growth of the church in the Global South is driven by the multiplication and flourishing of the "new" churches: evangelical, neo-Pentecostal, and the African Instituted Churches (AICs).[39] However, many of these are nontraditional churches. Few are sacramental or liturgical churches; most do not celebrate the Eucharist. The majority preach the prosperity gospel and are not particularly interested in ecumenism or the visible unity of the church. Believing in a rich spirit world, many stress spiritual warfare and exorcisms. In Africa some priests have adopted these emphases.

---

[39] See Thomas P. Rausch, "A New Ecumenism: Christian Unity in a Global Church," *Theological Studies* 78, no. 3 (2017): 596–613.

In 2013 the World Council of Churches produced a remarkable consensus text, *The Church: Towards a Common Vision*. It sees the church as a communion of churches, sharing a trinitarian faith, nourished by the word of God, strengthened by the sacraments, and guided by a mutually recognized ministry with teaching authority, a church nourished by the Eucharist and living in visible communion with other churches. However, many from the Global South find the text too Western, Eurocentric, and not sufficiently attuned to the experience of their new, largely Pentecostal churches.

"Cecil M. Robeck, Jr., who served as a member of the WCC Faith and Order Ecclesiology group, saw those assigned to his working group strongly slanted toward the ancient churches and those with episcopal government."[40] Robeck noted the document needed to address the issues of the churches of the Global South, "independent churches, megachurches, Pentecostal churches, African Independent churches."[41] Miroslav Volf argues that many ecumenical discussions have ignored the ecclesiologies of the free churches, even though they represent the largest Protestant groupings worldwide today.[42]

The more established churches cannot simply ignore these new churches of the Southern hemisphere, but relating to them will require a new, more inclusive ecumenism. These churches and communities are not interested in the theological dialogue and consensus statements that have so characterized the ecumenical movement since the end of the Second Vatican Council; nor are they prepared for them. More important for them is personal testimony, sharing stories about life in the Spirit, and a sense of mission based on gospel values. The Global Christian Forum, designed to bring into conversation groups not previously engaged in ecumenism, is one example of this. This is also the approach of Pope Francis, who favors walking, working, and praying together. The late Peter Hocken, with deep roots in the charismatic renewal, describes Francis as a

---

[40]Thomas P. Rausch, "Ecumenism for a Global Church: Can the Churches of the West and Those of the Global South Learn from Each Other," in *Leaning into the Spirit: Ecumenical Perspectives on Discernment and Decision-making in the Church*, ed. Virginia Miller, David Moxon, and Stephen Pickard, 199–215 (Switzerland: Palgrave Macmillan, 2019), 205.

[41]Cecil M. Robeck, Jr., "Panel Presentation on the Church: Towards a Common Vision," *Journal of Ecumenical Studies* 50, no. 2 (2015): 294.

[42]Miroslav Volf, *After Our Likeness: The Church as the Image of the Trinity* (Grand Rapids, MI: Eerdmans, 1998), 20.

"charismatic ecumenist." In the words of Austin Ivereigh, "He sees unity as firstly the work of the Spirit rather than an achievement of theological or institutional dialogue."[43]

While the WCC statement can serve as an ultimate goal of the ecumenical endeavor, it will not bring these new churches closer to the historic churches of the first millennium and the confessional churches of the Reformation. At the same time, to ignore Jesus's prayer for the unity of his disciples (cf. Jn 17:20–21) is to ignore the gospel.

The churches of the West and the Global South can learn much from each other.[44] The Southern churches may have something to teach those in the West. They have a strong sense of their evangelical mission, the gifts of the Spirit, and are vital communities. But as Philip Jenkins writes, these Global South Christians "retain a very strong supernatural orientation and are by and large far more interested in personal salvation than in radical politics."[45] They need to move beyond their health-and-wealth preaching, learn that faith and reason work in consort, and seek visible unity with other churches. The churches of the West may be more in touch with the church's historical tradition and with the social dimensions of the church's mission, but Enlightenment rationalism too often taints their theology and more attention to experience and to a sense for God's nearness is needed.

Unfortunately, there are few efforts to build a better relationship among churches in the Global South. The Vatican's Secretariat for Promoting Christian Unity has been in dialogue with Pentecostals since 1972, though not all Pentecostal churches support it. A similar dialogue with evangelicals of the World Evangelical Alliance has met off and on since 1977. There are a number of local dialogues with both evangelicals and Pentecostals in the United States, but little in the rest of the world. There has been some progress in bringing Catholics and Pentecostals together in Latin America, but mostly from the Catholic side.

The search for reconciliation and unity remains important. The church is bigger than any single church, and the gospel calls Christians to live in communion with one another. Can the bishop of Rome become not just

---

[43] Austin Ivereigh, "The Spirit of Peter: Could Francis Be Our First Charismatic Pope?" *America* 221, no. 3 (August 5, 2019): 23.

[44] See Thomas P. Rausch, "Ecumenism for a Global Church."

[45] Philip Jenkins, *The Next Christendom: The Coming of Global Christianity* (Oxford: Oxford University Press, 2007), 8.

a symbol of unity, but also truly its servant, without demanding that all the churches recognize his juridical authority? Authority is always greater when it is recognized rather than claimed.

Unity is for the sake of mission, "that the world may believe" (Jn 17:21). It calls for a conversion of Christians and their churches, so that they might recognize one another as brothers and sisters in the Lord. Ecumenism always begins in friendship. The extraordinary growth of Christianity in the Global South should bring Christians together; if it does not, they are not being faithful to the gospel.

Dialogue with Other Religions

Pundits and journalists are accustomed to proclaim the dying of religion, but it does not take much reflection to realize how many conflicts in the world today have religious roots, driven by various fundamentalisms. The term *fundamentalism* originates in a Christian context; conservative Protestants used it to defend what they saw as the fundamentals of Christianity against modern theology and a critical approach to scripture, often dismissed as "modernism."[46]

Peter Herriot notes five characteristics of the fundamentalist movement:

> The first and most basic distinguishing feature of fundamentalist movements is that they are *reactive*. Fundamentalists believe their religion is under mortal threat from the secularism of the modern world, and they are fighting back. . . . The remaining four distinctive features are all means to aid the ultimate task of resistance. First, fundamentalists are *dualist*. That is, they conceive of the world in binary opposites: God and the Devil, good and evil, truth and falsehood, etc. . . . Second, fundamentalists believe that their *holy book* . . . has supreme authority over what to believe and how to act. It reveals God's will for mankind. However, third, fundamentalists' interpretation of the holy book is *selective*. They choose specific ideas from it and emphasise them, often changing their traditional meaning when they do so. . . . Finally, they hold to a *millennialist*

---

[46]Torkel Brekke, *Fundamentalism: Prophecy and Protest in an Age of Globalization* (Cambridge: Cambridge University Press, 2012), 4. See also George M. Marsden, *Reforming Fundamentalism: Fuller Seminary and the New Evangelicalism* (Grand Rapids, MI: Eerdmans, 2018).

view of history, expecting God to fully establish His rule over the world at some future time.[47]

Peter Huff describes the standard criteria of fundamentalism as being antimodernist, emphasizing scriptural inerrancy, gender control, and minority consciousness.[48]

Fundamentalism is now a global phenomenon. It represents a response to modernity, heightened by globalization, on the part of many who fear change and the loss of power or privilege, whether religious, political, or gender based. Evangelical Protestants often condemn those without a personal relationship with Jesus to eternal damnation. Catholic fundamentalists substitute the magisterial text for the teachings of scripture, without interpretation or nuance, or reject liturgical change as contrary to tradition. Israeli fundamentalists, like those in Gush Emunim, lay claims to lands and properties not their own, and often resort to violence to gain both. Some ultraconservative Jews reject the existence of the State of Israel on religious grounds. Buddhists fundamentalists in Myanmar have forsaken the Buddhist message of peace to commit genocide against the Rohingya. Other Buddhists have resorted to violence against Muslims in Southern Thailand and Sri Lanka. Hindu fundamentalists in India have murdered Christians and Muslims, burned their churches and mosques, and forced low-caste converts to reconvert to Hinduism, all in the name of Hindu nationalism and in defense of the caste system.

Islamic fundamentalists in Africa and the Middle East, also referred to as radical or political Islam, include Boko Haram in Nigeria, al-Shabaab in East Africa, al-Qaeda in Afghanistan, Pakistan, Iraq, or the Sudan, and the Islamic State of Iraq and the Levant (ISIS)—to name just a few. They have murdered thousands and spread terror on three continents. Islamic fundamentalists in Afghanistan, Iran, and Saudi Arabia insist on laws denying women equality.

In much of Africa dialogue with Islam is still in its very early stages, and Europe is closely divided on relations with Islam. It is not the religion itself or its practices that many object to, but the social and political order that many Muslim countries seek to enforce, including the denial of freedom of conscience, forbidding religious conversion, denying the

---

[47] Peter Herriot, *Religious Fundamentalism: Global, Local and Personal* (London: Routledge, 2009), 2.

[48] Peter A. Huff, *What Are They Saying about Fundamentalisms?* (New York: Paulist Press, 2008), 141, citing Jay Harris, who reviewed these criteria.

full equality of women, and the treatment of religious minorities. These concerns should be part of any interreligious dialogue.

With so much religiously based conflict, interreligious encounter becomes increasingly important. Pope Francis emphasized this point during his visit to Morocco in March 2019; he stressed that authentic interreligious dialogue is a way to combat terrorism; "mere tolerance" is not enough. "While respecting our differences, faith in God leads us to acknowledge the eminent dignity of each human being, as well as his or her inalienable rights."[49] This is a message that all the religions should share.

Ecclesial Identity

A final issue concerns ecclesial identity. In my own experience most young Catholics are unfamiliar with their own tradition and with the protocols of ecclesial division; frequently they just ignore them. Many are comfortable with women or gay pastors, even if their elders are not. Unofficial eucharistic sharing is not unusual. Some speak of double belonging or post-confessional identities. A sense of community is more important than institutional identity. If couples are unable to have the "garden" marriage they want under Catholic auspices, they turn to Episcopalian or Methodist pastors, without considering themselves any less Catholic for that. In Nigeria, we noted that some Catholics attend both their own church and a Pentecostal congregation.

Thus, for some young people ecclesial walls today are porous, their ecclesial identity fluid. Some commentators describe church membership for many as a "non-binary relationship," inhabiting a "liminal space . . . of walking along boundaries of being neither in nor out, of neither staying nor leaving."[50] The easy crossing of denominational lines may itself be a sign of how much the ecumenical landscape has changed.

The evidence is not yet in as to how true this is in other countries, but Pope Francis seems to be less concerned about establishing clear lines of separation based on doctrinal differences. When he visited Morocco, he warned Catholics not to be concerned about making converts: "The paths of mission are not those of proselytism, which leads always to a cul-de-sac,

---

[49] Inés San Martín, "Pope Extols Interreligious Dialogue as a Means to Combat Terrorism," *Crux*, March 30, 2019.

[50] Mary M. Doyle Roche, "Lingering on the Margins: Church Membership Isn't Binary," *Commonweal*, June 2, 2019.

but of our way of being with Jesus and with others. The problem is not when we are few in number, but when we are insignificant, salt that has lost the flavour of the Gospel, or lamps that no longer shed light (cf. Mt 5:13–15)."[51] The challenge is to remain always open and welcoming without losing a sense for the gifts and convictions of our Catholic tradition.

Conclusion

And so we approach the end of this exploration of global Catholicism. With its numbers, its organization, its charitable ministries, and its rich legacy of social teaching, the Catholic Church is a transnational actor in an era of globalization and is increasingly less Eurocentric. But it is also a communion of diverse churches; it is present in different cultures, with different gifts, and facing different problems.

For some, globalization is seen as a threat; they fear that the forces leading toward globalization risk collapsing the uniqueness of their traditions, religions, cultures, and identities into a bland commonality in which everyone listens to the same music and drinks Coca-Cola. Around the globe, the emerging nationalist movements and fundamentalisms stand as a militant, often destructive opposition.

Others see globalization as foreshadowing a coming global community, rich in diversity but unified around common values. This was the vision of the Second Vatican Council, which in *Lumen gentium* describes the church as a quasi-sacrament, "a sign and instrument both of a very closely knit union with God and of the unity of the whole human race" (no. 1). The internet, like a common nervous system in a global body, can either further divide us or bring us together.

The churches around the world have much to learn from one another. Churches of the Global South seek to incarnate the gospel among the poor, enlivened with the experience of the Holy Spirit. Latin American liberation theologies show us how the gospel can empower those reduced to nonpersons by economic and social forces, revealing God's special concern for the oppressed and the disadvantaged. Churches in Africa sense our closeness to the natural world and the ways our ancestors continue to accompany us. Churches in India struggle to form a community that

---

[51] Deborah Castellano Lubov, "In Morocco, Pope Warns Religious to Not Be Discouraged by Being Few, But as 'Lamps' to Not Lose Their Light," Zenit, March 31, 2019.

ignores differences of caste, cult, or social status. Asian churches, often in the minority, hope to teach Christians how to live in harmony with those of different religious traditions; they challenge the individualism of Euro-American culture with a deep sense of familial and communal solidarity.

The diminishments of Western churches show the inadequacy of a Christianity that is merely cultural, calling attention to the importance of evangelization in an increasingly secular world. At the same time they struggle with difficult questions of race, class, gender, and sexuality that take seriously growing economic disparities as well as our embodied nature in a way that respects difference and emphasizes the importance of community. Most stress the compatibility of faith and reason. They argue that difference does not weaken our global community; it expresses its richness, like nature itself. For it was our common humanity that the Word assumed, while the Trinity itself shows forth unity in diversity.

This is the vision of Pope Francis for the Catholic Church. He teaches us that the realization of our deepest nature is relational. Stressing the manifold connections existing among all creatures, he writes in *Laudato si'*, "The human person grows more, matures more and is sanctified more to the extent that he or she enters into relationships, going out from themselves to live in communion with God, with others and with all creatures. In this way, they make their own that trinitarian dynamism which God imprinted in them when they were created" (no. 240).

Historically, Catholicism's unique charism has been precisely its ability to hold unity and diversity together in a creative tension. With the break between the Greek-speaking Eastern churches and the Latin West in the eleventh century, and even more with the Reformation in the sixteenth, the charism of unity was lost and the church continued to divide. Present estimates of the global number of denominations is forty-eight thousand. Islam, without any central teaching authority, is even more open to fracture, with each charismatic imam or mullah giving his own interpretation of the tradition, as we have seen so recently in the tragic example of the Islamic State of Iraq and Syria (ISIS).

Catholicism's hierarchical structure with its authoritative magisterium is a gift frequently unrecognized, helping to hold its diverse churches embedded in such different cultures together in communion. That charism of unity will be even more necessary in the future, as a once monarchical church, with all authority flowing from Rome, takes on the form of a decentralized, synodal church, no longer Eurocentric, less clerical, with greater lay involvement in its life. It will be a more ecumenical church, and it will continue its efforts to find common ground with the other great world religions.

The secular societies in which the church will continue to live will remain a challenge. Catholicism's religious leaders, theologians, and faithful will be called to find new ways to witness to the good news of the reign of God that Jesus proclaimed. Many people feel unfulfilled. They long for a lasting happiness or for greater meaning in their lives. They sense an emptiness in their hearts only God can fill. As Augustine writes: "You have made us for yourself, O Lord, and our heart is restless until it rests in you."[52]

This is what Pope Francis refers to as the joy of the gospel, the English title of *Evangelii gaudium*. In it he calls for a kerygma that expresses God's saving love, a kerygma

> marked by joy, encouragement, liveliness and a harmonious balance which will not reduce preaching to a few doctrines which are at times more philosophical than evangelical. All this demands on the part of the evangelizer certain attitudes which foster openness to the message: approachability, readiness for dialogue, patience, a warmth and welcome which is non-judgmental (no. 165).

Most important, the church itself and all Catholic Christians should strive to be more open to the Spirit that brings life and sometimes novelty, just as all Christians are called to live out more deeply their encounter with Jesus in their personal lives.

---

[52] Saint Augustine, *Confessions* (Lib 1, 1–2, 2.5, 5: CSEL 33, 1–5).

Index